Superfluous Things

Superfluous Things

*Material Culture and Social Status
in Early Modern China*

Craig Clunas

University of Hawai'i Press

Honolulu

First published 1991 by Polity Press in association with Basil Blackwell
Paperback edition published 2004 by University of Hawai'i Press
© 1991 Craig Clunas
© 2004 University of Hawai'i Press for preface to the paperback edition

Printed in the United States of America

08 09 10 11   7 6 5 4 3

Library of Congress Cataloging-in-Publication Data
Clunas, Craig.
Superfluous things : material culture and social status in early modern
China / Craig Clunas.—Paperback ed.
p. cm.
Includes bibliographical references and index.
ISBN-13: 978-0-8248-2820-2 (pbk. : alk. paper)

1. Social classes—China—History—17th century. I. Title.
HN740.Z9S6233 2004
305.5'0951—dc22
2004001199

University of Hawai'i Press books are printed on acid-free paper
and meet the guidelines for permanence and durability
of the Council on Library Resources.

Printed by Versa Press

Contents

List of Illustrations   vi

Acknowledgements   ix

Preface to the Paperback Edition   xi

Introduction   1

1 Books about things
   The literature of Ming connoisseurship   8

2 Ideas about things
   Themes in Ming connoisseurship literature   40

3 Words about things
   The language of Ming connoisseurship   75

4 Things of the past
   Uses of the antique in Ming material culture   91

5 Things in motion
   Ming luxury objects as commodities   116

6 Anxieties about things
   Consumption and class in Ming China   141

Conclusion   166

Appendix I Editors of *Treatise on Superfluous
Things*   174

Appendix II Selected prices for works of art and
antique artefacts c. 1560–1620   177

Notes   182

Bibliography of primary sources   197

Bibliography of secondary literature   199

Index   210

Illustrations

1) Exercises appropriate to the fourth month, one of the illustrations to the 'Discourse on being in harmony with the four seasons', one of Gao Lian's *Eight Discourses on the Art of Living*, 1591.

2) Table of *huali* wood, about 1600, with openwork panels carved in the shape of dragons between the legs. By Courtesy of the Trustees of the Victoria and Albert Museum, FE.18-1980.

3) An archaic bronze vessel of the tripod form known as *ding*, from a 1601 reprint edition of *Researches on Archaeology Illustrated* of 1092, *juan* 1, p. 17.

4) A handbill issued by the publishing house of Zi Yibin, complaining about the piracy of an edition of an unidentified text called the *Golden Ritual*, by a rival, Pan Jinshan. About 1590. The Hague, Koninklijke Bibliotheek, 133 M 63.

5) Hanging scroll on silk, painted about 1550, probably in Suzhou. The spurious signature is that of Li Zhaodao (fl. first half of eighth century), and there are spurious seals and colophons of the northern Song imperial collection (eleventh century), Ma Zhi (fourteenth century), Ke Jiusi (1312-65) and Wen Zhengming (1470-1559). By courtesy of the Trustees of the Victoria and Albert Museum, E.422-1953, Sharples Bequest.

6) Incense burner of white porcelain imitating Ding ware, made about 1550-1600. By courtesy of the Trustees of the Victoria and Albert Museum, Circ.130-1935.

7) An illustration to the drama *Ideal Love Matches* by Li Yu, showing an antique shop. After Fu Xihua (1980), no. 633.

8) The opening passage of the handscroll 'Dwelling in the Fuchun
   Mountains', painted between 1347 and 1350 by Huang Gongwang,
   showing the colophon by Dong Qichang and the seals of the
   Qing dynasty imperial collection. Collection of the National
   Palace Museum, Taiwan, Republic of China.

Acknowledgements

The poem 'Bogus Antiquities' (translated by Wai-kam Ho) on p. 111, and the 'Ranking of Antique Objects' (translated by Chu-tsing Li) on pp. 104–105 are reproduced by kind permission of the Asia Society Galleries from Chu-tsing Li and James Watt eds, *The Chinese Scholar's Studio: Artistic Life in the Late Ming Period*, Thames and Hudson, published in association with the Asia Society Galleries (New York, 1987). I am grateful also to Wai-kam Ho for his agreement to reproduce his work.

Preface to the Paperback Edition

The occasion of introducing the republication of a work which first appeared over ten years ago, and which was conceived well over fifteen, gives the author the opportunity to do a number of things. (As this is a photographic reprint of the 1991 edition, it should be admitted straight off that it does not give him a chance to correct any mistakes or errors of fact in the main body of the text). He ought properly to begin by thanking the University of Hawai'i Press, and in particular its editor Patricia Crosby, for their interest in bringing this work back into circulation and for their belief in its continuing scholarly relevance. He can also reflect on the intellectual processes and influences which led to the book's original composition. He can gauge its relationship to the wider field of the study of Chinese art and history. He can direct the reader's attention to new work done in the field since its first appearance and to the ways in which the conclusions of others would either support or contest the views which appear here. And finally he can indicate the extent to which the scholarship of the intervening years, whether by himself or others, would lead to a revised approach. Put bluntly, if I were to address this material again, what could or should be done differently?

Superfluous Things was written in the late 1980s in a particular intellectual context, that of the Victoria and Albert Museum's Far Eastern Department. The burden of objects, of the inventory, the list, of sorting and display, was an important issue in my daily routine; it was not just things in the abstract which demanded my attention, but things in a very real and present sense. As I have mentioned elsewhere, it was in the course of working on an exhibition of Chinese ivory carving, held at the British Museum under the auspices of the Oriental Ceramic Society in 1984, that I first encountered the Chinese text of the *Zhang wu zhi,* the 'Treatise on Superfluous Things', by Wen Zhenheng (1585–1645), which

forms both the starting point and the central material of this study of the culture of late Ming China. I used it then initially as 'raw data', scanning through it for mention of ivory objects which could be used to support the dating of individual pieces in the exhibition or, more subtly but no less problematically, to provide a 'context' for them in a wider Ming culture. My own formal training up to that point, largely within the reach of the text-based discipline of sinology, had led me without much conscious reflection to the view that the Chinese written record was the way to understand surviving Chinese things. This was added to a dissatisfaction with the way in which imprecise terms like 'scholars' taste' were used in both the museum and the art market to add lustre to objects presented to a viewing or buying public. If I read what Ming connoisseurs and con- sumers said at the time, I reasoned, I would know what they *really* thought about things. *Why* this procedure was intellectually problematic took a long time to dawn on me, but it did so in the arena of debate around the museum and its purposes, which was in the mid– 1980s loosely assembled under the heading of the 'New Museology' (after the pattern of the 'New Art History') and which elicited a range of responses from myself and certain close colleagues. What an object from the past 'really' meant, whether such a position was even tenable at all, was one of the key issues of the debate. But the central catalyst in my thinking was (as alluded to in the original introduction reprinted below) the range of people, ideas and writings made available to me through participation in the museum's then-innovative partnership with the Royal College of Art on a masters-level degree programme in the history of design. It was in trying to explain the relevance of Bourdieu or Foucault to students that I was forced to address the implications of this work (until then of little importance in my intellectual formation, which was one of a rather strictly sinological nature). Many of the scholars—Chandra Mukerji, Richard Goldthwaite, Jules Prown, Henry Glassie, Peter Burke, Lorna Weatherill—whose work on issues of material culture and consumption are cited here, passed through the course rooms as visiting speakers, and it was in listening to them that I was led for the first time to think about the nature of the sources *as pieces of writing,* rather than as mines of raw data. I realised that sitting at the back of the room interjecting, 'But what about *China!*' was of no value to them and limited satisfaction to me unless I were to put some of the Chinese material into the wider debate through publication. To an extent, therefore, this book was written for scholars of other parts of the world who might
be willing to engage with a truly comparative perspective. The optimism, perhaps naivete, of this appears only more striking as time goes by. With certain notable exceptions, it remains largely standard practice among historians of early modern (a term to which I shall return) Europe to dis-

cuss the evidence for the 'birth of a consumer society' in that part of the world without reference to any other. This tendency is the subject of a more recent and explicitly polemical piece of writing which revisits some of the issues in *Superfluous Things* from a comparative point of view.[1]

One of the great advantages of a job as a museum curator, the position from which the book was written, was that it allowed a certain side-stepping of, or at least strategic blindness to, disciplinary boundaries. This perhaps meant that the work, gratifyingly, was of interest to people occupying a range of disciplinary positions. A casual web-based search for the range of syllabi on which the book appears therefore reveals the following incomplete list: 'Decorative Arts of Late Imperial China'; 'Chinese Cultural History'; 'The Artist in Traditional China'; 'Consumer Society'; 'Art of China'; 'Material Culture in the History of Modern Japan'; 'Late Imperial and Modern Chinese History'; 'Chinese Social History'; 'Theories of Art in China and Japan'. The British Library subject index entry rather bizarrely reads: 'Social classes. China. History. 20th century [*sic*]'. What this diversity suggests is that the book can be situated as part of a loosening of the boundaries between, in particular, art history and social history, an intellectual development which has been much commented on, and which has been seen as positive or negative according to taste. The terms 'material culture' and 'visual culture' have both played a major part in providing a sort of strategic neutral territory on which both sets of specialists can meet. The increasing willingness of historians to take these realms of culture seriously has been part of the context in which this book and a subsequent volume entitled *Pictures and Visuality in Early Modern China* (London, 1997) have circulated.[2]

This means that at least some of the issues raised in *Superfluous Things* have continued to interest historians of Ming China, with a number of recent surveys addressing cognate issues. The 1994 work of John Meskill on Songjiang addresses 'the behavior and attitudes of the educated circle of one prefecture' in what he sees as an era of late sixteenth century change to a more commercialised society.[3] James Cahill's *Painter's Practice* (1994) put the authority of one of the founders of Western scholarship on Chinese art behind continuing investigation of the social history of Chinese art, its consumers and its practitioners.[4] Timothy Brook's 1998 volume, the best single-volume introduction to Ming social history, makes the links between commerce and culture explicit in its subtitle.[5] A salutary reminder that economic historians are by no means united in their interpretation of the types of economic change which cultural historians have to take on trust is provided by the work of Richard Von Glahn and Kenneth Pomeranz, to name the authors of only two of the most significant monographs to appear since 1991.[6] One of the most interesting developments in the field, and one only touched on sketchily in this book, is the issue of gender and material culture, which has been opened up by the work of Dorothy Ko, Wai-yee Li and Francesca Bray among others.[7]

Whether related to this book's appearance or not, one of the trends within scholarship in the decade or so since 1991 has been to draw attention to ways in which the claims made here for the distinctiveness of the attitudes to material culture in the late Ming period are or are not sustainable. This can be done very legitimately in at least two ways: by pointing to earlier manifestations of the relevant phenomena and by indicating that they did not effectively end with the fall of the Ming in 1644 but rather continued and even intensified in the succeeding Qing period. One of the central arguments of this book, picked up by reviewers and subsequent scholars, is that it was in the sixteenth century, above all in the later sixteenth century, that traditional elites saw their social position threatened and hence turned to the 'invention of taste' as a mechanism to stress not just the things possessed but the manner of possessing them. This is clearly an argument which is heavily indebted to the model of the late Pierre Bourdieu, and as such could be attacked on the grounds of the critiques of his work in general.[8] But it could also be modified on the grounds of empirical problems. Jonathan Hay among others has drawn attention to 'earlier manifestations of aestheticism' in China as grounds for caution regarding the distinctiveness of the equations of cultural capital and social status made here.[9] Ankeney Weitz has shown how the operations of the art market, the texts and the practices which make up its discourse at a much earlier period, require a revision of thinking on this issue, the central theme of Chapter 5 below.[10] And Kathlyn Liscomb's meticulous work on both the detailed contents and the wider implications of the tomb of the merchant Wang Zhen, interred in 1494 with his collection of paintings, shows us in the clearest possible terms that individual members of the merchant class were partaking of the trappings of the 'scholarly' lifestyle in the early Ming, well before the period in which Wen Zhenheng lived and wrote his 'Treatise'.[11] My own more recent work on the patronage networks in which Wen Zhenheng's great-grandfather, Wen Zhengming (1470–1559), enmeshed himself provide ample evidence for merchant collectors of paintings and antiquities in the first half of the sixteenth century.[12] It would therefore be wholly wrong to insist that the period around 1600 represents a material landscape of total novelty, or that the kinds of anxieties about the connections between things and status which are examined here were totally unknown at an earlier period. However, it is often the case that single transgressive acts do not so much challenge the rules as reinforce them. The occasional merchant with a fine collection does not threaten traditional types of scholar-gentry hegemony any more than the occasional female poet challenges patriarchy; indeed, quite the reverse. Moreover, there remains the issue of the degree to which observers alive in the late Ming *felt* that something novel was going on, and of the impulses which drove Wen Zhenheng and his contemporaries detailed here to write so much that was new about the details of what things were 'elegant' and what were 'vulgar'. There is always a risk of the historian becoming the prisoner of the sources. Certainly the texts one has read always seem more compelling as evidence than those one has not. This textual positivism al-ways makes the cultural historian, including the present author, a historian of discourse, but of a rather particular kind. This perception is sharpened in the case of the late Ming discourse of taste by Jonathan Hay in his 2001 monograph on the seventeenth-century painter Shitao, and in his discussion of 'modernity' as an issue in Qing China. He writes, *à propos* the present study:

> What made taste a compelling issue in the late Ming was the realisation that social status was not, after all, immutable; anything bearing on this sudden social fluidity was a matter of wide concern. The fall of the Ming dynasty inevitably rendered such rapid changes suspect, a shift reflected in the replacement of discourses of status advancement with discourses of social stability.... It would be a mistake, however, to infer from this shift in discourse the substance of sociocultural change (as opposed to its interpretation) had radically changed. At best it may have slowed down; more important, by 1700 it was a much more familiar and thus less noteworthy phenomenon.[13]

This puts more elegantly as well as more accurately than I did in 1991 the situation which prevailed in the half-century after Wen Zhenheng starved himself to death on the Manchu conquest of Suzhou in 1645. The text as published comes dangerously close to seeing the Qing period as some sort of 'step back' from a fluid and socially mobile late Ming, and the reader should consequently be on guard against any such sub-text. Recent monographs by Ginger Cheng-chi Hsü and Tobie Meyer-Fong have deepened understanding of the Qing context of luxury consumption in another city of the empire, Yangzhou, and reduced still further the plausibility of a loss of interest in such matters on the part of elites.[14]

In revisiting an earlier publication, one becomes very aware of what has been missed. These can be specific pieces of bibliography, as for example Chuang Shen's important 1970 article on Ming antiquarianism, a reading of which would have benefited the analysis in Chapter 4.[15] Or they can be more substantive issues of methodology. The single most important of this latter category is probably the work of Roger Chartier, whom I had not yet read at the time of writing this book. Chartier's attempt to 'close the false debate between the objectivity of structures and the subjectivity of representations' seems to take us a step, and a relevant step, forward.[16] So too does his central idea of 'appropriation', and his insistence that it is wrong to see intellectual or cultural divisions as following social boundaries, as scholarship in the Marxian tradition (including Bourdieu) would tend to do more or less mechanically.[17] It is probably a fair criticism of this book that it is unaware of the extent to which its two major points of reference, Bourdieu and Foucault, are ultimately incompatible with each other in their purest form. Perhaps a more nuanced body of work such as that of Chartier might point a way out of this dilemma. I feel this to be the case, even if my more recent work has made me wary of the term 'representation' as one too heavily indebted to its Platonic roots to be safely deployed in regard to images and texts within China.

Another major criticism concerns the historical object reified in this book's title as 'Early Modern China'. In an important polemic published electronically, the Danish scholar Søren Clausen has identified the problems inherent in this formulation, which I have now been guilty of foisting on the reader twice. He shows how the term 'early modern' China exists only by virtue of its relationship to the less threatening 'late imperial' China, as the 'glass-half-full/glass-half-empty' pairing of historiographical enquiry, and remarks of *Superfluous Things* that the 'basic structure of its argument' involves 'the idea of an internally-produced "early modern" trajectory of change in China that was somehow interrupted, perhaps due to the particularities of the Qing dynasty and the circumstances of its victory.'[18] He observes of *Pictures and Visuality in Early Modern China* that, *pace* its title, 'the analysis there has in fact parted ways with the EMC historiographical strategy', the term there being used more as a 'provocation' than a description.[19] This is a shrewd analysis, and its critique is on target; writing in 2003 I would like to think I would probably now be sensitive enough to the historiographic traps lurking under the surface of 'early modern China' not to use the term so casually. I would however wish to stick to its value as a provocation, or rather as a conscious move within a micro-politics of scholarly publishing, reading and reviewing practices. Books entitled '. . . in Ming China' will be received in a wholly different way from those which attempt, however crudely, to gate-crash the celebration of European exceptionalism which too often still passes for global history.[20] By putting *Superfluous Things: Material Culture and Social Status in Early Modern China* back into circulation, with its anachronistic title unaltered, the University of Hawai'i Press has made it possible for the arguments around its validity to go on for a new body of readers.

Craig Clunas
London,
December 2003

Notes

1   Craig Clunas, 'Review Essay—Modernity Global and Local: Consumption and the Rise of the West', *American Historical Review* 104.5 (1999), pp. 1497– 1511.
2   See, for example, the special issue of *Asia Major,* third series, 12.1 (1999), on 'the visual dimensions of Chinese culture'.
3   John Meskill, *Gentlemanly Interests and Wealth on the Yangtze Delta,* Association for Asian Studies Monograph and Occasional Paper Series, no. 49 (Ann Arbor, 1994), p. 5.
4   James Cahill, *The Painter's Practice: How Artists Lived and Worked in Traditional China* (New York, 1994).
5   Timothy Brook, *The Confusions of Pleasure: Commerce and Culture in Ming China* (Berkeley and Los Angeles, 1998).
6   Richard Von Glahn, *Fountain of Fortune: Money and Monetary Policy in China, 1000-1700* (Berkeley and Los Angeles, 1996); Kenneth Pomeranz, *The Great Divergence: China, Europe, and the Making of the Modern World Economy* (Princeton, 2000).
7   Dorothy Ko, *Teachers of the Inner Chambers: Women and Culture in Seventeenth-Century China* (Stanford, 1994); Wai-yee Li, 'The Collector, the Connoisseur and Late Ming Sensibility' *T'oung Pao* 81 (1995), pp. 269–302; Francesca Bray, *Technology and Gender: Fabrics of Power in Late Imperial China* (Berkeley and Los Angeles, 1997).
8   Jeremy Lane, *Pierre Bourdieu: A Critical Introduction* (London, 2000).
9   Jonathan Hay, *Shitao: Painting and Modernity in Early Qing China* (Cambridge, 2001).
10 Ankeney Weitz, 'Notes on the Early Yuan Antique Art Market in Hangzhou', *Ars Orientalis* 27 (1997), pp. 27–38.
11 Kathlyn Liscomb, 'A Collection of Painting and Calligraphy Discovered in the Inner Coffin of Wang Zhen (d. 1495 C.E.), *Archives of Asian Art* 47 (1994), pp. 6–32; 'Social Status and Art Collecting: The Collections of Shen Zhou and Wang Zhen', *Art Bulletin* 78.1 (1996), pp. 111-135.
12 Craig Clunas, *Elegant Debts: The Social Art of Wen Zhengming(1470–1559)* (London and Honolulu, 2004).
13 Hay, *Shitao,* p. 339; see also my review of this monograph in *Art Bulletin* 84.4 (2002), pp. 686–688.
14 Ginger Cheng-chi Hsü, *A Bushel of Pearls: Painting for Sale in Eighteenth-Century Yangchow* (Stanford, 2001); Tobie Meyer-Fong, *Building Culture in Early Qing Yangzhou* (Stanford, 2003).
15 Chuang Shen, 'Ming Antiquarianism, an Aesthetic Approach to Archaeology', *Journal of Oriental Studies* 8.1 (1970), pp. 63-78. I am grateful to Christer von der Burg for bringing this to my attention.

16 Roger Chartier, *Cultural History: Between Practices and Representations*, trans. Lydia B. Cochrane (Cambridge, 1988).
17 Chartier, *Cultural History*, p. 30.
18 Søren Clausen, '"Early Modern China": A Preliminary Postmortem', http://www.hum.au.dk/ckulturf/pages/publications/sc/china.pdf, p. 20 (accessed 19 December 2003).
19 Clausen, "Early Modern China", p. 22.
20 J. M. Blaut, *Eight Eurocentric Historians*, vol.2, *The Colonizer's View of the World* (New York and London, 2000).

Introduction

This is not simply a book about things. It is about some of the ways of looking at things in the China of the latter part of the Ming dynasty (1368-1644). It does, however, have its origins in the experience of working with surviving material objects, as a curator in the Far Eastern Department of the Victoria and Albert Museum. It was in the course of work on these objects that I first encountered what I initially interpreted as a literature of connoisseurship produced in the late sixteenth and early seventeenth centuries, the texts of which form the central source material of this book. The very close 'fit' between artefacts coming down to us from the period and the precise descriptions of them in these texts, which are often elegantly phrased but never willfully obscure, was very attractive. So attractive, in fact, that it initially acted to obscure the broader implications of the creation of a specialized discourse of objects in the late Ming. These texts, with names like *Eight Discourses on the Art of Living* or *Treatise on Superfluous Things*, have too often been read to shed light on those objects which do survive, principally paintings but also ceramics, jade carvings, pieces of metalwork, etc., and not enough regarded in their coverage of more perishable aspects of material culture. They have been generally used within the framework of the positivism which has continued to be identified as one of the chief weaknesses in museum presentations of the past.

However, 'things' have recently been judged to be too important to be left to curators and have increasingly attracted the attention of scholars working from within the broader disciplines of history and anthropology. The work of Mary Douglas and Baron Isherwood, particularly their *The World of Goods*, introduced to a wide audience the concept of a system of goods as a symbolic language, a way of sending and receiving messages about society and about an individual's place within it. Seeking to explain the growth of capitalism and a modern world-view, Chandra Mukerji's, *From Graven Images* has also made broad claims for the role which is to be allotted to material culture. She has written: 'Objects are carriers of ideas . . . [they] help to make autonomous forces out of ideas by remaining in the physical world long after their production . . . That it can be *both* a physical and symbolic constraint gives material culture a particular power over human action.'[1] Focusing on particular historical circumstances, Richard Goldthwaite's concept of an 'empire of things' in Renaissance Florence relates new patterns of consumption to a way of generating new and more complex social identities and posits for this period some of the nascent habits of consumerism which underpin the modern world-view. Simon Schama has brought some of the same ideas to bear on the Netherlands of the 'Golden Age', with an interpretation which again makes the relationship of consumers to the objects of consumption a moving force in broad patterns of change.[2]

Mukerji, Goldthwaite and Schama's ideas about the role of material culture as instrument as well as symptom of social change touch some of the same points as the American literature of material culture studies, a burgeoning discipline whose leading lights have been scholars like Jules Prown and Henry Glassie and which has had considerable influence over current curatorial practice in the United States and in Britain. The introduction to a recent anthology of these writings explicitly derives the greater degree of concern now felt by historians for 'material life' from the work of Fernand Braudel.[3] A weakness which a number of critics have identified in this school, however, is its tendency to see the meanings which are ascribed to items of material culture as being unambiguously fixed once and for all at the moment of production. More recently, the ideas of Arjun Appadurai and Igor Kopytoff have seemed to offer a solution to the historically divorced discourses of material culture (the province of the curator or archaeologist) and its 'context' (the province of the historian). Arjun Appadurai has written: 'even though from a *theoretical* point of view human actors encode things with significance, from a *methodological* point of view it is the things-in-motion that illuminate their social and human context.'[4] At the same time the justly controversial work of Pierre Bourdieu, for all its theoretical sophistication and methodological rigour, has underlined the importance of paying close attention to the precise forms of cultural practice within a given situation. They are not arbitrary choices.

So far, most of the theoretical work done on the 'consumption question' has rested on the empirical basis of historical investigation of the European and American traditions. This book, therefore, has two aims. One is to make historians of China consider more seriously the claims of the discourse of material culture upon their attention. Every member of the Ming elite made consumption choices, for example about clothes or about furniture, and it must, therefore, be a matter of legitimate concern to attempt to discover what conditioned these choices. The second aim is to draw the attention of those who work on the Western tradition to the existence of the Chinese world of goods, with its sometimes striking prefigurations of and parallels with early modern Europe. This needs to be done before the 'birth of a consumer society' becomes set as a new explanation for the 'Rise of the West'.

I encountered the literature on the consumption question in the West through teaching students on an MA course in the history of design, offered jointly by the Victoria and Albert Museum and the Royal College of Art. The course director, Charles Saumarez Smith and his students have been among my best teachers. One of the aims of this project was to see the extent to which the insights of design history (which typically takes the mid-nineteenth century as its point of departure) had validity for the very large body of pre-modern made goods which typically now comprise the collections of museums like the Victoria and Albert, as well as being the objects of discourses of connoisseurship centred around the art market. The claims of the 'new art history' to provide a form of access to this body of material were also worked through with students over a number of years, though here results were less satisfying, largely because, despite claims to reject the whole notion of an established canon, the majority of recent work remains centred on the same types of artistic practice as does the work it seeks to supplant. I have, therefore, sought in this book to find ways of talking about the deployment of luxury objects in late Ming China which were equally valid for categories like painting, with a highly self-conscious aesthetic of their own, and for clothing, where no such coherent framework of ideas exists ready made in the Chinese sources.

It was the V&A/RCA course, too, which brought into the Museum historians working on early modern Europe like Peter Burke, Lorna Weatherhill, Margaret Spufford, Keith Thomas and Peter Earle, with their most recent work on the compelling issues of luxury consumption and the social strategies involving the manipulation of luxury goods, art (however categorized) not excluded.[5] Their work seemed to hold out the possibility of better ways of understanding

Chinese goods in their full and original meaning, through the use of a comparative and methodologically informed framework. In particular, Peter Burke's brief account of the condition of seventeenth-century Japan, in his larger study of Renaissance Italian culture and society[6] seemed to demand a return of the compliment, through a comparative perspective on the China of the late Ming. I hope particularly that in my use of comparative material from early modern Europe I have not traduced the work of those historians on whose efforts I am wholly dependent and that I may be judged to have put something back into their enterprise through the provision of some material previously only available in Chinese.

The concept of an 'early modern period', from about 1500 to 1800, is a familiar one to historians of the West but is a less comfortable concept when applied to China. I am encouraged to make use of it by the example of the innovative Chinese historian Zhu Weizheng, whose book, *Zouchu zhong shiji*, *Coming Out of the Middle Ages* (introduced to me by Tim Brook), posits just such a turning point in the late Ming – early Qing.[7] It seems to offer a more fruitful way of looking at the period than does the now-hackneyed 'sprouts of capitalism' controversy, initiated in China in the 1950s, which subjected a limited body of evidence on historical changes in the relations of production during the sixteenth and seventeenth centuries to intense scrutiny, searching for signs of autochthonous roots for Chinese capitalism and confirmation of Marx's iron laws of history. The material which was recovered about the growth of a commodity economy, of a market for labour and about changes in a limited number of industries involved in processing agricultural raw materials was of great value, but of controversial significance. The same quotations were interpreted in diametrically opposed ways, and the same phenomena observable in the late Ming were searched for and found in periods as far back as the eleventh century, or even earlier.[8] The present study attempts to say something of relevance on this question, if only by taking attention away from the question of production and focusing it more firmly on consumption. I am well aware that this has become a 'fashionable' subject of historical enquiry but am at the same time convinced that it is an approach which can yield a fresh understanding of the period, if only because it is better documented and better articulated within the sources as a matter of concern to the literate elite of Chinese society.

I have not attempted a history of the late Ming empire, a political unit of broadly similar size to Europe with 150–175 million inhabitants in about 1600. It was roughly the same size in terms of conceptual geography, too, the speed of travel from the north to the south

being broadly equal to that from Venice to London. The secondary
materials for a study of China in this period which are available in
English are now comparatively rich and present no conceptual
problems to those coming fresh to the subject, who want to know
more.[9] There is also a considerable body of other synthesizing literature to which I am indebted, most of it of fairly recent production,
as the late Ming dynasty has shaken off its historically bad press as
an age of stagnation and decline.

The long reign of the Wanli emperor (1573–1620), during which
much of the source material of this book was composed, may have
been an age of increasing sclerosis in the heart of the bureaucracy,
but it was also one which saw the first integration of China into a
developing world economy and the consolidation of the kind of rural
order under which a quarter of the world's population were to exist
until within living memory. That rural order stemmed from a surge
in population, coupled with a decline in the size of the average
landholding which resulted from the eschewal of the principle
of primogeniture in the countryside. Not only were agricultural
products turned into commercial commodities on an unprecedented
scale, but there was a commercialization of state revenues, as both
taxation in kind and labour services were commuted to payment in
silver.

There was an expansion in the size of existing towns and the foundation of new towns, which created prosperous urban units whose
commercial importance as marketing centres was well out of proportion to their insignificance on the administrative map, which remained
static. The growth in size and complexity of the Chinese marketing
network at both a national and regional level was similarly not
matched by any 'rise of the merchants', since there was no guarantee
of prosperity for the individual entrepreneur and certainly no way of
translating commercial strength into political influence. That remained
firmly in the hands of the theoretical meritocracy of the officials,
sanctified by the award of degrees in the imperial examination system.
Under their control, the centralized imperial state took no part in
stimulating any 'modern' type of commercial activity and only an
intermittent part in exploiting it.

This book, as I have said, is deliberately not aimed solely at
sinologists. I have, therefore, tried whenever possible to underpin my
argument with work in western languages, allowing its validity to be
tested by the reader, and I am in the debt of the numerous specialists
on late imperial China whose writings are detailed in the bibliography
of secondary literature. A major weakness of which I am well aware
is that I have approached the work of Japanese sinologists only at

second hand, through its reflection in European languages. I have tried to limit the number of citations and keep them as simple as possible. All translations from Ming and Qing sources are my own, except where otherwise specified. In the latter case, I have standardized romanizations to the *pinyin* system for the sake of consistency, something for which I ask the forgiveness of other translators. In my own translations, I have silently altered the use of *hao*, *zi* or studio names to the principal *ming* by which a person is listed in the *Dictionary of Ming Biography* (cited as DMB) or other biographical sources, and I have standardized the literary names of cities, provinces and regions to those now obtaining on generally available atlases. This has been done to ease the path of the reader who is unused to these Chinese literary conventions, in the interests of establishing a better dialogue between specialists in different fields. The quantity of unfamiliar names is still daunting enough, and I have tried to give a biographical reference on the first appearance of any figure. Where possible, this is to DMB, and where it is not, a reference is given to the larger but less detailed Chinese language biographical dictionary *Ming ren zhuan ji ziliao suoyin* (cited as MRZJ). It is worth reminding the reader that in Chinese the family name comes first, to be followed by the personal name. *Wen* Zhenheng was a great-grandson of *Wen* Zhengming.

As well as the authors listed in the bibliography, I have benefitted from many general and specific pieces of aid. A British Academy/Chinese Academy of Social Sciences Exchange Scholarship in 1986 enabled me to study rare editions of the central texts in Chinese libraries, and I am grateful to the staff of the Institute of Literature, CASS (in particular its librarian Jiang Guangtian), the Suzhou Municipal Library, the Nanjing University Library and Nanjing Municipal Library. During that trip Professor Xu Shuofang of Hangzhou University discussed some of the issues withe me and helped me through the biography of Gao Lian's father, later sending me a punctuated transcription. I have been helped, too, by the staffs of the British Library's Oriental Collections and of the National Art Library. Peter Burke introduced me to Sabba di Castiglione and also to the importance of studying aesthetic terminology. Rose Kerr, Curator of the Far Eastern Collection, made the production of this book possible at the V&A through her generous and understanding management of my time as a member of her staff, as well as with many specific pieces of advice on Ming objects. Malcolm Baker, Tim Brook, Rupert Faulkner, Derek Gillman, Paul Greenhalgh, Andrew Lo, David Lowenthal (at whose seminar on 'The Uses of the Past' I first tried out the ideas in Chapter 4), Joseph McDermott, Liz Miller,

Charles Saumarez Smith, Jessica Rawson and Verity Wilson have all helped and encouraged me in a number of ways. Without them there would be more mistakes and misinterpretations than survive in the text, in spite of them. The broad outlines of Chapter 6 were presented as the Arts Club Annual Lecture at the V&A Museum in 1989.

1

Books about things

The literature of Ming connoisseurship

It is the central thesis of this book that the period of Chinese history from the middle of the sixteenth century to the fall of the Ming dynasty in 1644 was one in which the relationship between the manufactured things of the material world and the social order favoured by the power-holding elite was of particular concern to them. The placing of this concern in the foreground of public debate within this elite was achieved partly through the actual practices of social interaction (through the clothes they wore, the gifts they gave and the vessels they chose to use at table) but also partly through the production of texts which were published, sold and circulated through the literate minority of society. Although writing about *things* was in no sense an innovation of the late Ming period, the greatly increased quantity of material being put into circulation, either as new work or as reprints of earlier writings, was unprecedented and points to a heightened awareness of the production and consumption of luxury goods as an arena for potential social conflict, if not correctly handled.

These texts have been mined by collectors and dealers within the Chinese art market almost since their production. In recent years they have provided some of the underpinning for the commercial strategy within the Western art market for Chinese antiques whereby 'scholar's taste' can be invoked to broaden the canon of marketable goods beyond the traditionally dominant area of Chinese ceramics. Western curators have also in recent years used these texts not just to provide identifications of individual objects or classes of objects within museum collections but to provide the 'background' or 'context' currently required to legitimize the museum's self-definition as an essentially 'academic' project, contrasted with that of the market-place. The present author came across the texts discussed below, like

Treatise on Superfluous Things or *Eight Discourses on the Art of Living*, while engaged in this sort of work and could equally be accused of using their contents in this simplistic way, as if they 'told us what things were like'. They have been little studied as texts in their own right, as consciously constructed attempts to reduce the confusion of the Ming world of goods to order. When studied at all, they have been excerpted and truncated in ways which give undue prominence to our present concerns and gloss over those parts, in some cases the majority of the text, which fail to answer immediate needs. For example, the connoisseurship of swords is prominent in these texts, but since swords have no place in the art market or in the standard museum presentations of Chinese culture, this material is simply elided.

The first Western scholar to get to grips with this body of material was, typically, the great Dutch sinologist Robert van Gulik, whose comments are still worth quoting extensively:

> Copious material relating to Chinese connoisseurship . . . can be extracted from books of a special genre, viz. compilations meant as guide-books for the scholar of elegant taste. Such books describe the interior in which the refined lover of art and literature likes to live. They deal with the furniture of his library, the brushes and paper, ink and incense he prefers, the art treasures he likes to contemplate and the books he likes to read . . .

He identifies as the founding text of the genre the *Dong tian qing lu ji, Record of the Pure Registers of the Cavern Heaven*, written in the first half of the thirteenth century by Zhao Xigu (1170–1242). As Zhao's work set much of the pattern for the much larger number of texts of this type which would be published in the period covered by this book, it is worth looking at its contents and the kinds of topics it covers. There are ten sections, covering antique *qin* zithers, antique inkstones, antique bronze vessels, curious rocks, table screens, brush rests, water vessels for the desk, antique manuscripts and calligraphy, antique and modern rubbings of stone inscriptions, and antique paintings. The mix of antique and contemporary items is what sets Zhao's *Record* apart from the larger number of purely antiquarian texts being produced at the same time (some of which are discussed below in Chapter 4), as does the sense that these are objects for possessing. Van Gulik goes on:

> The genre continued to be popular till the end of the Ming dynasty, thereafter interest in the subject declined . . . The men who

compiled these handbooks borrowed freely from each other, quoting *verbatim* entire passages. Since such passages are as a rule not marked, one can locate them only by a careful comparison of the texts preserved. This labour is often rewarded. Usually a writer who incorporated a statement made by one of his predecessors in the field would make slight changes in the wording so as to make the passage agree with his own argument. Thus a comparison of the various versions of a statement on some aesthetic principle will bring to light controversial points that would otherwise remain unnoticed.[1]

Van Gulik's point about the Ming as a high point of this kind of writing is even more strongly taken when it is remembered that his earliest Song dynasty example was in fact only first published in the late Ming (having previously circulated in manuscript), in an encyclopedic collection of texts printed somewhere between 1607 and 1620, the *Shuo fu, Tales Within a City Wall*.

Tales Within a City Wall is a *congshu*, 'collected writings' or 'collectanea', a form of literary artefact with its origins in the late twelfth century, common in China from the Ming period, though rarer in the Western tradition.[2] In the absence of any sort of legal protection for intellectual property, and in the context of a flourishing and commercially organized publishing industry, it was standard practice to issue large, multi-volume sets of writings by different authors, gathering together a number of texts connected by some common denominator, be it subject matter, geographical proximity of the authors involved, or some other criterion. Many *congshu* were simply reissues in a uniform format of a number of rare printed or manuscript items in the library of a given bibliophile, and it is this aim of scholarly preservation which has usually been seen as the main point of the enterprise.[3] However, the profit motive was behind at least as many Ming *congshu*. It was the same motive which led to the frequent 'piracy' and retitling of constituent texts from one *congshu* to another and to the association of the names of nationally or locally known cultural leaders with these texts, in an attempt to increase their saleability.

All these factors mean that the question, 'What is a book?', is a difficult one to answer in the late Ming context. The major traditional bibliography of *congshu*[4] often vastly overestimates a writer's oeuvre by the simple device of listing all of his works as they appear in the contents pages of these numerous collectanea, without making it clear that these may be just chapters or sections of larger, integral works dismembered and republished as if they were independent texts. Very few books, and certainly very few books on the arts, have been transmitted from the Ming to the present as integral wholes, without undergoing incorporation or disintegration in the *congshu* format at some stage in their biographies. Not to have done so at all, or to have done so only rarely, is in some sense an index of a work's rare and peripheral status to the generality of discourse on these subjects.

This is, for example, the case with the only Ming work on the connoisseurship of artefacts to have been subjected to anything like a full critical study, though it is a study dominated by a search for the 'purest' early text, rather than by a concern for the degree of influence this text may have enjoyed through republication. This is the *Ge gu yao lun*, *Essential Criteria of Antiquities* by Cao Zhao, an author from the lower Yangtze city of Songjiang. The book was first published as an integral work in Nanjing in 1388, during the very first years of the Ming dynasty. The full translation, with critical and bibliographical study, of this work by Sir Percival David is well known and supplies the material for the following discussion.[5] Its availability in English makes it by far the best known piece of Ming connoisseurship literature in the art market and in Western museums. David's concerns were essentially those of the object-centred connoisseur and collector, seeking in the written record for confirmation or contradiction of views held about surviving pieces.

As its name would suggest, the *Essential Criteria* takes little cognizance of contemporary material culture and is largely occupied with valued products of earlier periods. It opens with a study of archaic bronzes, proceeds through 'ancient painting', calligraphy, rubbings of calligraphy (the largest single section by a long way), ancient *qin* zithers, ancient inkstones, precious objects (largely natural curiosities but also including worked jades), metals, ancient porcelain, ancient lacquer, textiles, rare woods and rare stones. It then acts as a minor sort of *congshu* in its own right, reprinting a number of short texts of antiquarian interest from the Song dynasty (960–1279), before concluding with 'studio objects' and various detailed studies of early imperial patents, seals, tallies and other impedimenta of imperial government.

In a number of ways, the *Essential Criteria of Antiquities* sets a pattern which is to be replicated in a number of later texts. Firstly, it shows a concern with 'authenticity' (*zhen*) as the major value of the enterprise of connoisseurship, over more overtly aesthetic values. The author's preface makes this plain.

> Whenever I came upon an object [of interest], I would search
> through all the books and illustrated catalogues [at my disposal] in

order to trace its origin, evaluate its quality and determine its authenticity before I laid it aside . . . There are certainly some among the younger gentle-folk of today who are interested in this lofty pursuit; but unfortunately, despite a genuine love for such things, these people lack discernment.[6]

Another topos in this kind of literature is the author's self-presentation as a person of detachment and indifference to worldly affairs, keen only to save the well-meaning from falling into error. Given the almost total lack of independent biographical material on Cao Zhao himself, we are at liberty to posit this as the donning of a familiar and acceptable cultural role, rather than unvarnished fact. What we know of his social status is largely negative; he is not recorded as a bureaucratic degree holder, the major formal distinction of status in Ming China, nor does he have any other recorded writings to his credit. His position as a member of the cultural elite can be inferred, but we are not in a position to say anything about his economic or political status. And to award him the title 'scholar' loosely is to extend this term to mean simply, 'literate person', an unacceptable degree of imprecision.

Thirdly, there is throughout an anxiety about forgery, inauthenticity and fraud which suggests that as early as the fourteenth century, at least in the most commercially developed parts of the empire, all the major types of luxury commodity which presented themselves through the market-place were potentially unreliable. Hence, the social message about their owners which these objects might be expected to carry was potentially unreliable, too. Thus, the texts offer the justification for their own existence in the necessity for searching out reliable information on which to make judgements about things. There are parallels here with what the American anthropologist Clifford Geertz has identified as the 'bazaar-style' economy, where accurate commercial information is hard to find and where those who wield it possess considerable power and prestige. Such a fixation on the search for reliable information is typical of any situation where the quality and correct financial value of goods is not standardized, precisely the sort of situation which pertains in any market for antiques, or where non-intrinsic criteria like 'fashionability' govern the major part of the value of goods.[7] What is distinctive about China, however, is *not* that there was an uneven distribution of knowledge about how to deploy consumption to achieve social ends. Such knowledge exists in all societies and is unevenly distributed in all cases showing social stratification. The Chinese distinctiveness lies in the very early reduction of this type of knowledge to a commodity, published in a book and hence available in the market-place to any player wanting to enter the search for ways of transforming economic power into cultural power.

Despite being a clear forerunner of much later work, the *Essential Criteria of Antiquities* of 1388 generated few immediate successors, although it was significantly expanded in a republication of 1459. The *Gu qi qi lu, Record of Curious Ancient Vessels*, written in 1508 by Lu Shen (1477–1544; DMB, 999–1003), appears in bibliographies as if it were a work of the same precisely documented type, but it is rather a collection of miracle tales about extraordinary happenings associated with numinous ancient objects, a genre with a long history. David has located five Ming texts which note or cite Cao Zhao's *Essential Criteria*, but three of these are bibliographies and do not support his conclusion, for the Ming period at least, that 'the frequency with which KKYL [*Essential Criteria*] has been referred to should be sufficient to show its value'.[8] However, it remained in print as an active player in the decades of most intensive attention to writing on this sort of subject, those between about 1590 and 1630, a more detailed look at which forms the body of this chapter. Appearing as an integral text in the middle of the sixteenth century, in a *congshu* of 1596, and twice again on its own in about 1600 (making four republications in fifty years), it formed part of an explosion of publishing interest in the fields of what might loosely be called luxury consumption, encompassing not just high-status and high-value works like painting, calligraphy and early bronzes, but also a whole range of contemporary products necessary to the presentation of self in elite life.

No less enigmatic, if rather better documented than Cao Zhao, is the author of a work which in its history subsequent to its first publication in 1591 exemplifies the shifting and unstable nature of the Ming text, and also the shifting and unstable nature of the Ming authorial persona, as viewed through the traditional bibliographical apparatus and its development in modern sinological practice. The book in question is called *Zun sheng ba jian, Eight Discourses on the Art of Living*, and it was written by a man called Gao Lian, whose problematic social status and personal/cultural connections provide a microcosm of the very complex context for Ming writing on cultural topics. To put it at its crudest, Gao Lian's authorial persona has disintegrated over the centuries into its constituent parts, even as his writings have been dissected, retitled and incorporated into different published settings. To reintegrate him into the whole person seen by his contemporaries is not an easy task, but one of considerable importance.

Once again it is easiest to begin with negatives. Gao Lian held no
degree and, hence, no place within the political power structure. We
do know that he was a resident of Hangzhou, living on the shores of
the fashionable West Lake, probably the leading focus of elite tourism
in the whole of China at this period. The only clear dates associated
with his life are 1581, when a collection of verse appeared in his name,
1590, when (according to the preface by an otherwise unknown Taoist
priest named Li Shiying) he completed the manuscript of *Eight Discourses*, and 1591, when it was published. The evidence of the prefaces
is that he was still alive at the time of publication, and the form of
titling of the book, as *Ya shang zhai zun sheng ba jian, Eight Discourses on the Art of Living from the Studio where Elegance is
Valued*, using the name given to a studio within his own residence,
suggests that, as was not uncommon at this period, the publication
was undertaken at his own expense and possibly by itinerant block-
carvers and printers working in his own home and under his direct
supervision. We know a little about Gao's family background from
the tomb inscription which he caused to be written for his deceased
father Gao Jigong, choosing to employ one of the most prestigious
writers and cultural figures available, Wang Daokun (1525–1593;
DMB, 1427–30).

It is Wang's fame as a writer which has ensured the survival of this
conventional eulogy, incorporated into his collected works,[9] rather
than the prominence of the subject. This very fame was by the late
Ming a type of commodity, as Wang made his living after the aban-
donment of his political career by writing to order such 'epitaphs,
birthday notes, poems and prose for others, particularly for merchants'. He was, literally, the best that money could buy, though
clearly in a context where the financial element of the transaction had
to be masked by the forms of elite civility and reciprocal services
between friends and equals. The text makes explicit the fact that Wang
Daokun was a client of the Gao family and lived with them over a
possibly extended period. It would, however, be very unwise to posit
a relationship of close personal friendship between Wang Daokun and
Gao Lian, his patron of the moment, on the basis of what may well
have been a very standard type of arrangement.

The epitaph which Wang provided gives Gao Lian's father an
impressive but unprovable line of descent of great antiquity, as the
descendant in the fifteenth generation of a sixth-century empress,
whose family had taken up residence in Hangzhou at some unspecified
time in the distant past. He became extremely wealthy through the
lucrative trade in supplying grain to the state and was esteemed by the
relevant high officials for his probity and reliability. Following the

birth of Gao Lian, his only son, to a concubine, he began to take an interest in the appurtenances of elite culture, acquiring a library and forming a collection of antique bronze vessels. His son was 'broadly learned and rich in knowledge, consorting with a multitude of famous gentlemen'. However, an attempt to convert the family's economic position into political power failed when Gao Lian was unsuccessful in the examination system. His father then set him up with a primary wife, named Miss Zhang, and a secondary wife also called Miss Zhang (though written with a different character) and died leaving him a considerable fortune and a quantity of conventional exhortations.

On the basis of this fairly standard eulogy, we can make one characterization of Gao Lian as a rich merchant, with a sufficient degree of cultural tastes and accomplishments to make him presentable to the cultural elite, and someone whose family had a reputation as liberal patrons. It is, however, very difficult to quantify Gao Lian's degree of cultural involvement in elite activities, other than on the basis of the evidence he himself presents. Some arguments can be advanced *ex silentio*. Gao did not himself paint, or at least has left no recorded works of painting or calligraphy from his hand. This is not of itself that surprising. Although histories of Chinese art sometimes succeed in giving the impression that facility with the brush was the birthright of everyone above a certain social level, even the most cursory mapping of collections of artists' biographies onto the names of the top level of the cultural/political elite of a given year, categorized as those three hundred individuals passing the highest level of the examination system, shows that a more than family-based reputation for artistic achievement was in fact quite rare.

Perhaps more surprising is the fact that seals or colophons by Gao, which would record his ownership of or at least exposure to these works, do not appear on recorded works of art, with one exception. There can be no sense here that his social position as a merchant debarred him from participation in the quintessential elite pastime of art collecting and appreciation, since not only had all social, as opposed to economic, barriers to owning pictures dissolved by the sixteenth century, but some of the most important connoisseurs of the day were from a background in trade. And, indeed, Gao's own writings on painting suggest an acquaintance with, and a history of ownership of, a number of significant works and a familiarity with most of the objects deemed worthy of attention in Ming art-historical discourse. The most prominent example of the merchant as collector is Gao's possibly rather older contemporary Xiang Yuanbian (1525–1590; DMB, 539–44), whose collecting was financed by a lucrative chain of pawnshops; yet he was on terms of social ease with members of the landholding classes and owned a number of the most important early samples of painting and calligraphy to have survived to his day.

The sole recorded work to carry evidence of its having been in Gao Lian's collection does not, by contrast, appear to have been in any way an important or distinguished painting, a large hanging scroll showing the conventional subject-matter of two herd boys and a water buffalo. Nor are Gao's comments in the colophon, in which he uses the jokey 'Master Gao states . . .' formula discussed below, anything other than banal and conventional.[10] There is another glimpse of Gao Lian in the role of art collector in the diary of Feng Mengzhen (1546–1605; DMB, 343), who enjoyed a distinguished official career before retiring to the West Lake at Hangzhou in 1597. He was closely connected to Gao Lian's client Tu Long (see below), by virtue of their both having obtained the highest level degree in the same year, 1577. This was a type of relationship particularly pregnant with meaning among the Ming scholar bureaucracy. He talks of a visit to Gao Lian in his home, and records that works of art were looked at, in the following terms (the date involved must be somewhere between 1599 and 1602):

On the seventh day of the second month, when the weather had just cleared up, I climbed Master Gao's tower to gaze upon the snow upon the mountains. My host produced a copy of the 'Wangchuan Villa' by Guo Zhongshu [910–977], and an 'Illustrations to the Odes of Lu and Shang' by Ma Hezhi [active twelfth century] to show me. Both were pieces I had been hoping to appreciate all my life, and my heart and eyes were both delighted to an unspeakable degree. When I left him, I made this note in recognition of a rare experience in connoisseurship.[11]

Feng's record of this encounter with Gao Lian as the owner of valuable early works of art tells us something about Gao's social role and the circles in which he moved, and it is of some use, too, as a testimonial to his aesthetic standards. Feng Mengzhen was not particularly renowned as a writer on painting. His own collected writings show that he only very rarely provided colophons for the work of others. However, his views can be given some weight by the fact that he owned at least two of the most important works of art in circulation in the Ming period. These were the painting, 'Rivers and Mountains after Snow', generally accepted at this date as being from the hand of Wang Wei (701–761), and a piece of calligraphy, the 'Clearing Weather after Sudden Snowfall Letter', believed to be among the most important surviving pieces by Wang Xizhi (303–361), who enjoyed unquestioned pre-eminence as the greatest calligrapher of all time.[12] Feng Mengzhen is also of significance to this account, as the second of these fabulous treasures, a concentrated package of wealth but also of cultural power in Ming terms, turns out to form a crucial link between the milieu of the merchant's son Gao Lian and the scion of the great landholding family Wen Zhenheng, author of *Treatise on Superfluous Things* and imitator of Gao's writings.

Histories of literature give us a different Gao Lian, again, from the possessor of a number of valuable works of art. Here, he has an abiding reputation as a poet and dramatist, responsible for more than one collection of verse and for two surviving dramas, one of which, *Yu zan ji, The Jade Hairpin*, is still in the repertoire to this day. In many ways a conventional romantic drama telling of the star-crossed love of the archetypal brilliant young scholar for a Taoist nun, it has been read in this century as a prefiguring of themes of social criticism in Chinese literature, 'one of the first open literary presentations of sexual mores and related social problems in the Ming'.[13] Contemporary theatrical criticism was relatively uncomplimentary about Gao Lian's talents, one writer placing him in the fifth out of six possible rankings, probably on the grounds that he was simply adapting an earlier work, and another grading him merely as 'lower middle'.[14] At the same time one of the few detailed studies of the audience for and reception of drama in the Ming period hints that *The Jade Hairpin* was a work of a kind 'presented in small market towns and at local fairs, performed by low-ranking troupes of itinerant actors' and viewed with extreme disfavour by the local and regional political authorities in their role as guardians of morality.[15]

A third Gao Lian can be constructed round an alternative set of concerns, and this is Gao Lian as one of 'a group of scholars, largely of Taoist inspiration, who sought no office and lived in seclusion, cultivating plants and writing about them in order to console the heart in bad times and nourish the spirit'.[16] Elsewhere in Joseph Needham's magisterial *Science and Civilisation in China*, the same man is variously an 'encyclopedic amateur', a 'Taoist naturalist' and a 'distinguished scholar, who lived in retirement and devoted himself to studying everything which could promote the health of mind and body'. Although this is in many ways as reductionist as the image of Gao Lian, 'the merchant' or 'the playwright', it does at least address him in the terms in which he chose to present himself in the prefaces to *Eight Discourses on the Art of Living* (or *Eight Disquisitions on Putting Oneself in Accord with the Life-Force* in Needham's typically more 'Taoist' version).

There is also evidence that the perception of the book at the time of its publication had at least as much to do with medical topics as with aesthetic. The edition of *Eight Discourses* now in the British Library carries the publisher's mark of the Zhongdetang, a book business established in the early sixteenth century by the Xiong family at the major publishing centre of Jianyang, Fujian province. The bibliographer Wang Zhongmin has demonstrated how this publisher specialized very much in medical books, in which it had an empire-wide reputation.[17] In much of what follows it is inevitable that Gao Lian will be presented to the reader as if his writings, and in some sense he himself, were 'about' the elements bearing on the study of material culture which they contain. The alternative of referring to 'the merchant – playwright – failed examination candidate – medical specialist – patron of writers – Taoist – connoisseur Gao Lian' is not attractive. The number of alternative personae which were simultaneously, not sequentially, in play must be born in mind for anything like a plausible assessment of the relationships between the personal status of the writer and the objects of his study to emerge.

As its title suggests, there are eight sections, of roughly equal size, which make up *Eight Discourses*. They are:

1 Discourse on sublime theories of pure self-cultivation;
2 Discourse on being in harmony with the four seasons;
3 Discourse on comfort on rising and resting;
4 Discourse on extending life and avoiding disease;
5 Discourse on food and drink;
6 Discourse on the pure enjoyment of cultured idleness;
7 Discourse on numinous and arcane elixirs and medicines;
8 Discourse on remote wanderings beyond the mundane.

Those areas of immediate concern, and which will be quoted and referred to elsewhere in this study, are largely drawn from Discourse 3, dealing with surroundings of contemporary manufacture (furniture, writing utensils, equipment for travelling and the whole of what we would call 'interior decoration'), and Discourse 6, covering the collection and connoisseurship of works of art, paintings and bronzes, but also lacquer and ceramics. Discourse 6 in particular has been quoted extensively since its publication, its comments frequently abstracted as *dicta* on a broad range of issues of connoisseurship.[18] If we allow the category of material culture to be extended to include areas like food and medicine (as it certainly should be), then it will be seen that the achievement of harmonization of self with the life-force *through things* was a central concern of the work, if not one explicitly stated.

The apparatus of prefaces in *Eight Discourses* is, in fact, more concerned with establishing the wider cosmic connections of the project and deliberately draws the reader away from the material world to an avowedly higher plane. The first preface is by Tu Long (1542–1605; DMB, 1324–7), like Wang Daokun a figure embodying cultural prestige at the highest national level and, like Wang too, a pensioner of the Gao family in Hangzhou. His approval serves, in effect, as a testimonial to the value of what follows, even if as an economic dependent of the author he cannot be viewed as a totally independent witness. A second preface is by an otherwise unknown Taoist priest, Li Shiying. He was perhaps attracted to the area by its associations with the Taoist patriarch Ge Hong (283–343), the scene of whose own enlightenment was very close to Gao Lian's home on the banks of the West Lake. Li relates his own spiritual autobiography and the steps by which he received a series of dream visions and instructions from luminaries of the Taoist faith, beginning in 1571 and ending with his meeting with Gao Lian in the autumn of 1590, when Gao showed him the manuscript of the *Eight Discourses*. He at once saw the larger cosmic significance of this work and gives a brief characterization of each of the eight constituent treatises in suitably macrocosmic terms. For example, the 'Discourse on the pure enjoyment of cultured idleness', 'roams at will among the hundred things, and thereby nurtures the heavenly harmony'. Gao's own preface is, as conventions demanded, similarly couched in the most general of terms and written in the most abstruse of language, a style far removed from the relatively prosaic writing found in the body of the text.

The various Dicourses all take the same format, with citations by early authorities on the subject under discussion quoted first, followed by the author's own views. These views are framed by an ironic rhetorical device which is quite startling in the Ming context,[19] the use of the formula *Gaozi yue*, 'Master Gao states . . .' to introduce each new topic. Here, there is a not very subtle parody of the diction of the Confucian classics, something which would have been unacceptable in any more rigorously 'high-cultural' context. It has an edge of self-mockery, as of one not caring whether he was taken completely seriously or not.

It is extremely difficult to make more than broad inferences about the popularity or degree of dissemination of a given text in the Ming period. A fortuitous piece of evidence from the eighteenth century suggests that in some cases the 'edition' of a work published by its author could be as little as 120 copies.[20] However, the fact that *Eight Discourses* was produced in at least three editions between 1591 and 1620 suggests that there was a ready market for the kind of material which it contained.[21] Any successful work would immediately be pirated and reissued by competing publishers, and there is no reason to think that was not the situation with these three editions. Following this spurt of publication there was to be no further edition until 1810.

However, another index of popularity is the reappearance of individual sections of the larger work, retitled as independent texts, within a number of *congshu* of the period. And importantly, the sections to receive this treatment were predominantly not those on Taoist techniques of exercise or meditation but those on material culture. Thus, a standard bibliography lists Gao Lian as the author of works devoted to inkstones, noodles, soups and the interior arrangement of a dwelling in the mountains, when, in fact, these are all elements of the *Eight Discourses* shorn of their original setting. Gao Lian, despite the shadowy circumstances of his own life, thus becomes in the late imperial period a very pervasive presence of a certain kind, the very model of the secluded scholar, disengaged from worldly affairs. Alexander Wylie, whose *Notes on Chinese Literature*, originally of 1867, still gives a very good impression of a sort of basic bibliography of work available in the nineteenth century, has Gao Lian as the author of 'a treatise on objects of vertu', 'a book of receipts for the manufacture of artificial perfume', 'a treatise on the distillation of spirits', 'a treatise on the Epidendrum', and a number of short works of culinary interest.[22] The macrocosmic claims, the great wealth derived from trade, even the popular if rather salacious drama have by now all been stripped away. It is the writer about things who has endured.

Something of the same process has affected the other writer to be considered in detail here. Wen Zhenheng (1585–1645), author of the *Treatise on Superfluous Things* (dated here to about 1615–20). He belonged to a different and much younger generation than Gao Lian and, in terms of social class and family background, was almost as distinguished as it was possible to be. It would be little exaggeration to say that the Wen family enjoyed greater personal prestige, at least in the Yangtze valley area, than did the imperial family in distant northern Peking itself. It was a prestige composed of a powerful mixture of ancient lineage, cultural achievements in the most esteemed fields, great wealth founded on the most socially acceptable form of riches, namely landholding, and the political leadership of the elite on the regional level. Wen Zhenheng was born to a massive inheritance of influence and a principal role in what might, on the model of early modern Britain, be called the 'Wen family interest', the network of relatives, friends and clients which formed the family's power base in its native city of Suzhou. The modern Chinese word *guanxi*, 'connections' sums up the continuing and pervasive role of this kind of personalized tie in Chinese society, more nebulous yet often more powerful than the formal ties of family or lineage. Wen's treatise on elite material cultural not only embodies the confidence which he owed to such a position, but also, by the network of other significant figures which it includes as 'honorary editors', it makes manifest the composition of this network of connections and reveals the degree to which participation in debates about taste and style was accepted as a legitimate form of elite activity.

Although the family traced a connection to a famous thirteenth-century patriot and prime minister, and beyond that to the hoary antiquity of the Han dynasty, its prominence in the Ming period can be seen as stemming from Wen Zhenheng's great-grandfather Wen Zhengming (1470–1559; DMB, 1471–4), who is now probably most famous as a painter and as the living embodiment of the amateur 'scholar gentleman' ideal in artistic production. In his own time, however, it was probably at least as much his poetry which made him famous, and it is likely to have been his writings which impelled the imperial court to offer him a post which he held on fairly desultory terms in the 1520s. Two out of his three sons were distinguished as artists, and artistic distinction continued to run in the family.[23] One of them, Wen Zhenheng's great-uncle, was given the task by the court of cataloguing the huge art collection of the disgraced Grand Secretary Yan Song when it was confiscated by the state on his fall from power in 1562. The next generation, that of Wen Zhenheng's father and uncles, was distinguished more for its participation in the exercise of political power at the regional and provincial levels, as the type of local officials who ensured the interpenetration of the landholding local elite and the power-wielding political elite.

With his own generation, the family made its first transition into political importance at the national level, in the person of his elder brother Wen Zhenmeng (1574–1636: DMB, 1467–71). Wen Zhenmeng's early career, passing at first place in the highest of the civil service examinations only at the tenth attempt, demonstrates the crucial necessity of a wealthy family background in the lengthy process of achieving examination success. This triumph was nearly blighted, however, by the ascendancy of a hostile political faction, led by the eunuch Wei Zhongxian, and he returned home in 1624, spending the next three years out of office. This was not to be his only period of retrenchment in the turbulent court politics of the late Ming, where he was identified as a leading member of the 'Restoration Society' faction, and he did not reach the highest ranks of the bureaucracy until the 1630s.[24] He enjoyed the supreme bureaucratic post of Grand Secretary for just three months in 1635, after his brother, younger than him by eleven years (almost a generation in a situation of very early marriages), had completed the *Treatise on Superfluous Things*. He was the owner of what is still among the most lovely of the celebrated gardens in his native city of Suzhou. Known in his day the 'Medicine Patch', it is preserved from the crowds by its site in the once fashionable but now less visited north-west quarter of the city, down narrow streets inaccessible to tourist buses.[25]

Wen Zhenheng, then stood from his birth in 1585 at the intersection of a number of nexuses of economic, cultural and political power. It was unlikely that any member of the regional or even national elite should not know who he was and what he represented, both in cultural politics and in terms of factional alignment. Both in painting and in poetry the tradition he embodied may have seemed a bit old-fashioned, newer trends having captured the aesthetic high ground, but the prestige was undimmed, as can be seen by the impressive array of authorities marshalled to give their imprimatur to his literary efforts and by the leading role he assumed in a major crisis of confrontation with the agents of imperial government in 1626. This was the mass demonstration of resistance staged by the population of Suzhou, led by its most prominent members, to attempts by the eunuch-controlled 'Eastern Depot' to seize an official, Zhou Shunchang, popularly held to be incorrupt and an active opponent of the moral dissoluteness of the dominant faction at court. In this unprecedented display of cross-class solidarity in the late Ming (which, nevertheless, did not prevent Zhou's arrest and subsequent execution) Wen Zhenheng assumed a spokesman's role, expressing the corporate grievances of the local elite to the agents of central power and later recording the event in written form.[26]

Wen Zhenheng never achieved formal political power through the examination system, though in later life he, like his great-grandfather, was given what may have been a largely ceremonial place in the central bureaucracy as a polisher of the literary style of documents. It is not impossible that his seeming non-participation in the competition for bureaucratic office reflected not so much an aesthetically founded distaste for the mundane affairs of the world as the deployment of a strategy for maintaining the power and prestige of the Wen line, whereby the eldest son ventured on the risky world of politics, while his younger brother nurtured the family base in Suzhou, at the heart of the network of landholding which underpinned their position.

Much of what we know about the detail of Wen Zhenheng's own life history comes from an account, valuable in that it stresses those parts of his activity which were most worthy of esteem in the eyes of his peer group, written shortly after his death in the sixth month of 1645, by his daughter's grandson, Gu Ling, at the request of his second son Wen Guo.[27] Indeed, the account opens with the dramatic circumstances of that death, a man of sixty fleeing from his native city to the shores of Lake Yangcheng to escape the armies of the invading Manchus and expiring there after several days of coughing blood. Later sources make it clear that Wen actually committed suicide by starvation, choosing as many of the elite did to die with the Ming dynasty. (Suzhou was not a particularly resolute centre of resistance, and the majority of the upper class surrendered eagerly to the Manchus, as protectors against a rising tide of violent peasant unrest aimed at themselves.)

Gu then recites the illustrious Wen family pedigree in great detail, before beginning with the facts of Wen Zhenheng's life – his birth in 1585, his precocity in literature and his early love of travel, both of the latter being to an extent formulaic in a young man of good family. In 1621 he was made a *zhusheng*, holder of the lowest rank of examination degree, and moved to the city of Nanjing, more of a political centre than Suzhou. The following year saw his brother's major examination triumph at the highest level, which he conspicuously failed to emulate in an unsuccessful attempt on the second level *juren* degree in 1624. We are told that he then abandoned thoughts of preferment, 'selected a troupe of singing girls, directed a group of musicians, and roamed among beautiful mountains and waters'. An allusion is made to his brother's fall from political power around this time and to an attempt to offer Wen Zhenheng a court position, which he declined.

It was only after his brother's death in 1636, and following the statutory year's mourning, that he was again nearly absorbed into the bureaucratic structure. Narrowly avoiding a posting to Longzhou, a town in Shaanxi province in the underdeveloped north-west, on account of his reputation as a *qin* zither player and calligrapher, he received a more congenial appointment in Peking, as a Secretariat Drafter.[28] However, the supposedly 'literary' scope of his duties did not preclude his involvement in factional politics, and he was actually imprisoned in 1640 as an associate of the disgraced Huang Daozhou (1585–1646: ECCP, 345–7), a key figure who had been closely involved with his late brother as an opponent of eunuch power around the emperor. In 1642, as peasant rebellion and Manchu incursion swelled and the Ming dynasty slithered towards collapse, Wen

Zhenheng received an attachment to one of the armies defending Peking but returned home on leave. He thus avoided (perhaps intentionally) one of the most notable military fiascos of the Ming dynasty's last agony, when the crucial fortress of Jizhou fell to the Manchus on 5 January 1643.[29]

He had intended to return to court in 1644, but on the nineteenth day of the third month (24 April in the Western calendar) the peasant rebel armies of Li Zicheng took the capital, the emperor hanged himself, and as Gu Ling puts it in a monumental understatement, 'matters turned out to be unusual'. The members of the official class in Suzhou turned to Wen as their natural leader, and he appeared once again to be facing active involvement in politics when a Ming dynasty prince was set up as emperor in Nanjing, summoned him to court and conferred the honorary title of 'Child Nurturess'[30] on his late mother, Madame Shi. At this critical point, 'those holding the reins of the state were old drinking and versifying companions' of his, but he significantly refused to involve himself in the faction-ridden hothouse of the doomed Southern Ming court, despite the prominent role in the Nanjing government of Huang Daozhou and other close associates of his late brother, and took no office, going to his martyr's death as a private citizen.

Having first placed on record, as was only proper, the public Wen Zhenheng (from which there is yet the very significant omission of his leading role in the Suzhou riot of 1626 in defence of Zhou Shunchang), Gu Ling goes on to give an account of the private man. Again the terms are those of the gentlemanly ideal; tall and erect of stature, fastidious in his preferences for bright windows, cleanliness, swept floors and the aroma of incense. He variously had residences, with their essential gardens, just outside Suzhou to both the east and west of the city, as well as a home within its walls. One of these rural estates was still being constructed for him at the time of his death, and he never had a chance to visit it. In addition to these, there was a property in Nanjing. Eight literary works of his, much of them poetry, are listed as having been published in his lifetime, including the *Treatise on Superfluous Things* and *The True Story of the Proclamation*, an apologia for his role as leader of gentry resistance to the eunuchs, together with two completed but unpublished works and a quantity of drafts. Finally, as is again standard with this genre of eulogy, we are told of his wife, née Wang, a granddaughter of Wang Zhideng (1535–1612; DMB, 1361–3), a key figure in the 'Wen family interest'. She bore him one son, Wen Dong, who acquired the initial *zhusheng* degree, while an unnamed concubine bore him Wen Guo, the commissioner of Gu's memorial, who maintained his father's aesthetic interests as poet and painter.

This then is something of the total context into which the *Treatise on Superfluous Things* must be installed, as one component in a life which was remembered by contemporaries at least as much for its significance in factional politics as for its commitment to excellence in the creation of aesthetic values. In a Ming context, indeed in the context of the Confucian value-system in which the elite were brought up, there was no real distinction between the personal and the public, the political and the aesthetic. It is precisely because of this inter-locking of values that so much time was spent on nurturing self-images of withdrawal, of disengagement and of lack of interest in mundane affairs. But we risk finding only the palest reflection of our contemporary concerns in a work like *Treatise on Superfluous Things*, if we wrench it from its context and forget that its author was not some romantic loner but a man who, at least in later life, risked his life in a very public confrontation with the state and who spent time in prison as the victim of the vicious political infighting of the late Ming court.

No attempt has yet been made to date the *Treatise* and to position it not only within Wen's total literary output but in relation to the social and political currents of the early seventeenth century. It will be argued here that it is a work of his relatively early years, probably produced before his first public 'political' involvement of 1626 and certainly before his first period of formal office holding. To demon-strate this, we need to look in detail at the layout of the book, and in particular at the involvement as honorary editors of a number of luminaries from the world of late Ming literature and politics.

The work as a whole is described as being 'collated' (*jiao*) by one Xu Chengrui, about whom nothing is known except negatively. No biography of him can be found, and he was not a holder of the highest level *jinshi* degree. He was perhaps no more than a representative of the publisher. It is provided with a preface signed by Shen Chunze, a native of the neighbouring centre of Changshu, a holder of the lowest level *zhusheng* degree, and principally known as a painter and calligrapher.[31] He describes himself in the preface as a 'friend and junior' (*you di*), though this does not necessarily imply that he was actually younger than Wen Zhenheng (born in 1585). Each of the twelve chapters into which the work is divided then deals with a different theme, and each is described as being 'approved' or 'estab-lished' (*ding*) by one of eleven separate figures. The degree of personal contact between these people and Wen Zhenheng may well have varied significantly, along with their degree of actual input into the text. At the least, these illustrious names were no more involved than are the political and cultural heavyweights who appear on the 'Committees

of Honour' for important exhibitions held in our major museums.
The twelve chapters of the *Treatise on Superfluous Things* are:

1   Studios and retreats;
2   Flowers and trees;
3   Water and rocks;
4   Birds and fish;
5   Calligraphy and painting;
6   Tables and couches;
7   Vessels and utensils;
8   Clothing and adornment;
9   Boats and carriages;
10   Placing and arrangement;
11   Vegetables and fruits;
12   Incense and teas.

The editors of these twelve chapters, which between them cover most
of the material surroundings of the Ming upper class, are detailed in
Appendix I. The distribution of these names across the twelve chapters
may have some now undiscernible pattern to it, but equally it may be
fortuitous. For example, Li Liufang, credited as 'editor' of chapter
3 on 'Water and rocks', did indeed create a very fine and renowned
garden for himself, but Shen Defu, the commentator on 'Calligraphy
and painting', could in no sense be considered the most distinguished
artist in the list. However, although it was far from unknown in the
Ming period for the names of famous scholars, artists or officials to
be attached to books by unscrupulous publishers, the assumption has
been made here that these men, all of whom save one were senior to
the author and most of whom like him were resident in the province
of Southern Zhili (the modern Jiangsu), did consent to the appearance
of their names in the published version of *Treatise on Superfluous
Things*.

Genuine impressive names were an even more powerful aid to a
book's sales than faked impressive names. Given that, it should be
possible to narrow down, at least to a degree, the period of Wen
Zhenheng's life in which the text was composed. James Watt's dating
of 1637[32] seems too late, if the evidence provided by the dates of the
'editors' is to be admitted. One certain *terminus ante quan* is provided
at 1622, the year in which Pan Zhiheng, editor of chapter 2, died. This
date seems to be confirmed by internal evidence in the text, where Wen
Zhenheng, in a discussion of contemporary calligraphers, gives Dong
Qichang the title *tai shi*, literally 'Grand Scribe', the familiar Ming
term for a member of the Hanlin Academy.[33] This would not have

been appropriate after Dong's promotion which, again, took place in 1622. However, even this gives a problem with regard to Song Jizu, editor of chapter 10. As a *jinshi* of 1553, he cannot have been born much later than the very early 1530s. If he was 20 when he took this highest degree, then he would have been an extremely venerable ninety-two years old in 1625. Another possible argument in favour of an earlier date of writing is that the author's brother, Wen Zhenmeng, was away from the Jiangnan region for much of the early 1620s, either taking the *jinshi* examinations in Peking or embarking on his political career in the capital.

The date *after* which the text was finished can arguably be established by the omission of Wang Zhideng, who died in 1612, when Wen Zhenheng was, by the western style of reckoning, twenty-seven years old. Given the nature of the relationship between this much older man, the grandfather of the author's wife, and Wen Zhenheng, we might reasonably expect him to have been called upon to give the work his imprimatur. That he did not do so argues for a dating after his decease, and it therefore seems likely on balance that the *Treatise on Superfluous Things* was completed in the second half of the 1610s, the declining years of the Wanli era, when its author would have been in his early thirties.

The subsequent publishing history of *Treatise on Superfluous Things* is in many ways much simpler than that of the work of Gao Lian. The original Ming edition, here posited as a work of the period *c*.1615–20, is now a very rare work, indeed, and one which I have not had the opportunity to study. The text, similarly, does not seem to have undergone the same process of dismemberment as that suffered by Gao's *Eight Discourses*. Only one section appears as an independent text in a *congshu*, and that is chapter 10, 'Placing and arrangement', which is reprinted in its entirety as 'Placing and Arrangement of the Pure Studio' (*Qing zhai wei zhi*) in a well-known collection, *Shuo fu xu*, *Tales Within a City Wall, Continued* (*juan* 27) of 1646, just subsequent to Wen Zhenheng's death.

This, however, should not be taken as meaning that the text received a poor reception, as a number of manuscript versions of potentially late Ming or early Qing date are preserved in various libraries, including one in the Percival David Foundation of Chinese Art, London, which emanates from the collection of a famous bibliophile named Qian Zeng (1629–after 1699).[34] Indeed, it was to a manuscript that the editors of the massive Imperial library project were forced to turn, when they catalogued the *Treatise* as part of their attempt to record all literature then deemed worthy of transmission, between 1773 and 1782. This again was a transmission in manuscript form, and it was not in fact until 1853 that a full printed edition was published, as part of a *congshu* from a Cantonese publishing house. At least seven more late Qing and Republican period editions appeared, ensuring the work a high profile in the present century's perceptions of the late Ming. However, the accessibility of the text to modern scholarship has been immeasurably increased by the fact that it is one of relatively few Ming works of this type of literature to have been the subject of a full critical and annotated edition.[35]

If the foregoing hypothesis about the dating of *Treatise on Super-fluous Things* is correct, then less than thirty years separate it from Gao Lian's *Eight Discourses*. However, an even more direct connection between these two texts, and between the cultural milieu of Hangzhou and Suzhou, can be drawn if for a moment we consider the question of Wen Zhenheng's sources. As van Gulik pointed out, there is no such thing as complete originality in this area of Chinese literary production, the name of the game being as much elegantly modified but unattributed citation as it is independent creation *de novo*. The very concept of this sort of precedent-free expression of personal tastes was a polemical position in the world of Ming literature, held by the Gong'an school centred on the brothers Yuan and opposed by more traditionalist writers. In some ways it is more helpful to think of Ming connoisseurship literature in its entirety as constituting a single 'text', repeated and reaffirmed by a number of separate individual writers.

Post-Renaissance European concepts of 'plagiarism' and 'originality' are here of very little help as tools of analysis. That said, it is still possible from within the Chinese bibliographical tradition to make statements regarding the degree of dependence of one published text upon another. The eighteenth-century editors of the *Si ku, Four Treasuries*, Imperial Catalogue were exercising these possibilities when they drew attention to the fact that a considerable amount of Wen Zhenheng's material was drawn from a work called *Kao pan yu shi*, or *Desultory Remarks on Furnishing the Abode of the Retired Scholar*, by Tu Long (1542–1605), whom we have encountered already as a client of Gao Lian in Hangzhou in the 1590s, and as a personal friend of Wang Zhideng, elderly patron of the young Wen Zhenheng in Nanjing in the early 1600s. The possibility of a direct encounter between Tu Long and Wen Zhenheng in Nanjing in the last years of the former's life certainly cannot be ruled out. However, a closer look at Tu's *Desultory Remarks* reveals a connection between it and the writings of Gao Lian and Wen Zhenheng which in one sense compli-cates the picture but in another simplifies the question of textual transmission, by reducing the 'core' amount of information we are dealing with, even as it multiplies the number of times that same information is redistributed.

Desultory Remarks on Furnishing the Abode of the Retired Scholar takes the form of 15 *jian* or 'treatises', using a word cognate with but not identical graphically to that used for the titles of Gao Lian's sections. These treatises are; Calligraphy and books, Rubbings, Paintings, Paper, Ink, Brushes, Inkstones, *Qin* zithers, Incense, Tea, Potted plants, Fishes and birds, the mountain studio, Necessities of life and dress, and Utensils of the studio. The first edition of the complete work is that contained in one of the most prestigious of all late Ming *congshu*, the *Bao yan tang bi ji* of 1606, supposedly based on the holdings of the library of Chen Jiru (1558-1639; ECCP, 83-4). The value of Chen's massive reputation was such that his is the name most frequently attached fraudulently by publishers to works aimed at the upper end of the book market.[36] Possibly even the majority of the books on which his name appears as editor or author are falsifications on this point.

A very close similarity has long been noted between Tu Long's *Desultory Remarks* and a work entitled *Jiao chuang jiu lu, Nine Records from a Banana-shaded Window*, attributed to the great merchant – collector Xiang Yuanbian (1525-1590). Despite the dismissal of this latter work as a forgery based on Tu Long by the editors of the Imperial Catalogue, the most widely available brief biography in English of Tu Long repeats the canard that the plagiarism must be the other way round, with a genuine work by Xiang being foisted on Tu Long. The grounds given for this are as follows.

> Judging from the expensiveness and rarity of most of the articles mentioned in the book, it seems unlikely that T'u could have had the means to afford them, the patience to evaluate them, or the temperament of describe them. It may well be the work of a collector, affluent and devoted, someone like Hsiang Yuan-pien.[37]

In fact, the close textual analysis of the contemporary Chinese scholar Weng Tongwen has established without a doubt that it is the Xiang text which is a forgery, probably of the early Qing period, one of a number of pieces of literature on connoisseurship which make use of his reputation as a collector to improve their attractiveness to the reader.

However, Weng goes one step further, by analysing the contents of Tu Long's work in turn, and what he comes up with is proof of the degree of dependence of the *Desultory Remarks* of 1606 (a year *after*, it should be remembered, the death of its supposed author) on Gao Lian's *Eight Discourses* of 1591, with its preface by Tu Long.

The sections in *Desultory Remarks* on paper, ink, brushes, inkstones, *qin* zithers, incense, fishes and birds, and utensils of the studio (eight out of fifteen chapters) are shown by Weng to be completely taken from Gao, with no more than a cursory rearrangement of the material. He shows, too, that the chapters on calligraphy and books, rubbings and paintings draw very substantially on Gao's wording with the addition of material culled from other writers, principally the book collector and bibliographer Hu Yinglin (1551–1602; DMB, 645–7), the official and man of letters Wang Shizhen (1526–1590; DMB, 1399–405) and the writer on art Zhang Yingwen (fl. 1530–1594; DMB, 51), who we will meet again as the author of another key text on collecting. The chapter on tea can be shown similarly to be identical to a text by Zhang Yingwen's son Zhang Chou (1577–?1643).[38]

Deficiencies in the text available to him meant that Weng was not able to study the sections on potted plants, on the mountain studio, and on the necessities of life and dress, yet when the comparison is made, it becomes apparent that they, too, have no independent existence but are just rehashes of material included in the *Eight Discourses*. At this point it might be objected that Tu Long was in fact the author of the *Eight Discourses*, acting as the hired pen of his wealthy patron. This argument might be sustainable if we did not fortuitously known enough about Gao Lian's education and other attainments as a poet and dramatist to make it seem on balance unlikely. However, it is certainly the case that Tu Long's phantom work on connoisseurship and elegant living enjoyed an afterlife every bit as widespread as its source. The individual treatises of the *Desultory Remarks* appear with great frequency in a number of Ming and Qing *congshu*, a testimony not to their intrinsic independent value as sources of Tu Long's ideas (which is nil) but to the continuing lustre attached to his name in subsequent centuries, by contrast with the more shadowy Gao Lian.

This lengthy diversion into the byways of bibliography may not seem to be strictly relevant, but its importance to the main discussion can be briefly summarized. The eighteenth-century editors of the Imperial Catalogue were quite correct to point out the dependence of Wen Zhenheng's *Treatise on Superfluous Things* (*c.* 1615–20) on Tu Long's *Desultory Remarks on Furnishing the Abode of the Retired Scholar* (1606). However, they missed the fact that the independent content of this latter work is very small, and that Wen Zhenheng thus depends very directly on the relevant sections of Gao Lian's *Eight Discourses on the Art of Living* (1591). What we are faced with is, in effect, one 'text', its author being Gao Lian, which is being transmitted three times. It is largely irrelevant to the present thesis whether the *Desultory Remarks* are actually 'by' Tu Long at all (for what it is worth, I am inclined to suspect they may not be).

What is important is that the state in 1606 of the market for writing of this kind meant that it was a reasonable commercial proposition to attach the name of this very famous and recently dead writer to material which was, in fact, over a decade old and which was the work of his very much *less* famous patron, the presumably also deceased Gao Lian. Without attempting to unravel the details of the textual transmission, made deliberately more obscure by the marketing strategies of Ming publishers, we can accept that a body of work was in existence which had as many structural similarities between texts as differences of detail between them. These differences of detail do certainly exist, as van Gulik pointed out, and some of them will be noted in the following chapter, but it would still not be indefensible to talk about a homogeneous tradition of writing about material culture, however confusingly multifarious its manifestations may at first sight seem.

One further example of the genre which needs to be taken into account, not just for its contents but for the personal connections of its author, is the *Qing bi cang, Pure and Arcane Collecting*, by Zhang Yingwen, with a preface by the author dated 1595. Together with *Eight Discourses on the Art of Living* and *Treatise on Superfluous Things*, this was for the editors of the eighteenth-century Imperial Catalogue an archetypal example of this sort of writing, and the three works appear sequentially in it, receiving the same sort of criticism from the changed cultural environment of nearly two centuries later. It is perhaps worth pausing at this point to look at these criticisms and to get some sense of how the connoisseurship literature of the late Ming appeared to writers within much the same cultural framework but with a very different ordering of cultural priorities. Of *Eight Discourses on the Art of Living* they have this to say:

> The book solely records those things necessary for passing the time in leisurely idleness, and its headings and categories frequently stray into trivialities, unable to go beyond the clichés of late Ming 'Minor appreciation' literature (*xiao pin*). It is the the fount of much of the writing of Chen Jiru and Li Yu. Its mistakes are quite numerous, as in taking Zhang Ji for a painter of the Yuan period when, in fact, he lived in the Song and taking Fan Shi as a recluse when, in fact, he served as Governor of Lujiang. However, its use of sources is extremely rich, and it may be of some value in textual research, while it has detailed discussions of ancient vessels and an

occasionally useful collection of medical prescriptions. Compared to those who engage in 'pure talk', he is to a degree better.[39]

On Zhang Yingwen, the verdict is this:

> The body of the text is modelled on that of *Pure Registers of the Cavern Heaven*, and the wording frequently follows that of the discussions of earlier authors . . . without noting his sources, he adheres to the Ming habit of extensive unattributed quotation . . . there is some useful material in his extremely detailed accounts of the detection of falsehood, of the ranking of works of art, collecting and mounting. At the end he records works he has owned and seen . . . subsequently his son Zhang Chou wrote *Qinghe's Listing of Calligraphy and Painting*, (*Qinghe shu hua biao*), listing thirty-one works under Zhang Yingwen's name. Now the present text was written when Yingwen was on his deathbed, and he could not have added so much to his collection. Chou's listing is done simply to exaggerate his wealth, and cannot be trusted.[40]

The entry on Tu Long is briefer than either of the above and contents itself with noting: 'This treats in a miscellaneous fashion of the pure pleasures of the studio . . . its various topics are rather trivial.'[41] Typically, the lengthier entry on Wen Zhenheng's *Treatise on Superfluous Things* begins with a retelling of its author's distinguished ancestry, and his martyr's death, before commenting:

> In general it deals with matters of leisure and enjoyment, with niceties and trivialities. It has a distant source in Zhao Xigu's *Pure Registers of the Cavern Heaven* and a more immediate model in Tu Long's *Desultory Remarks*. Late Ming recluses and artists made much of each other over these matters, the so-called 'pure presentation' (*qing gong*). There were, indeed, those who, through dissembling words about 'elegant connoisseurship', in fact only increased their air of vulgarity. However Zhenheng's family had been renowned over generations for their painting and calligraphy, and he himself was steeped in the arts and distinct from the throng . . . Furthermore, he died a martyr for his dynasty, as a beacon of righteousness; thus, whatever comes from his hand ought to be valued and not allowed to be lost. Hence, a special attempt has been made to record and preserve this work here.[42]

The implication is quite clear that Wen Zhenheng's work on 'trivia' is saved for posterity purely on account of its author's social position and moral qualities, not for any intrinsic merits in the text.

By contrast, Zhang Yingwen (fl. 1530–1594), the author of *Pure and Arcane Collecting*, remains a somewhat shadowy figure, sandwiched between a father and an uncle, who had distinguished official careers, and a son, Zhang Chou (1577–?1643; DMB, 51–3), who left behind copious writings on artistic theory together with important accounts of works of art viewed by himself. Zhang Yingwen was clearly wealthy and, as a resident of Suzhou, was socially on a par with the family of Wen Zhenheng. He was apparently related by marriage (though in what degree is not clear) to Wen's grandfather or great-uncle. There was also a connection with Wang Zhideng, whose family was itself closely intertwined with the Wen clan as we have seen, since *Pure and Arcane Collection* carries an undated preface which reveals that a daughter of Wang Zhideng was married to Zhang Chou. Hence, Zhang Chou's wife was an aunt by marriage of Wen Zhenheng. It was Zhang Chou who edited and collated his father's work after his death, as the preface dated 1595 informs us. The work, however, remained unpublished until the later eighteenth century, the copy used by the imperial cataloguers being a manuscript one in the collection of the Bao family of Suzhou.

The book is divided into two *juan*, or chapters. The first of these is further subdivided into twenty 'discussions' on the following topics: jades; ancient bronzes; calligraphy; famous paintings; inscriptions on stone; ceramics; seals of the Jin and Han dynasties; inkstones; rare rocks; pearls and precious stones; *qin* zithers and swords; famous incenses; crystal, agate and amber; inkcakes; paper; printed books of the Song dynasty; embroideries and woven silk tapestries of the Song dynasty; carving; antique papers and silks (for use in painting and calligraphy); mounting and collecting of pictures. The second chapter contains ten 'accounts' on more specialized topics, mostly to do with the connoisseurship of painting: famous collectors, the recognition of seals, famous collections of rubbings and their transmission, famous instances of copying, curious treasures of the past culled from literature, famous *qin* zither makers, brocaded silks of the Tang and Song period used in mounting pictures, famous makers of inkcakes, a bibliography of famous treatises on connoisseurship topics, 'An account of what I have collected and what I have seen'.

It can be seen from this list that there is a slightly different focus here from that seen in Gao Lian or Wen Zhenheng, read in their entirety. The emphasis is placed, as the title clearly states, on collecting as an activity, and hence largely on objects which were either genuinely or were accepted as antique. Zhang Yingwen's work contains nothing on contemporary clothing, on furniture or on the utensils thought suitable for the consumption of food, tea or alcohol.

It is, thus, more of a continuation of a work like the fourteenth-century *Essential Criteria of Antiquities* (reprinted at least once in Zhang Yingwen's lifetime, and again in 1596 just after his death) than a true analogy with *Treatise on Superfluous Things* or *Eight Discourses on the Art of Living*, though it may have seemed so at a distance of nearly two hundred years, in the 1780s. A quantity of the material contained in the book is translated in a chapter devoted to Zhang Yingwen as the archetypal Ming collector, in Michel Beurdeley's rather unfocused compilation of material on 'the Chinese collector'.[43]

Gao Lian, Zhang Yingwen, Tu Long (or 'pseudo-Tu Long') and Wen Zhenheng may appear now, with the benefit of ordered bibliographical hindsight, to be the key players in the creation of a literature of material culture in the decades from 1590 to 1630. This appearance could be illusory. Certainly, there is some evidence that Gao Lian and Tu Long were publishing 'successes', but the extreme rarity of first editions of Wen Zhenheng and the non-publication at all of Zhang Yingwen must make us cautious in constructing a world of Ming books about things solely on the basis of named authors. However, the contention that there was a boom in publishing this sort of literature can still be sustained simply by looking at what was being published or republished over this period. No claims for completeness are made for what follows. However, a chronology, incorporating the texts already discussed but bringing in some of the other major literary landmarks in this area might run as follows:

> *c.* 1550 *Essential Criteria of Antiquities* republished.
>
> 1591 *Eight Discourses on the Art of Living* first published. Two, possibly three more editions before 1620.
>
> 1595 *Pure and Arcane Collecting* complete and circulating in manuscript.
>
> 1596 *Essential Criteria of Antiquities* republished.
>
> *c.* 1600 *Essential Criteria of Antiquities* republished.
>
> 1603 Publication of the collection *Ge zhi cong shu, The Investigation of the World*, containing texts on a very wide variety of subjects and of very various dates, but among them *Essential Criteria*, as well as a number of contemporary Ming works on vessels necessary for tea drinking, on food, and on ten treasured items in the 'mountain studio' of Gu Yuanqing (1487–1565; DMB, 570).
>
> 1606 *Desultory Remarks on Furnishing the Abode of the Retired*

Scholar published as one of the twenty-one texts in part I of the collection *Bao yan tang bi ji*, associated with the name of Chen Jiru. This includes several important pieces of the material culture literature, including the *Ping shi*, *History of Vases*, a treatise on flower arrangement by the poet, essayist and aesthetic theorist Yuan Hongdao (1568–1610; DMB, 1635–8).[44] Part II, published in the same year, prints several treatises on painting, among them Wang Zhideng's account of the painters of Suzhou.

1607–1620 Serial publication of the first sections of the *Tales Within a City Wall* collection,[45] including one of the earliest printed versions of the Song work on connoisseurship, *Record of the Pure Registers of the Cavern Heaven*, of *c.* 1200–50). The forty-six sections of the 'Continuation' of 1646 include in its twenty-seventh part the chapter on 'Placing and arrangement' from *Treatise on Superfluous Things*.

1615–1620 Conjectural date for completion and publication of Wen Zhenheng, *Treatise on Superfluous Things*.

1615 Part III of *Bao yan tang bi ji* includes works on food and plants, as well as Zhang Chou's work on flower arranging *Ping hua pu*, *Manual on Vases and Flowers*, dependent to a very great degree on Yuan Hongdao's *History of Vases*.

1615 *Cheng shi cong ke*, *Master Cheng's Collected Prints*, a collection of nine works on the correct consumption of tea and alcohol, together with one work about painting.

1617 *Xian qing xiao pin*, *Minor Writings on Elegant Leisure*, contains writings on tea and painting, among other subjects.

1629 *Shan ju xiao wan*, *Minor Enjoyments of Dwelling in the Mountains*, published by the Changshu book collector and literary entrepreneur Mao Jin (1599–1659; ECCP, 565–6). Its ten texts include Yuan Hongdao's *History of Vases*, and Ming works on chess, tea, incense and a curious arrangement of dining tables, along with earlier pieces of writing on orchids, rocks, inkstones (by Mi Fu) and the oldest text on bronze collecting, the *Ding lu*, *Record of Tripods* by the Liang dynasty (AD 502–557) author Yu Li. This collection, with two additional texts (neither of them contemporary) was reissued somewhere around 1654 with the title *Qun fang qing wan*, *Pure Enjoyment of a Myriad of Fragrances*.

These are all texts which can be dated with a degree of accuracy, usually on the basis of prefaces (though these are not invariably reliable). In addition, there are a number of equally important collections of texts which can be dated generally to the period *c*. 1600–1640, but no more precisely than that. They include:

Shui bian lin xia, By the Waters, Beneath the Trees: a collection which makes use of several pieces of Gao Lian and Tu Long, removed from their original context and retitled. Among them are Gao's *Shan zhai zhi, Record of my Mountain Studio* (taken from Treatise 3), his work on wild plants suitable for use as foodstuffs, and Tu's thoughts on goldfish and on incense.

Chong ding xin shang pian, Recompiled Texts on Connoisseurship: Here we have almost a full roll-call of the prestigious writers in this sort of field; Gu Yuanqing, Yuan Hongdao (the *History of Vases*, as well as his *Shang zheng, Regulations of the Goblet* on wine drinking), Zhang Chou on flower arranging, Gao Lian in inkstones, Pan Zhiheng (one of the commentators, it will be remembered, on Wen Zhenheng's *Treatise*), Wang Zhideng and many others on paintings, tea, food, prostitutes and all the other luxury commodities available to the late Ming man of fashion and wealth. The presence within the one purchasable commodity (a book) of information on a very wide spread of other commodities appears to justify the project of treating upper-class consumption as a continuum. To extract the information on the high-status activity of painting, or on areas such as ceramic collecting which modern patterns of consumption have retrospectively raised in status, while ignoring the concerns with food, gambling and sex, is to grant anachronistically privileged positions to some areas of elite concern and lose in the process any hope of understanding the bigger picture.

Ju jia bi bei, Necessities for the Householder: a considerable proportion of this collection consists of work by Gao Lian over a wide range of concern. The arrangement of the collection is in seven large sections, being: family management, familial instruction, household economy, health, observation of taboos, food and drink, the arts.

With this manual for the householder we enter a conceptually different world from that of the great Suzhou magnate, living in the city on the basis of rents from land he may never have been. We enter the world of the late Ming small landlord, the local elite scattered across the vast area of the empire, whose sense of continuity of interest with the regional and national elites was such a key factor in ensuring social stability and gentry hegemony. This text acts to demonstrate a very important transition between the higher levels of the ruling class, symbolized by the kinds of writers whose works are excerpted here, and the world of the Ming 'encyclopedia for daily use' (*ri yong lei shu*). These encyclopedias, whose most flourishing period exactly coincided with the boom in the publication of connoisseurship literature around 1580–1640, have been studied by Sakai Tadao for their role in the dissemination of elite values to a much wider, though still literate audience while Timothy Brook has demonstrated their importance in spreading another type of necessary commercial information, accurate accounts of routes across China.[46]

Necessities for the Householder may remain in essence a *congshu*, a collection of texts by named authors, and hence within the 'high' literary tradition. However, it betrays by its internal arrangement and by its name that it is at least as closely related to something like the ten chapter *Ju jia bi yong shi lei quan ji*, *Complete and Categorized Essentials for the Householder*, an encyclopedia which is undated and which may have its origins as far back as the Yuan dynasty but which was certainly in circulation around 1600, as a number of surviving late Ming copies prove.[47] It was only one of a number of such books and the cognate genre of almanacs, the production of which was expanding very much at the same time as the literature on luxury consumption.[48] Here, no separate authors are credited for the sections, and the work's 'sales pitch' depends on the authority or literary reputation of a body of contributors but on the intrinsic accuracy and usefulness of the information it contains.

In the broad sense *Complete and Categorized Essentials* is very much about material culture, about the personal management of a small estate, about the taboos to be observed when raising a new building, about how to raise chickens and make soya sauce. The association of this text with an under-studied class of petty rural landowners, prominent at no more than the county level, is suggested by the recovery of a copy from the grave of a man named Shi Zhenshi who was buried in 1631 at Taicang in Jiangsu province.[49] Shi Zhenshi's tomb was a very modest one, containing only a few personal items of adornment, copies of deeds relating to land ownership and four books, of which *Complete and Categorized Essentials* is one. In several respects it is a close relative of the *Hausvaterliteratur* of contemporary central Europe, books like Coler's *Oeconomia* of the 1590s with their instructions on moral as well as on animal husbandry.[50]

But the Chinese version also contains considerable quantities of material on how to imitate the material surroundings of the elite, with one whole section on 'Necessities of the Studio'. A reading of this suggests that there no actual barriers by about 1600 to the spread downward of the luxury artefacts of the rich. The market mechanisms were in place to ensure that brushes from Anhui province or ceramics from the great potteries of Jingdezhen were available across the the empire to those who could pay for them. Crucially, the networks of information were also in place, through the medium of books like the encyclopedias of daily use, to ensure that no one was excluded from participation in the market for luxury commodities on the grounds of ignorance of how to consume appropriately. For a certain stratum of the Chinese elite, the baffling and unreliable information networks of the bazaar had given way to elements (only some elements) of the consumer culture. The operation of this proto-consumer culture will be examined in the rest of this book, and in the next chapter through a closer look at some of the contents of the material culture literature discussed so far and the ideas about self and society they promote.

The specialist treatises discussed above are, however, far from being the only kind of Ming literature to shed light on the creation and consumption of luxury goods. Considerable use will also be made of the rich seam of Ming *biji* literature, the genre of miscellaneous notes which many members of the elite used to record interesting, instructive or merely entertaining anecdotes, stories about the inner workings of the political system, or their thoughts on a wide variety of social or artistic topics.[51] The form, which flourished particularly in the late imperial period, remains much exploited by those working in almost every field of traditional Chinese studies but under-investigated by historians of literature. Thus the *biji* have tended to be used as if they were fascinating but unstructured heaps of raw material, and little attention seems to have been paid to the extent, if any, to which their loose, baggy form might profitably be treated as a structure embodying a coherent viewpoint. Some of them, such as Shen Defu's invaluable, *Random Gatherings of the Wanli Era*, contain material germane to the present study in identifiable sections, while others have it scattered throughout what can be very lengthy works.

Deliberately sparing use has also been made of Ming imaginative literature, in the form of the prose fiction which in the late sixteenth century was getting into its stride as one of the glories of traditional Chinese culture. Here, the most useful work, almost a crash-course in Ming civilization, is the lengthy but unflagging *Jin ping mei*, known in English usually by the name *The Golden Lotus*. Despite being ostensibly set in the twelfth century, this anonymous masterpiece is generally held to reflect social conditions and attitudes in the decades immediately preceding its probable first publication in 1617. It deals with life in the mansion of the polygamous, upwardly mobile, vulgarian Ximen Qing, whose strategies for social and sexual gratification, and whose ultimate downfall, are laid out in unflinching detail.[52] The novel, too, is a consumer luxury of the late Ming which, like the guides to elegant living, mirrors as well as embodies the social patterns in which it circulated and was enjoyed.

2

Ideas about things

Themes in Ming connoisseurship literature

In order to convey in as short a space as possible some sense of the types of issues raised by the literature discussed in the preceding chapter, there follows a selection of extracts taken from Wen Zhenheng's *Treatise on Superfluous Things* of about 1615–20, one drawn from each of the twelve chapters into which the book is divided. I would remind the reader at this point that no claims are being made for the originality or intrinsic interest of this material as opposed to that of other contemporary texts nor for its value as a guide to Wen's personality or individual psyche. The ideas contained in what follows are in the main generally accepted commonplaces across a number of separate texts, and in several cases their wording is even identical to that found elsewhere. The entry on how to store picture scrolls is, for example, found in exactly the same words in Tu Long, who in turn derives it from Gao Lian.

The chapters all take more or less the same format, with an introductory general statement and a number of individual entries, that number ranging from ten in the case of the shortest chapter, 'Clothing and adornment', to fifty-eight in the case of the longest, 'Vessels and utensils'. A typical entry would be of about seventy Chinese characters, though some are as short as thirty, while the longest, concentrated in the 'Calligraphy and painting' chapter, can reach just over a thousand characters. An example of the introductory statement, that from the chapter on 'Tables and couches', is also given below. Some chapters also contain 'General discussions' of a number of topics. Each of the extracts translated below forms a complete entry in the text, with its own title.

Chapter 1: Studios and retreats

The teahouse: Build a structure of one column's span, adjacent to a mountain studio, and set therein the tea utensils. Train a boy to the exclusive service of tea, so that the whole day may be spent there in pure talk, the chilly night spent in sitting there in a dignified attitude. This is the first priority of the recluse, which cannot be dispensed with.[1]

Chapter 2: Flowers and trees

Camellias: Sichuan camellias (*Camellia japonica*) and Yunnan camellias (*Camellia reticulata*) are both valuable, and the yellow ones are particularly hard to obtain. People often match them together with magnolia, since they bloom at the same season, and the white and red make a dazzling show. This is rather vulgar. There is another variety called 'Drunken imperial concubine' (*Camellia japonica var. anemoniflora*) which opens when the snow is on the ground and is particularly attractive.[2]

Chapter 3: Water and rocks

Lake Tai rocks: Those Lake Tai rocks which come from under water are valuable, where long years of buffeting by the waves have pierced them through and turned them into caverns and hollows, reticulated on every side. Those from the mountains are called 'dry rocks' and have a dull, unlustrous surface. They can be faked up into the water-pierced rocks and have an elegant appearance only after a number of years when the traces of the chisel have completely disappeared. The artificial mountains which are so valued in Suzhou are all made of these rocks. There are also smaller rocks which have been long submerged in the lake and which are dredged up by fishermen in their nets. These are rather like *lingbi* or *ying* rocks, but they have an inferior tone and do not ring clearly when struck.[3]

Chapter 4: Birds and fish

Parrots: Parrots are capable of speech and, thus, must be taught short poems and harmonious phrases. They must not be allowed to hear the chattering of the market-places, well-heads and villages, a violent assault upon the ear. Their bronze perches and feeding jars must all be elegant and curious. However, these birds, just like golden pheasants, peacocks, collared finchbills and turkeys, are all categorically things of the women's quarters; they are not among the necessities of the recluse.[4]

Chapter 5: Calligraphy and painting

Storing paintings: Paintings should be stored in caskets of fir wood, with absolutely no use of lacquer or glued paper linings internally, lest they seep out and stain the picture. In the fourth or fifth month, you should unroll every piece and give them a brief sight of the sun, then return them to their boxes at a distance of ten or so feet from ground level, to prevent foxing. Generally, when displaying pictures, they should be changed every three to five days, to prevent both fatiguing the eye and damage by dust. When taking them down, first whisk the dust off both sides of a scroll, so that the surface will remain undamaged.[5]

Chapter 6: Tables and couches

Tables and couches: When the men of old made tables and couches, although the length and width were not standardized, they were invariably antique, elegant and delightful when placed in a studio or room. There was no way in which they were not convenient, whether for sitting up, lying down or reclining. In moments of pleasant relaxation they would spread out classic or historical texts, examine works of calligraphy or painting, display ancient bronze vessels, dine or take a nap, as the furniture was suitable for all these things. The men of today make them in a manner which merely prefers carved and painted decoration to delight the vulgar eye, while the antique pieces are cast aside, causing one to sigh in deep regret.[6]

'Natural' tables [i.e. tables with a top made from one solid plank, as opposed to a framed top of several pieces]: 'Natural' tables are made of some grained wood, such as *huali* (*Pterocarpus sp.*), *tieli* (*Mesua ferrea*) or *xiangnan* (*Machilus odoratissima*). The length should not exceed eight feet, nor the thickness of the top five inches. The end flanges must not be too sharp, but smooth and rounded, which is the antique pattern. Those which have stretchers between the feet at ground level, like a Japanese table, are even more curious. They

should not have four legs like the pattern for a writing table. Some are set into supports of old tree roots. Otherwise, use pieces of thick, wide timber like that of the top, hollow them out and carve them lightly with designs such as cloud scrolls and *ruyi* heads. They must not be carved with such vulgar patterns as dragons, phoenixes, flowers, and grasses. The long, narrow ones made recently are abominable.[7]

Chapter 7: Vessels and utensils

Incense burners: The bronze *ding* and *yi* vessels of the Three Ages and of the Qin and Han dynasties and those ceramic vessels of *Guan* ware, *Ge* ware, Ding ware, Longquan ware or Xuande ware are objects of connoisseurship and are not convenient for daily use. The most suitable are the rather larger bronze incense burners dating from the Xuande reign (1426–35), and those cast by the Jiang family in the Song dynasty are also acceptable. However, it is unacceptable to use temple burners, or those of gilt white brass, or those in the shape of pairs of fish or of elephants. Particularly to be avoided are all the vulgar forms such as the 'eight precious emblems', 'Japanese landscapes' or 'hundred nail head' burners cast by the bronze-workers of the Pan and Hu families at Yunjian, as well as the recently made ceramic burners of Jian ware or of porcelain decorated in five colours. Antique blue-green Boshan incense burners can be used sometimes, while wooden tripod burners are acceptable in the mountains, and stone ones are solely acceptable for Buddhist worship. All the rest are not worth considering. The tripod vessels of the ancients all have stands and covers, and nowadays people make these of wood, with ebony being the best, though *zitan* wood and *huali* wood (*Pterocarpus sp.*) are also acceptable. Avoid the vulgar shapes like water-caltrop flowers or mallow flowers. The knobs of these lids should be Song dynasty jade buttons, mythical animals or sea beasts, and of a size appropriate to the incense burner. Materials like agate and crystal can be used if they are old.[8]

Chapter 8: Clothing and adornment

Bed curtains: Bed curtains for the winter months should be of pongee silk or of thick cotton with purple patterns. Curtains of paper or of plain-weave, spun-silk cloth are both vulgar, while gold brocaded silk curtains and those of *bo* silk are for the women's quarters. Summer curtains can be of banana fibre, only these are not easy to obtain. Curtains of blue fine gauze from Suzhou, or curtains of patterned towelling are also acceptable. There are those which are made of silk for painting, with landscapes or monochrome ink paintings of plum blossom on them, but these all achieve vulgarity while striving for elegance. Then there are some particularly large curtains, known as 'sky-covering curtains'. To sit or lie inside them in the summer months, with tables, couches, cupboards or shelves, is rather suitable, although not in the antique style. In the months of cold one should place curtains of cotton over the window frames of the studio, but only blue or purple can be used.[9]

Chapter 9: Boats and carriages

Small skiffs: A small skiff should be just over ten feet long and about three feet wide. It can be set on a pond or lake, sometimes speeding along in mid-current, sometimes tethered in the shade of willow trees to a meandering bank, where you can fish with a pole, enjoying the moon and chanting with the breeze. Make a long awning of blue cotton, attached to the gunwales at both sides, held on two bamboo poles at the front and tied round the two stern posts at the back of the boat. One boy is enough to row it.[10]

Chapter 10: Placing and arrangement

Placing vases: Depending on the style of the vase, set it on a Japanese table of appropriate size, using bronze in the winter or spring, porcelain for the summer and autumn. Vases for the reception hall should be large; those for the studio should be small. Value bronze or ceramic, and hold gold and silver cheap, avoiding those with ring handles, or which come in pairs. Flowers should be emaciated and curious; they should not be over-complicated. If using a cut branch, then it must be selected to be curious and antique. If there are two, then their relative heights must be suitable. It is particularly important to have no more than one or two varieties, since too many gives the appearance of a wine shop. This does not apply to a small vase with an arrangement of autumn flowers. In placing flowers do not burn incense with the windows closed, lest the smoke blight the petals. This is particularly the case with narcissi. Nor should flowers be placed on a painting table.[11]

Chapter 11: Vegetables and fruits

Mandarin oranges: Mandarin oranges from the region of Lake Dongting are particularly sweet, while those from Xinzhuang have no juice and need to be peeled with a knife before eating. There is another variety with an even thicker skin, called *miluo* mandarin oranges which are particularly fine. The little ones are called 'golden mandarins', and the round ones 'golden beans'.[12]

Chapter 12: Incense and teas

'Tiger Hill' and 'Heaven Pond' teas: 'Tiger Hill' is of the most refined quality, supreme throughout the empire, but unfortunately very little is produced and that is mostly commandeered by the officials. The humble mountain dweller, if he gets hold of one or two potfuls, considers this a rare treat, but its flavour is in fact inferior to that of 'Cen' tea from Changxing in Zhejiang. As for 'Heaven Pond' tea, that which comes from the area around Longchi is fine, but that from Nanshan is picked very early and has a slight flavour of grass.[13]

These few brief extracts can only give an outline of the sort of ideas contained in *Treatise on Superfluous Things*, ideas which are conveyed in language which is, in the context of the total range of Ming prose, relatively direct and easy to understand, even at times suggesting something of the patterns of elite speech. (The question of the vocabulary used is discussed in more detail below.) Although selections from this and related texts have been translated before,[14] and however valuable these renditions are, they suffer from the common weakness of privileging one type of object of the discourse of Ming connoisseurship at the expense of studying that discourse itself. The concentration on painting and on ceramics in the choice of what use to make of the total texts has to an extent skewed our perception of what those texts are 'about'. Subjects such as dress and food, areas where there is no contemporary connoisseurship or market for the goods, have received much less attention, certainly not as much as their positioning within the text would justify.

Looking, then, at the total picture of Ming elite material life given in Wen's *Treatise*, to what extent does it match James Watt's description of it as 'encompassing the full range of objects organised as a reflection of spiritual values'?[15] What does it, in fact, include, how does it categorize, and how do those categories match those of other, differently focused, contemporary descriptions of the material world?

Clearly the objects described by Wen omit several important categories of artefact. There is no mention of any sort of productive technology, either the tools of the artisan or, more significantly, of the peasant population on whose labour Wen Zhenheng depended for his wealth. This elision of any mention of production may hardly seem surprising, but it is not inevitable. The contemporary almanacs and householder's manuals do deal with questions of production in the same way as they give instruction on how to ape the consumption patterns of the higher levels of the elite. They situate production and consumption in the same space. We may be seeing represented here one of the almost imperceptible lines of fission within the larger ruling class, between those who could literally afford not to know where their wealth came from and those who by intimate involvement in the supervision of hired labour could be expected to be personally interested in how to effect repairs to a plough, or manufacture noodles.

The twelve categories of the *Treatise* can also be compared profitably with the much longer list of headings given in a very important but under-utilized text entitled *Tian shui bing shan lu, A Record of the Waters of Heaven Melting the Iceberg*. Although not published until the early eighteenth century, in the context of a *congshu* collection of rare manuscript texts,[16] this is a reliable account of the breakdown of elite material culture through the eyes of the lower reaches of the bureaucracy. It is, in effect, a total inventory of the property of a man named Yan Song (1480–1565; DMB, 1586–91), who as a Grand Secretary from 1542 to 1562 was one of the effective leaders of the national political elite. Having long been a focus of hostility within the official world, he was dismissed from office and died in disgrace, his entire property being forfeit, as was standard, to the state. His fame, or rather his infamy, as one of the most vilified men of the dynasty seems to have ensured the survival of the inventory made of his property long enough for it to be printed as an object of historical curiosity. (The allusion in its curious title is to the effect of imperial wrath in melting the gross bulk of Yan Song's over-mighty position.) Although it has been suggested by at least one author that it was exaggerated by his political enemies, the bland bureaucratic language in which it is written is not that of prurient excitement but rather of a dispassionate listing of seemingly inexhaustible riches.

In any case, it seems unlikely that the categorization is markedly eccentric, and this provides useful comparisons with that in the more self-conscious connoisseurship literature, both in the actual headings used and in the order (presumably reflecting some at least unconscious ranking) in which they appear. Certainly of quite major significance is the division of the inventory into two sections, the first being of material simply absorbed into the storehouses of the Imperial Household Department and the second being of material converted by sale into its monetary value. The two groupings are as follows:

I: Material confiscated by the state

Gold (i.e. gold in ingot form)

Vessels and dishes of pure gold

Silver

Silver vessels

Jade vessels

Jade belts

Belts of gold-inlaid tortoiseshell, rhinoceros horn, ivory and incense wood

Belts, bracelets and other items of gold filigree

Vessels, chopsticks, etc. of gold-inlaid mother of pearl, rhinoceros horn, ivory and tortoiseshell

'Dragon eggs' (pearls?)

Hats, hair-nets and other items encrusted with pearls

Pearls, precious stones and amber

Coral, rhinoceros horn, ivory and other items

Precious and rare vessels and bibelots

Antique water-measures and other items

Minerals and cinnabar

Incense materials

Bolts of woven, gold-patterned satin, spun silk cloth, self-patterned twill, openwork silk, gauze silk, plain weave silk, *gaiji*, velvet, brocaded silk, cloth of feathers, *kudzu* cloth (*pueraria hirsuta Matsumoto*) and cotton

Male and female woven, gold-patterned silk clothing in various colours

Antique and modern famous *qin* zithers

Antique inkstones

Elegant writing accessories

Screens and folding screens

Beds inlaid with marble and mother of pearl, etc.

Antique bronzes

Bronze cash and notes

'Veritable Records', Classics, Histories, Philosophy, *Belles-Lettres* and other books

Rubbings of inscriptions on stone and works of calligraphy

Antique and modern famous paintings, handscrolls and album leaves

II Material converted into its money value (the categories here have been simplified)

Textiles

Garments

Fan pendants

Vessels of bronze and pewter

Books

Writing accessories

Couches

Bedding

Sedan chairs

Furniture

Utensils of wood, lacquer, ceramic, etc.

Musical instruments

Shrines

Weapons

Property, further subdivided into houses, land, livestock and stored grain

The Yan Song inventory list, in that it is by its very nature an attempt to list everything in the possession of the disgraced grandee, turning him from a free, agent who might be expected to present himself through things in the terms most agreeable to his elite peer group into an essentially passive object of the state's wrath, provides a valuable cross-check on the more self-conscious presentation of Wen Zhenheng in the *Treatise on Superfluous Things*, some two generations later. Clearly, however, there are continuities. Yan Song's landed interests may of necessity have been recorded with some precision, but they are recorded last, deprived of the prominence to which the crucial nature of landholding as a source of wealth in Ming China might have been expected to entitle them. Other similarities and dissimilarities will emerge in the course of this study.

One important element of continuity, however, lies in the use of language and in the degree of precision of description used by both sources. There was clearly a Ming readership for lists of things. A third example would be the *Wan shu za ji, Miscellaneous Records of the Administration of Wanping County* of 1591, with its enumeration of every sheet of paper, stick of ink and table frontal to be used in the examination process, and its careful count of pewter as opposed to ceramic wine ewers to be used in the 'mounting' and 'dismounting' feasts offered to examiners and successful candidates.[17] That such precision should exist in an inventory or a manual of bureaucratic procedure is only to be expected and is, indeed, paralleled by the language of contemporary inventories from early modern Europe, though they tend not to make as many separate categories of goods as do the compilers of the Yan Song document, being preoccupied with more broadly-defined significant groupings such as 'plate'. Only an exceptional document such as the 1607–11 inventory of the *Kunstkammer* in Prague of the Emperor Rudolf II displays the same degree of subdivision.[18] However, the precise specification of dimensions (not in terms of 'large' or 'small' but of standard units of measurement), of materials, of form and of decorative schemes is common to both the literary text and the administrative document in China.

This is, thus, a language very far from the typical rhetoric of Western art history (and also of most Chinese types of writing about pictures), language which has been characterized by Michael Baxandall as 'ostensive', that is, as operating by 'showing', in a rhetorical posture of pointing out features of the representation which only receive their full degree of meaning when juxtaposed with the object itself or with an accepted reproduction of it.[19] The 'descriptions' of pictures in Vasari, for example, would not enable us

to reconstruct the artefact of the painting in a situation where we
lacked any surviving evidence for the visual appearance of either that
object or of other objects of the same class. However, Wen Zhenheng's
works not only enable us to attempt a reconstruction of certain
elements of the Ming material world which no longer survive (the way
displays of fruit were laid out on plates, for example, something not
based on visual sources, or some types of lacquered furniture of which
no examples have come down to the present); they allow us to pluck
out from the poorly differentiated mass of material in museums and
circulating in the art trade objects which fit his forensically exact
descriptions and describe them as 'clearly the kind of thing he had in
mind'.[20] Without this degree of precision in his descriptions, Wen
Zhenheng would be of no more value to the museum/market complex
now than is Sabba di Castiglione, a rather earlier Italian writer whose
work touches on issues of taste which in some ways parallel that of
the Chinese writer, but who employs very different types of language
in sustaining the essentially social nature of distinctions between
things.

The Lombard nobleman Sabba di Castiglione (1485–1554) was a
relative of the better-known Baldassare Castiglione, the author of the
most widely known of all Renaissance conduct books, *The Courtier*
of 1528. He is remembered by western historians principally as the
author of a set of *Ricordi* of 1546, addressed to his nephew, a group
of 134 short essays on subjects as diverse as choosing names for
children, ingratitude, the clerical life, how children ought to behave
in front of their parents, and the end of the world. The book was
extremely popular in sixteenth-century Italy, going into eleven
editions between 1546 and 1584. Art historians in particular have been
attracted by Ricordo 109, *Cerca gli ornamenti della casa*, which gives
advice on interior decoration in a manner which has some interesting
points of comparison and contrast with a writer like Wen Zhenheng.[21]
What is immediately apparent is the much greater degree of
imprecision involved:

> Others decorate and ornate their halls with hangings of Arras and
> Tapestries of Flanders made with figures, foliage or greenery; rugs
> and moquettes from Turkey and Syria, barbaresque carpets and
> tapestries; painted hangings by good masters; Spanish leather
> ingeniously wrought; others decorate them with new, fantastic and
> bizarre, but ingenious, things from Levant or Germany, subtle
> inventress of beautiful and artistic things. I favour and praise all
> these ornaments, too, because they are a sign of judgement, culture,
> education and distinction . . .[22]

Here, there is a heavy reliance on generalities, 'ingeniously wrought', 'beautiful and artistic things', as against Wen's precision of colour, from, decoration and dimensions. Ricordo 13, *Cerca il vestire*, is similarly restricted to generalities on the appropriate dress of a gentleman. And it must be remembered that the *Ricordi* are in no way devoted exclusively to material culture in the manner of Wen's *Treatise*. The oft-quoted remarks on ornamenting the house are placed between an entry, *Cerca la cupidita delle richezze*, and one entitled *Cerca il tiranno*, both classic humanist topics which are far removed from a concern with the things of the material world.

The unwillingness to descend to specifics in the matter of material goods is a constant of early modern European conduct books. Sabba di Castiglione has been referred to so often because he is unusually detailed in this respect. There is nothing comparable in the *Civil Conversation* of Stefano Guazzo, another international best-seller, written in 1574 and published in an English edition in 1586.[23] Guazzo is concerned with what makes 'gentrie' or a 'gentleman' in terms of the distinction between blood alone and blood plus 'virtue'. Wealth and conspicuous consumption are an important part of 'liberality' and can add to the esteem in which a gentleman is held, but there is no guidance offered as to what exactly wealth is to be spent on. Later, when deploring the growing tendency of rich peasants to attire themselves unsuitably like gentlemen, to the degree where 'a man can discern no difference in estates', he recommends that the lower orders should be forced 'to wear such apparel as may be at least different from gentlemen, if they will needs have it as costly'. His readership is presumed to be acquainted with the dress of a gentleman, without the need for specifics. A native English example of the genre, Henry Peacham's *Compleat Gentleman* of 1622 (and, thus, closely contemporary with the *Treatise on Superfluous Things*) is also willing to allude but not to describe. His chapter 15, 'Of reputation and carriage' includes advice on clothing, but again only in terms of the broadest generalities.[24] His language elsewhere, like that of all early modern European writing on the question of luxury consumption, is that of morality and of humanist idealism and not in any way comparable to the material precision of the Chinese writings.

This precision of language, good enough to serve as an identifying label for surviving types of object after some four hundred years, may partly be the answer to a question which has never, to my knowledge, been posed. Why is a book about things, like the *Treatise on Superfluous Things* or the relevant sections of *Eight Discourses on the Art of Living*, not illustrated? Not only was the technology easily available to publishers (illustration in wood block was essentially the same technology as that used to print the text of a book), but the period of the late sixteenth – nearly seventeenth century was one which saw a massive increase in the publication of illustrated books of all kinds; not just literary works like novels, plays and collected volumes of poetry, but reprints of the major Song treatises on archaeology, religious works and books of popular moral instruction, books on geography and travel, volumes of reproductions of paintings, works on technology and medicine, botany and natural history, and accounts of foreign peoples are just some of the categories produced.[25]

Gao Lian's *Eight Discourses* does, in fact, contain a number of illustrated pages, which serve in the treatise on preventative medicine to show various therapeutic exercises akin to yoga (Plate 1). There are also a couple of illustrated pages showing how to pack a travelling case. But there is no use of pictures when it comes to the sections on contemporary material culture, such as furniture, or on antiques. The obstacles to the use of such pictures can only have been ideological, rather than technical, since there exists one rather curious text from a slightly earlier period which does juxtapose pictures of things, some of them contemporary, with written commentary on them. This is *Shi you tu zan, Illustrated Praises of my Ten Friends*, written towards the end of his life by the Suzhou author Gu Yuanqing (1487–1565; MRZJ, 949), contained in the *congshu, Tales Within a City Wall, Continued*, not published until the last decades of the Ming dynasty.[26] It describes the following ten possessions, listed as the author's inseparable 'friends': a slate table-screen, an 'ancient pottery vessel', a jade-handled whisk, a speckled-bamboo couch, a gourd water vessel, an iron *ruyi* (a sort of ornamental sceptre, but with no ritual significance), a bamboo flute, a bamboo staff, a jade chime and an inkstone. The picture of each item is followed by a brief and simple description, incorporating precise measurements (the couch is 1 ft 2 in off the floor, 7 ft long by 3 ft 5 in wide), then by a more florid and literary 'encomium' (*zan*), which is quite unlike anything seen later in Gao Lian or Wen Zhenheng. This unusual text stands on its own without imitators, as a hybrid of the very old tradition of 'poems celebrating objects' (*yong wu shi*) and the developing late Ming interest in a precise verbal fixing of the material world.

Both the meticulous and archetypally bureaucratic listing of object after object found in the Yan Song inventory and the more mannered phrasing of Wen's *Treatise* are structurally equivalent in one crucially important way, which is quite distinct from Gu Yuanqing's celebration of ten favourite possessions. They are not so much about things as entities in themselves, but as entities in opposition to other entities. On the linguistic model, they do not so much provide us with a complete grammar of Ming objects as with a number of significant features which allowed one utterance to be distinguished from another by contemporaries. Wen Zhenheng in particular rarely introduces an object except to state what it is *not*. Here in the pre-industrial world of goods of the Ming elite is a clear parallel to the situation described by Adrian Forty as intrinsic to the more complex world of the nineteenth century in Europe and America:

> To look at the ranges of goods illustrated in the catalogues of nineteenth-century manufacturers . . . is to look at a representation of society . . . For, like any representation, be it in the form of painting, literature or film, this strange and cumbersome master-piece created by manufacturing industry not only corresponded to what was seen to exist, but, without recourse to language, metaphor or symbolism, also showed people social boundaries and distinctions that might otherwise have been invisible to them, or to which they might have been indifferent . . . to know the range of different designs was to know an image of society.[27]

With the always crucial *caveat* that, in the case of Ming China the overwhelming majority of the population concerned itself not with choices about consumption but about whether it could consume enough of the necessities of life to avoid, death, there is nothing in Forty's formulation which is not applicable to the minority of the population living above subsistence level, that minority itself being the subject of further very complex social stratification and differentiated access to power. That differentiation of access was made manifest by differentiated choices in the range of commodities to be consumed. Forty, however, seems to me to place too much emphasis on the role of manufacturing as against consumption, particularly as his basic thesis holds up equally well in the context of China, where the accumulation of political, economic and cultural power on the part of elite consumers far outweighed the resources of the relatively weak producers, un-centralized, unorganized and relatively unconscious in their responses to the demands made on them by their customers, as we shall see. The distinctions which Wen Zhenheng enunciates are not those made manifest to him by the actions of producers of clothes, or tables, or incense burners. Rather they are the product of elite consensus about the way 'things ought to be', both in the precise and the figurative senses. It is the separate grounds, the different poles of opposition along which the configurations of objects were negotiated, on which Wen and his contemporaries made these distinctions that will form the subject of the remainder of this chapter.

One of these poles of opposition, present as much by virtue of its deliberate exclusion as by and explicit statement, is male/female. Adrian Forty again has highlighted this as one of the more important cleavages through society made manifest by different sorts of goods in Europe from the nineteenth century.[28] It seems to be the case, however, that prior to this period of European history this social distinction was not one which was constantly manifested through society in the form of different male and female material cultures, except in the case of garments, and of types of object only ever used by one or the other sex, such as weapons or cosmetics. There does not appear, in seventeenth-century Italy, for example, to have been such a thing as a 'woman's chair' or 'man's cup'. (The point is not that such differentiation did not exist, but that it was not raised to the level of conscious pronouncement). However, as we see above in the case of 'Parrots' and and 'Bed curtains', Wen Zhenheng is prepared to state explicitly that certain types of object, or certain sub-types of object, defined either by material, decoration or both are not suitable for use by men at all.

This of itself may not seem very startling. Ming China was a society strictly segregated on gender lines, a segregation which extended even to close blood relations in the same family. Those whose dwellings were large enough to allow it divided them strictly into a male part of the house (at the front) and female quarters, with very little crossing of the boundaries between except by the male master of the house. This crossing of boundaries, potentially dangerous in its mingling of the male *yang* and female *yin* principles, would most probably occur largely in the private quarters of the women, where sexual relations would be likely to take place. Thus, it seems powerfully symbolic that most of Wen Zhenheng's anxieties about possible upsets to the natural order of things, through male misappropriation of objects and types of material or decoration intended for women, should be focused on the bed or the bedroom.

In additional to his comments on bed curtains already quoted, his chapter on furniture contains a differentiation of the type of beds more suitable for women, while another more general entry on 'Bedrooms' in the 'Placing and Arrangement' chapter explains the necessity for great simplicity and plainness there, lest the slightest touch of 'prettiness' produce an effect more suitable to a woman's room. Balustrading carved with an openwork pattern which we know as the swastika (a common Ming decorative motif) was suitable only for women's quarters, being not very 'antique or elegant',[29] He does not manifest these sort of worries with regard to, for example, dress. There, he simply disregards the clothing of women altogether, and the general 'Clothing and adornment' stands, by a process also observable in Western writing, for the specific '*Men's* clothing and adornment'. No fear of the female is felt here, where boundaries are clear cut.

There is, however, evidence from sources other than Wen Zhenheng that the boundary between men's things and women's things was felt more widely than his concentration on the area of greatest danger would suggest. A much-quoted entry in *Essential Criteria of Antiquities* uses it in its description of what it calls 'Syrian ware', the copper vessels decorated in cloisonné enamelling which were at the time of writing a recent import from Islamic west Asia: 'I have seen pieces such as incense-burners, flower vases, boxes and cups, which are appropriate for use [only] in a woman's apartment, and would be quite out of place in a scholar's studio'.[30] If we look more broadly, there are further suggestions that the sexual segregation made concrete in the upper-class dwelling by a division into men's and women's parts of the house was echoed by a distinction between men's and women's things. This is often clear as much by omission as by statement. For example, Wen Zhenheng's chapter on furniture, when dealing with storage, is interested only in the storage of books and works of art. Any other from of cupboard or coffer (and we know quite a lot about the various types in existence in his day from the numerous surviving examples) is simply not worthy of notice, as the sole concern of women and servants.

Similarly, it seems likely, on the basis of graphic rather than textual evidence, that women never sat on the typical high-backed armchairs of the period when men were present. This was not an absolute rule, but a distinction based on precedence, as the most important or aged woman in an all-female grouping would make use of such a seat in the absence of any men. One particular type of low-backed armchair may, as the etymology of its Chinese name suggests, have been destined specifically for the use of women. There are even more tantalizing hints of a separate women's attitude to things in the case of furniture, where items such as chests of clothing, and more particularly the large canopied beds which dominated the women's quarters of the house, formed part of a woman's dowry, publicly carried through the streets to her intended husband's home at marriage. These pieces of furniture remained the woman's property, available to be removed by her on any dissolution of the marriage.[31] A woman's bed acted very much as a symbol of her status within the household, its quality serving to differentiate primary from secondary consorts within the polygamous family unit.

Decoration, too, could act as a way of marking some things off as the exclusive provenance of women. Despite the existence of a number of famous female scholars, poets and artists at the period – one of the most famous of all, Wen Shu (1595–1634) was a cousin of Wen Zhenheng[32] – the more general position appears to have been that women even in wealthy families were not taught to read, or at best had only a little functional literacy which still denied them access to the more prestigious written traditions. If this was in fact the case, then the non-verbal methods of presenting to women paradigms of behaviour and expressions of cultural norms deemed appropriate to their subordinate position assume much greater importance, beside better-studied ways of inculcating these norms, principally the theatre, other performing arts, such as those provided by hired story-tellers, and the practice of religious cults.[33]

Judging by the evidence of surviving Ming artefacts, women were constantly exposed to objects which carried messages reinforcing the view that their principle social function was as the bearers of male children who could carry on their husbands' ancestral lines. Textiles decorated with the motif of the 'Hundred Boys' have been found in the tomb of the principal wife of the Wanli Emperor (r. 1576–1620), showing a degree of consensus right up to the highest levels of society about what a woman should aim for. Plants symbolic of fecundity, such as the lichee, decorated the cosmetic boxes used by women, while a particular kind of lacquer box, employed probably for the exchange of horoscopes between the bride's and the groom's family in the course of marriage negotiations, was invariably decorated with the same few scenes (anecdotes drawn from history and literature), at least one of which was a classic instance of the appropriate ritual formality ideally prevailing between man and wife.[34] This was, indeed, a material culture for the women of the Ming period, but it cannot be taken for a material culture *of* Ming women, whose distinctive cultural patterns are submerged in the silence to which their subordinate status consigned them.

To switch rather arbitrarily from a distinction between things on the basis of the gender of their ultimate users to one based on the conditions of their production, one of the most prominent seen in the literature is that of geography, of where a thing was made. This is a criterion on which to rank objects which had a particularly venerable pedigree in China, going back at least as far as the late Bronze Age text, the fifth-century BC *Tribute of Yu* chapter of the even older *Classic of Documents* purporting to describe the particular products, both raw and manufactured, of the nine divisions of the empire presented by his subjects to the mythical emperor Yu the Great, tamer .of the primeval flood and inventor of the crucial technology of water management. The enumeration of the 'special products' (*te chan*) or 'famous products' (*ming chan*) of the different parts of China remained a feature of official historiography right through the early imperial period, enjoying a prominent place in the dynastic histories and in other sorts of quasi-official writing. Several of the famous descriptions written in the thirteenth century around the fall of the Southern Song capital and commercial centre of Lin'an, the modern Hangzhou, lovingly list the production centres for the best teas, silks or other luxuries.

Wen Zhenheng's entry on types of tea comes from within this tradition of writing about 'famous products'. However, he also displays to the fullest possible extent something which was only beginning in the Song period, but which had reached an advanced stage of development by the sixteenth century, and which has attracted a great deal of attention on the part of Marxist scholars working from the 'sprouts of capitalism' hypothesis, and that is the formation of a national market in luxury manufactures. The networks of commercial activity, but also of commercial information, had by his day reached the point where products of a particular locality could enjoy a reputation on an empire-wide (which is to say a continental) scale. Merchant networks centred on Anhui, south of the Yangtze, and on Shanxi province in north-central China were, for example, able to circulate the products of the great ceramic kilns of the town of Jingdezhen throughout the empire and beyond. Merchant handbooks were published listing the particular specialities of each province, in conventionalized terms like 'an abundance of bamboo, wood, lacquer and tallow is concentrated in western Zhejiang', or of Jiangxi 'the region abounds in bamboo, arrows, gold, lacquer, copper and tin', together with hints on the best markets for these products.[35]

Thus, it is hardly surprising that we get from such a sophisticated consumer as Wen Zhenheng statements like 'Hangzhou brushes are best for painting', and the assertion that the best contemporary paper is made in Anhui province.[36] In the case of the carved stones used for grinding cakes of ink to manufacture the essential medium of writing and painting, Wen lists a great number of localities specializing in different types of stone, from eight separate Ming provinces ranging from nearby Zhejiang to Guangdong in the deep south and Gansu in the remote north-west of the country. As a type of luxury of particular interest to the scholar class (and, thus, by extension to all who imitated their lifestyle), inkstones were particularly finely differentiated as to place of manufacture, but all types were equally available through the workings of the commercial process in the late Ming. They were available not only to the very wealthy group of Suzhou families of whom Wen Zhenheng was a representative but also

to the much humbler type of local gentry who may have formed the
readership of the almanac literature and the householders' manuals.
Thus, *Complete and Categorized Essentials for the Householder*
includes in its section on the 'Necessities of the studio' the information
that the best bristles for brushes are from Panyu county in Southern
Guangdong province, while the most famous brush-makers are concentrated in the two prefectures of Xuanzhou and Changzhou in
Anhui province.[37] This represents a diffusion of knowledge about
'special products' which to this day has continued to be sustained by
oral transmission, as well as by written guide books of many different
kinds.

One particular type of geographical discrimination well represented
in the *Treatise on Superfluous Things* is that of exotica, of manufactured goods from beyond the boundaries of the Chinese empire. This
was quite different from the importing of exotic raw materials, which
had a history of centuries, if not millennia.[38] Nor were these merely
occasional, chance curiosities in the later sixteenth and seventeenth
centuries but a systematically imported and significant sector of
luxury consumption. The list of 'tribute goods' (as international trade
was disguised in Ming official ideology) given for the Wanli period
in the *Riben kao*, *Study of Japan*, by Li Yangong and Hao Jie lists:
'sprinkled gold cupboards, sprinkled gold writing tables, painted gold
cosmetic boxes, sprinkled gold portable boxes, plastered gold painted
screens'.[39] Taken cumulatively, the evidence for the prevalence,
above all, of Japanese luxury goods in the fashionable late Ming
interior is a powerful corrective to simple characterizations of Ming
culture as 'nationalistic', or relatively unreceptive to foreign influences.

Despite the fact that for much of the sixteenth century coastal
China and the prosperous Jiangnan region were preyed on by the
wokou, 'Japanese pirates' (many of whom were, in fact, renegade
Chinese under Japanese leadership), the minds of the rich do not seem
to have poisoned against Japanese objects in their own homes. It is
simply not true for the Ming elite that, in the words of what has until
very recently been one of the most widely read undergraduate text-
books in Chinese history, 'Alien rule had inspired hostility towards
alien things in general. Gradually this view hardened into a lack of
interest in anything beyond the pale of Chinese civilization.'[40] In
addition to turkeys from the New World to be kept as pets, woven
matting from Portuguese-held Malacca on the Malay peninsula, and
paper and brushes from Korea (all three being semi-processed goods
rather than manufactured luxuries), Wen gives a great deal of notice
to importations of high-craft objects from Japan, principally in the
fields of lacquer and metalwork. His account of Japanese swords may

be a venerable literary topos, quoting the Song dynasty scholar Ouyang Xiu (1007-1072), like his praise of Korean lanterns which similarly goes back to *Record of the Pure Registers of the Cavern Heaven*, but his mention of religious texts in Tibetan (certainly unreadable but adding an elegant air of Buddhist scholasticism) is more likely to be based on contemporary practice. The same is true of Japanese bronze hand-warmers, bronze rulers, steel paper-knives and scissors, and from the same country, lacquered incense boxes, wrist rests, inkcake boxes, dressing cases, tables, cupboards and display shelves (the Japanese *tana*).

There is no hint of a patronizing tone in Wen's enthusiasm for these foreign goods:

> Japanese caskets are of black lacquer with inlaid gold and silver sheet. The large ones measure over a foot. Their hinges, pins, and locks are all marvelously curious and ingenious. They are highly suitable for storing antique jades, precious objects and small scrolls of the Jin and Tang dynasties. There is another sort which is rather larger, of an antique and elegant pattern, with designs such as diamond diapers and 'strings of beads'. They are as light as paper and can also hold scrolls, aromatics, medicines and bibelots. It is advisable to have several ready for use in one's study.[41]

Indeed, as was to be the case with seventeenth and eighteenth century European customers, the quality of Japanese lacquering was held generally to be pre-eminent, being mentioned often by Gao Lian and praised as 'supreme' in Zhang Yingwen's *Pure and Arcane Collecting* of 1595.[42] Wen Zhenheng also mentions folding fans as an item of fashion, and these too were regularly imported from Japan, having been introduced from there to China in the early part of the fifteenth century. Although no surviving pieces of Japanese lacquer of the relevant period have been identified in China (they surely rest unnoticed in the stores of China's great museums), some of these fans, which are either Japanese in manufacture or else very precise Chinese imitations of Japanese manufacture, have been recovered by archaeologists from tombs of Ming date.[43]

This receptiveness to exotica on the part of the elite adds depth to the eagerness with which high officials, and the imperial court itself, embraced the gifts of clocks, engravings, prisms and other European imports, when they were offered by the first generation of Jesuit missionaries in China, led by the famous Matteo Ricci (1552-1610; DMB, 1137-44). This episode is often recounted as proof of China's fascination specifically with the scientific advances of the West, when

it may fit more comfortably into a pattern where goods from overseas could be a familiar and a desired category, regardless of
the nature of the individual items involved. Novelties were not a
novelty.

The distinguishing of objects on geographical grounds was, as we
have seen, a very long tradition in China. However, a more distinctively Ming innovation was the new importance attached to the name
of the manufacturer as a ground of distinction, something which is
seen in its typical form in the entry on 'Incense burners' quoted above,
with its reference to the Pan family and the Hu family of Yunjian,
the modern Songjiang. This type of 'trade marking' of manufactured
goods was not unknown in earlier centuries, particularly in the highly
commercialized world of the late Song period in the thirteenth
century. The kilns in Henan province making painted ceramic pillows
frequently marked their products with formulae like 'Made by the
Zhang Family', implying a degree of customer recognition of at least
some of the better known sources of supply.[44] On luxury lacquers,
decorated with incised gold, dating from the same period, these
maker's marks could become quite elaborate, sometimes giving the
purchaser detailed information on the place of manufacture, presumably as a primitive form of advertising: 'Finest quality work by
Nian Wulang of Xinwujin, Wenzhou' or again, 'Finest quality work
by Jie Qishu, of the alley by the T-shaped bridge in Wenzhou, [made
in the] *geng shen* year'.[45] The famous detailed descriptions of the
thirteenth-century capital city at Hangzhou are also full of details
about named manufacturers of all sorts of everyday and luxury good,
a street-by-street directory of the longed-for but vanished delights of
its sophisticated urban milieu, driven by a powerful nostalgia in which
no detail is too insignificant to be allowed to perish in the horrors of
the Mongol conquest.

The situation prevailing from the late sixteenth century was slightly
different, in that a considerable number of craftsmen in a much
broader number of areas of work started to achieve national recognition and status, where the addition of their name alone was sufficient
to add value in the market-place to a manufactured object. So Shen
Defu can take notice of the fact that folding fans in the fashionable
Japanese style by Shen Shaolou or Liu Yutai (these are just names now
and cannot be connected with any surviving object) sell for one ounce
of silver, while those by Jiang Sutai can fetch three or four ounces.[46]
This had been a phenomenon unknown in, say, the fifteenth century
(the question of the value attached to painters' names is, as we shall
see, quite a different matter) which was, nevertheless, relatively
common after the Jiajing reign (1522–66). It was felt by elite consumers

at the time to be something of a novelty and worthy of comment and record.

One of the longest and most explicit notices of what was felt by a typical member of the upper classes to be happening in the whole area of the luxury trades is found in the *biji* writings of Wang Shizhen (1526-1590; DMB, 1399-405).[47] I will have occasion to refer to it again for its claims about how the fashion mechanism was operating, but it is for what it has to say towards the end of the passage about the role of leading craftsmen that it is worth quoting extensively here:

Once it was Song dynasty painting which was valued, but in the past thirty years there has been a sudden emphasis on the men of the Yuan, so that the value of a Ni Zan (1301-1374) or of a Shen Zhou (1427-1509) from our present Ming dynasty has shot up tenfold. In the field of ceramics, once it was Ge ware and Ru ware which were valued, but in the past fifteen years there has been a sudden emphasis on wares of the Xuande reign (1426-35), so that the value of those of the Yongle (1403-25) and Chenghua (1465-87) reigns has shot up tenfold. Probably it was the men of Suzhou who began this, and the men of Anhui province who brought it on. It is an extraordinary thing. Nowadays, the jades worked by Lu Zigang, rhinoceros horn pieces worked by Bao Tiancheng, silver worked by Zhu Bishan, pewter worked by Zhao Liangbi, fans worked by Ma Xun, inlay work by Zhou Zhi (all of whom are from Suzhou here), and then the goldsmithing of Lu Aishan, the agates worked by Wang Xiaoxi and the bronzes worked by Jiang Baoyun (both from Shexian in Anhui province) – all these are several times the price of ordinary pieces. This sort of person gets as far as sitting with the gentry. Recently, I gather that this fashion has entered the palace, and its rise is not yet at an end.[48]

The same mixture of fascination and unease about the fluidity of social boundaries can be seen in the writing of Zhang Dai, who consciously prolonged the style and the concerns of the late Ming 'minor appreciation' (*xiao pin*) writer into the following Qing dynasty:

The matchless skills of Suzhou are: Lu Zigang's jade carving, Bao Tiancheng's rhinoceros horn work, Zhou Zhu's inlay work, Zhao Liangbi's comb making, Zhu Bishan's gold and silversmithing, Ma Xun and Lotus-leaf Li's fan-making, Zhang Jixiu's *qin* zither-making and Fan Kunbai's making of three-string guitars. All of them have been without rival for a hundred years. But the excellencies of their craftsmanship and their efforts have reached a level of competence in their arts. Their qualities and contrasts fit them

for the piercing discrimination of true connoisseurs of later ages.
How could an ordinary artisan achieve this? They are skills, but they
approach the Way (*Dao*).[49]

Elsewhere Zhang muses on the strange social effects of the much
despised artisan skills and seems to be groping towards a recognition
of the very relative, culturally defined nature of the 'menial crafts':

> Bamboo, lacquer, bronze and ceramics are menial crafts. Yet look
> at Bamboo-worker La of Jiaxing, the lacquered bamboo of Wang
> Er, the *meilu* bamboos of Suzhou's Qiang Huayu, the lacquers and
> bronzes of Lacquerer Hong and Bronze-worker Zhang of Jiaxing,
> and the ceramics of Wu Mingguan from Huizhou – all of these men
> have brought renown and elevation to their families simply on the
> basis of bamboo, lacquer, bronze and ceramics. They themselves
> sit as equals and exchange greetings with members of the gentry.
> There is nothing under the sun which is not of itself sufficient to
> ennoble someone; it is simply that people will consider them as
> 'menial'.[50]

These lists of famous craftsmen are largely formulaic and can be
repeated from other sources of the period. The repetition of a few
names again and again, together with disquieting details such as the
uncertainty over whether the otherwise totally unknown Zhao Liangbi
made pewter vessels or combs, should cause us just to pause and
consider exactly the degree of elite involvement in the patronage of
named craftsmen which they imply. For with the exception of these
casual mentions of the same names which are endlessly repeated in
the form of lists of famous craftsmen, we actually know next to
nothing from independent contemporary sources about the scope of
their activity. Indeed, we do not really know if they were craftsmen
at all.

Most of the names on a list like that of Wang Shizhen are simply
that, names. We know of no surviving pewter pieces (or combs, for
that matter) from the hand of Zhao Liangbi, no agates by Wang
Xiaoxi, no bronze vessels by Jiang Baoyun. However, there do exist
in circulation today silver objects with the signature of Zhu Bishan,
jades with that of Lu Zigang and bronzes similarly attributable to the
equally renowned metal worker, Hu Wenming. They raise as many
serious doubts as they provide answers with regard to the question of
the extent to which elite notice of previously despised artisans involved
an actually transformed relationship within society. The fact that they
were noticed at all, in fact, seems more likely to be a factor of the

increased need of the elite to fix bench-marks of discrimination between different types of goods than of any more relaxed social atmosphere.

For a start, not all of the names are contemporary with their rise to a prominent position in the late Ming connoisseurship literature. Zhu Bishan the silversmith was, for example, first recorded by a contemporary Tao Zongyi (*c.* 1316–*c.* 1402) as being active in the middle of the fourteenth century, and the most famous surviving objects attributed to him are all dated in a way which would accord with this. Late Ming lists of silversmiths are only able to repeat the same four names as Tao, showing that no more figures in this craft had registered on the consciousness of the elite in the intervening two centuries. And, indeed, it can be shown that objects with his signature but which stylistically cannot have been made before about 1580 were in circulation in the late Ming.[51] Zhu Bishan was *the* silversmith, sufficiently well known to give a higher profile to the craft even if no more contemporary names were necessary. This core name, one famous personage who was of himself sufficient to stand in for the whole craft, was a necessary part of fixing any given type of craft on the hierarchy of elite esteem.

Some forms of making, principally bamboo carving and the carving of seals (closely related to calligraphy) were prestigious enough to attract gentleman-practitioners and, thus, escape the stigma of the artisan's humble status altogether. Li Liufang, the commentator on chapter 3 ('Water and rocks') of the *Treatise on Superfluous Things* enjoyed a contemporary reputation as a bamboo carver without it damaging his social standing in the eyes of his peers. At the opposite end of the hierarchy were those crafts where not a single name of a producer is recorded in the writings of the consuming class. The outstanding examples of this are probably furniture making and the manufacture of clothes. As we have seen from the extracts quoted above, clothes and furniture existed in the same continuum of consumption as other areas which (on first sight, at any rate) are better documented. Fine clothes and fine furniture were an important part of the presentation of an upper-class persona to the world, yet we do not have the name of a single Ming tailor or a single Ming cabinet-maker. In the middle of this scale of values came those luxury trade like silversmithing, bronze casting and jade working, where it seems to have been necessary for the operation of the discrimination between the acceptable and the unacceptable that there be a name to which praise or blame could be attached, but without there having to be the full spread of names which would follow from a fuller engagement with the actual processes of manufacture.

Lu Zigang plays this role for jade carving, but once again the contemporary evidence for his activities is surprisingly slight, by contrast
with his reputation, sustained throughout the Qing period and into
the modern art market-place, as the finest jade worker of all time.
There is in existence a box with his signature dated 1562, which if
genuine would have to place his birth some way before the mid-point
of the century. He appears as a contemporary in the passage by Wang
Shizhen (who died in 1590) quoted above, and in a poem by Xu Wei,
dead in 1593. The 1642 edition of the *Gazetteer of Taicang Prefecture*
records him as a native of that district, with the words;

> Fifty years ago there was of this prefecture a certain Lu Zigang,
> whose skill at carving (jade) with the knife remains unsurpassed to
> the present. Jade hairpins by him sell for fifty or sixty ounces of
> silver each. The skill was not handed on at Zigang's death.[52]

This may be a meagre quantity of documentation on which to build
an artistic biography, but it is still a lot more than we know about
Hu Wenming the worker in bronze, equally famous in later centuries.
With the exception of the notices, not all of them complimentary, by
arbiters like Wen Zhenheng (and it has been shown that he is less an
authentically original voice than the mouthpiece of a consensus), there
is a bare notice in a very suspect gazetteer of his native district of
Songjiang, supposedly of Ming date but remaining in manuscript until
the middle of the eighteenth century. There are a larger number of
pieces ascribable by inscription to him and also to his son or to the
continuer of his workshop style, one Hu Guangyu.[53]

Through what I have just written, as well as through almost all of
the modern writing about the Ming 'decorative arts', runs the assumption that Lu Zigang and Hu Wenming were individuated artistic per-
sonalities, single, artistically conscious wielders of the knife, the
abrasive wheel, the cauldron of molten metal. The emergence of these
and other 'names' at this particular period has been linked not only
with the gradual freeing of the artisan class from the restrictions
placed on them by the 'service' system of the early Ming, whereby they
had been compelled to spend regular periods in the unpaid employ of
the state. As a part of the growing commercialization of the period,
the state from about 1550 more or less abandoned the attempt to
enforce these obligations in favour of a straight purchase in the
market-place of the goods and services it required.[54] It has also been
linked with the development of a concept of 'individualism', rather
as the growing practice of signing pictures in Italy after about 1500
used to be seen by Western art historians as the rise of an essentially

individualist, typically 'Renaissance' attitude to artistic creation, by contrast with a 'medieval' model in which the anonymous creators worked much more closely to the specifications of patrons, or of doctrinal necessity, in the case of works destined for a religious clientele.

The parallel with early modern Europe is interesting and can be extended a little here. Certainly, it has been asserted that it was only from about 1520 that the name of the maker added significantly to the immediate or subsequent value of the work, just as was the case with Shen Defu's fans.[55] Interpretations of the meaning of this phenomenon in the West, however, have long veered away from the idea of a burgeoning 'individualism' towards seeing it as, in fact, the very opposite. Works were signed to show that they met the standards of a hierarchically *administered* but collectively working enterprise, with the signature being not that of the artist as individual hero but of the entrepreneur who guaranteed the quality of the output, regardless of the quantity of actual creative or executive labour he put into each separate piece.[56] This perception is coming to dominate much of contemporary work on the luxury trades in early modern Europe, as some of the most famous names in the history of the decorative arts are reassessed, on the basis of a close study both of archival material and of surviving objects.

The 'individual artist' model of craft production in this formative period in the history of the European decorative arts was imported almost wholesale from the more developed study of western painting, and its decline has followed some way behind the recognition of the major role of the workshop in the production of single and multiple images in Europe. Michael Sonenscher's work on the luxury trades of eighteenth-century Paris demonstrates that literally no type of object was ever made by a single pair of hands, and he shows that the immense reputations of 'artists' like the cabinet-maker Jacob and the *vernisseur* Guillaume Martin depended principally on their skills not only in managing the work of a shop of up to fifty people, but in manipulating the networks of credit and commercial information necessary to deploy the skills of a much larger network of sub-contractors and outworkers. Close investigation of the archives of Parker and Wakelin, the late eighteenth-century London goldsmiths, has similarly shaken any lingering confidence in the belief that a work bearing their mark is in any meaningful sense 'made by', rather than co-ordinated by, them.[57]

There are, inevitably, no archival sources which would shed light on the workshop practices of Lu Zigang or Hu Wenming, in late sixteenth-century China. Several factors, however, point to the strong possibility that the model of the workshop leader as co-ordinator rather than individualist creator which is now being widely established for Europe holds good there, as well. The division of labour was certainly very well established in those Chinese craft workshop contexts which we are able to study at all, most notably in the huge ceramics producing centre of Jingdezhen in southern-central Jiangxi province, the largest industrial complex anywhere in the world prior to the eighteenth century. There, a single piece of porcelain could pass through a very large number of hands in the course of its manufacture in workshops which, when not operating directly to the order of the state and for the supply of the court, were dominated by merchant entrepreneurs largely originating from Huizhou, a highly commercially developed locale of neighbouring Anhui province. They in fact controlled ordering, manufacturing and marketing.[58] Indeed, it seems quite likely that the otherwise unrecorded Wu Mingguan of Huizhou, who in Zhang Dai's words quoted above 'brought renown and elevation to his family' on the basis of his ceramic products, was just such an entrepreneur, a workshop chief who might well 'sit down with the gentry', without ever having had clay under his fingernails or having wielded a brush charged with cobalt pigment.

The scale of ceramic production might be argued to be a special case, but there is equally compelling evidence for the division of labour in much smaller kinds of workshop. Two good examples are the Cantonese workshops in the eighteenth century, which were engaged in painting to the commissions of Western merchants in enamels over the glaze on ceramic 'blanks' already imported from Jingdezhen, and the ateliers in the same city one hundred years later, which produced watercolours on paper, again as export commodities destined for the European and American markets. A figure like Guan Lianchang, the owner of one of the most successful of these export painting enterprises, may well have provided models for his workers to copy and adapt, but he cannot be regarded as the executor of the vast number of works surviving which bear his workshop stamp of 'Tingqua'.[59]

What this brief survey of the conditions of production of Ming luxury artefacts inexorably leads us towards is the thesis that the distinctions of name visible in writing like that of Wen Zhenheng, of this bronze-maker against that bronze-maker, for example, are not distinctions between the recognizable and recognized artistic styles of individuals but between what are essentially trademarks, the names of enterprises which might owe their origins to a nameable individual but which continued to employ that name well beyond an individual's lifetime. The problem we are faced with, if we reject the model of individual patron – client relations lying behind the apparent rise in the practice of recording craftsmen's names, is why a few names should be recorded, repeated endlessly and hardly ever augmented. Lu Zigang *is* jade carving. Hu Wenming *is* bronze-casting.

This problem is even more perplexing when we consider that, in fact, the conditions of production often provided the ideal conditions for the recording of craftsmen's names, due to the common practice of workers in the capital-starved luxury trades often taking up residence in a patron's home and working there on expensive raw materials supplied by him. This can certainly be shown to have happened in jade carving. The inventory of Yan Song's property contains a significant amount of uncut jade in boulder form, awaiting the hiring of skilled hands to turn it into something decorative or useful. Zhang Dai records how an uncle of his got hold of a piece of particularly fine jade and hired a craftsman to turn it into a cup in archaic style.[60] The word used for 'hire' (*mu*) carries the meaning that he took the craftsman, whose name is quite pointedly *not* recorded, into his own household.

Similarly, silversmiths would come and make jewellery in a client's house and to his immediate oral specifications, while cabinet-makers, too, seem to have been in the habit of bringing tools and timber to the client's house and working there under his supervision.[61] We even have one piece of evidence for a bronze-caster named Pan working in the home of our own Gao Lian, but the mention of his name seems here to have as much as anything to do with verifying the amazing tale of his capture by Japanese pirates, subsequent artistic training in bronze-working in Japan and return to China.[62] The immediacy of the contact between customer and maker may well have been of crucial importance for the nature of pre-modern Chinese design, but what it does in the present context is make more, rather than less, curious the fact that Lu Zigang is more or less the only Ming jade carver whose name survives. Does his fame really rest on the measureless superiority of his products, or is it more likely to be related to some necessity within the Ming system of object distinction and discrimination for *a* name, any name, in a given craft? The answer may well lie in the field of the grandest and most prestigious kind of luxury commodity, painting.

Put bluntly, I would argue that the late Ming was a period when a number of luxury trades came within the ambit of a system of discrimination which had long been applied to paintings when in their commodity state. Names, even a very few names, were essential to the operation of this mechanism. This was far from having always been the case. Such few remnants of Chinese painting as survive from the first millennium AD show that it was quite common for major images to remain unsigned, despite the existence of a developed art-historical literature which was for the most part arranged on biographical lines, after the model of the extended collections of biographies arranged by type to be found in the standard dynastic histories.[63] It was not the case that it did not matter who had executed a picture, but rather, the fact of that execution was not overwhelmingly determined by explicit signature of the work (this is in some ways analogous to the situation in pre-quattrocento Italy). However, by the Song period (960–1279), with the full formation of an accepted body of canonical work and the working out of a more broadly aestheticized set of criteria for quality in painting, the singularization of the work, made explicit by the signature and seals of the artist, came to the fore. A modern scholar has written:

> China's artistic tastes have over the last six hundred years veered increasingly towards name-association. Moving away from a direct encounter between man and art, collecting became a social relationship between famous artists and fame-seeking collectors. When an artwork is produced for admiration, 'by whom' is the first concern: visual appraisal of its intrinsic excellence is given almost secondary importance. In such relationships the collector joins a fraternity of cultural elites: he associates (and becomes associated in turn) with ancient cultural heroes, with their character, talent and prestige. This has become the primary relationship, the function of collecting.[64]

As soon as names started to matter, there appeared the topos in art-historical writing that the average viewer was too dependent on these name identifications, too willing to be impressed by a famous signature. The distinction at work here was supposedly between an inferior perception on the part of those who needed to see the name of a famous artist before appreciating a work's quality and those connoisseurs of a superior perception who were not reliant on such obvious devices. Shen Gua (1031–1095) was among the first of many to complain that, of those pretending to an appreciation of painting, 'the majority rely on names alone'.[65] By the Ming period, anecdotes supportive of this abound, and it forms an important litmus test of the difference between 'us' (the author and the reader) and 'them' (the undiscriminating, excluded mass). Shen Defu puts it this way: 'In ancient times famous paintings put no stress on signatures or inscriptions, but the men of today are credulous, and invariably mark down the price of an unsigned work.'[66]

Wen Zhenheng himself provides several examples, one of which refers to the regularly unsigned work of the court painters of the Song imperial 'academy':

When people nowadays see an unsigned painting they at once add a signature on the basis of its subject matter, in search of a high price. So they see an ox and it must be by Dai Song, see a horse and it must be by Han Gan, and so on. This is particularly laughable.[67]

In his general discussion on painting at the head of chapter 5 of the *Treatise on Superfluous Things* he carefully makes a distinction between those unsigned works which, by their pre-eminent aesthetic qualities, are 'clearly by the hand of a master' and those works of a 'vulgar brush' which yet bear a pretentious signature 'added later'.[68] Interestingly, the possibility of a genuine but poor work by a 'famous name' is never admitted. And having made his obeisance in the direction of this time-honoured position, he goes on to do what seems to have in fact been the more common Ming position when faced with the task of discriminating between pictures; he lists acceptable and non-acceptable names. Or rather, he lists mostly acceptable names, with a few significant exceptions in the other direction. His list of painters to be collected is very broad, indeed, encompassing all of the famous names of the Song and Yuan periods, professional masters of the sixteenth century and, in prominent positions, his own distinguished ancestors, Wen Zhengming, Wen Jia and Wen Boren, with the words, 'these are all famous masters whom you cannot be without. It is not appropriate to preserve the work of anyone else, and if you have, it is not appropriate to bring it out to show people.'[69]

There is of course a voluminous literature on Ming art history in both Chinese and Western languages, and a number of distinguished syntheses exist. But these are by their very nature likely to concentrate on painting as if it were a totally different type of artefact, inhabiting a sphere of pure aesthetics unconnected with other kinds of luxury consumption. They are also likely to concentrate on what seems at the time innovative, interesting and culturally enriching, at the expense of what seems conventional, trite and unmotivated by deeper personal motives. Thus, a reading of the secondary literature on Ming art history can convey an impression of a period of intense aesthetic debate and cultural ferment, of struggle over the definition of the canon and of a very polarized discourse, split between those who saw the ultimate roots of meaningful painting as lying in the Song period (960–1279) and those who saw the exemplars of good practice as being the painters of the subsequent Yuan dynasty (1280–1367). The struggle between those who preferred Song models, one of the last of whom was none other than Gao Lian, and those who revered instead the Yuan, their standard bearer (and ultimate victor in the process of defining a canon) being the celebrated practitioner and theoretician Dong Qichang, can in this reading come to seem like the most prominent feature of the discussion of painting in the late Ming.[70]

Yet in Wen Zhenheng, writing, if I am correct, in about 1620, and who was connected to the circle of Dong Qichang through his acceptance of patronage by Li Liufang and Lou Jian, there is no sign of these supposedly titanic battles. His casual acceptance of Song and Yuan masters as equally desirable may well reflect a more prevalent elite attitude, where those thought worthy of record were also thought worthy of esteem. Only the despised 'wild and heterodox' school of six relatively obscure painters, condemned in identical terms by Gao Lian, Tu Long and Wen Zhenheng, existed as a necessary foil to the very much larger roster of those who could be safely and uncontroversially owned and shown to one's peer group.[71] Advanced aesthetic debate was left to the very few.

There is by implication a certain amount of polemic on the art of painting in Wen Zhenheng, though it may be ultimately traceable to family loyalty. By stating that collecting of paintings should cease with 'the famous masters of the Longqing reign' (1567–72, i.e. the generation of his own father and uncles), and expressing the view that, 'as for the gentlemen working with dot and colour in recent times, I have not dared to criticize them lightly',[72] he was quite obviously snubbing Dong Qichang and his school, the grouping which succeeded not only in stamping their impress on all subsequent Chinese painting practice and theory but in substantially restructuring everything that had gone before them, by their deployment of the theory of a 'northern'/'southern', professional/amateur, inferior/superior dualism stretching back into the Tang period. This attitude clearly was not enough to damage his relations with Li Liufang or Lou Jian , and it may simply emanate out of a familial loyalty to the stylistic tradition embodied by his own family and by his native city of Suzhou, by 1620 no longer in the national vanguard of painting practice (or at least so it seems to us now, given Dong's realignment of the canon; it may not have seemed so then). Wen Zhenheng does include contemporaries in his list of distinguished calligraphers, with none other than Dong Qichang topping the list.

If we, then, leave aside the particular freight of social and aesthetic meaning with which they were endowed and look at paintings, both ancient and contemporary, in circulation in the late Ming period as simply being one type of rather special commodity, some continuities and some disjunctions in Wen Zhenheng's treatment of the question of 'names' emerges. At the most basic level, names of makers were a way of identifying and categorizing things. This is obvious, but it needs stating. Names could in particular travel with an object through a whole series of encounters in the market-place, being turned several times into a commodity again, when the name would continue to function as an index of value independent of the status of the seller or of the purchaser. Names were, with the exception of the 'wild and heterodox', used principally to say positive things about painting but could be used to identify other types of artefact negatively. Names were applied differentially to different types of goods, with some very important types (e.g. luxury textiles) remaining formally nameless, although they may have been identified at the point of sale with the name of the enterprise responsible for making them. A very limited number of names, often no more than one to a craft, became established in the closing decades of the sixteenth century and remained constant not just through the Ming period but on into the succeeding Qing. The existence of at least one name was, it appears, sufficient to allow these goods, like jades and bronzes, to be the objects of the sort of discrimination which had been applied to paintings for centuries, the sort of discrimination which we see them undergoing in the pages of Gao Lian and Wen Zhenheng.

The grounds of discrimination discussed so far, being those of appropriateness to gender, geographical origin of the product and name of the craftsman responsible, are suggestive of some of the ways objects were thought about in the late Ming. Another major line of cleavage, that between the 'antique' and the 'modern' was so important that it warrants separate treatment in a following chapter. But these are far from being the only qualities which Wen Zhenheng isolates in categorizing things, and particularly in categorizing manufactured goods. He makes distinctions very freely on the grounds of form, of material, of decoration and of appropriateness as to placing both in space and in time. An example of each of these relatively easy to grasp distinctions shows his style of working very plainly and can be drawn out of the extracts quoted in full at the head of this chapter. So with form, an incense burner in the shape of a pair of fishes (or with fish-shaped handles) or in the shape of an elephant (and surviving examples of the latter do exist, to confirm that we are dealing with a discourse about the real world) can never be acceptable. Even greater precision of form and decoration is seen in the entry on 'natural tables', where the panels between the legs must not be carved with 'such vulgar patterns as dragons, phoenixes, flowers, and grasses'

(Plate 2). When it comes to material, an otherwise acceptably shaped incense burner can be vetoed if it is made from ceramics from the province of Fujian , which in the context almost certainly means the white porcelain of Dehua. Decoration, too, can make a correctly formed object of the right material fail, as when the 'vulgar patterns, like dragons, phoenixes, flowers and grasses' bring down a 'natural table'. Finally, the entry on 'Placing vases' demonstrates the twin criteria of appropriateness, both as to place (large in the reception hall and small in the studio) and season (bronze in winter and spring, porcelain in summer and autumn). A great deal of the irony in the novel *The Golden Lotus* seems likely to stem from the wanton flouting of these criteria of taste by the rich but unspeakably vulgar hero. His wealth enables him to purchase, for example, famous paintings, but he then hangs them in sets of four on all the walls of his 'study', a thing explicitly criticized by Wen Zhenheng. The seasonal criterion, one for which no explicit parallel can be drawn in the West, was of particular importance. It is referred to time and again, and one extensive section of the chapter on painting is devoted to the types of picture appropriate to different times of the year, not just according to season but according to individual months.[73]

I would now wish to argue that any attempt, and several have been made, to extract a set of constant underlying aesthetic principles, valid for the entire body of Ming 'scholars', from these multifarious types of distinction is bound to fail. It might be objected that there are certain general principles enunciated in Wen Zhenheng's *Treatise*. For example, he tells his readers to 'Value bronze and ceramic, and hold gold and silver cheap . . .', but this is simply with regard to the placing of vases, and cannot be taken as expressing a broad distaste for the use of precious metals in other contexts, most notably in the context of the dinner table. We have a statement from another late Ming writer, in the context of a *biji* collection, that the use of ceramic cups for wine was a sign either of great poverty or, on the part of those who could afford precious metals, a sign of an ostentatious and unattractive puritanism. It was quite in order for the same man to praise a contemporary for the elegance of his silver tableware.[74] Or again, at one point Wen Zhenheng appears to lay down a general law with regard to subject-matter in decoration, stating: From of old there is the saying that, 'First come "sword rings" (a type of abstract spiral decoration), second come flowers and grasses, and third come human figures.'[75]

The comment is made, however, apropos of a particular kind of small lacquer box for the storing of incense, on surviving examples of which all these three types of decoration are indeed found, though they do not necessarily appear on other classes of artefact. It is, therefore, dangerous to assume that he is here positing a general rule, rather than a particular principle applicable only to incense boxes.

What is certainly not a safe practice, for example, is to make a statement to the effect that the 'culturally conservative literati', of whom Wen Zhenheng is here identified as one, preferred two specific types of ceramic 'to all other ceramics'.[76] The two types in question are both crackle-glazed wares of the Song period, which are not in fact the most frequently mentioned in a positive context in Wen's chapter on 'Vessels and utensils', but that is beside the point. What is not beside the point is that there are also copious *negative* references to all the most supposedly favoured types of ceramic ware, if they are of the wrong shape or utilized for the wrong purpose. It is, in fact, quite untenable to point to a general class of surviving Ming objects, or to an individual piece, and label it as one which 'Wen Zhenheng considered to be elegant'. Even if we can ascertain his views on the form, material and decoration involved and find all of those 'acceptable', we cannot match his criteria of suitability. The project of understanding the meaning of late Ming material culture purely on the basis of a taxonomy of objects cannot succeed.

> Every essentialist analysis of the aesthetic disposition, the only socially accepted 'right' way of approaching the objects socially designated as works of art, that is, as both demanding and deserving to be approached with a specifically aesthetic intention capable of recognizing and constituting them as works of art, is bound to fail.[77]

What, then, is the object of the discourse of the *Treatise on Superfluous Things* and the texts which it replicates and modifies? The answer must surely be that it is a discourse about society, about things-in-motion as a model of, not how that society *was*, but of how it was perceived by the literate elite. It will by now have become obvious that I am reading *Treatise on Superfluous Things* very much in the light of Pierre Bourdieu's work on *Distinction*, and in particular in the light of his detailed working out of the implications of the perception that, 'Social identity lies in difference, and difference is asserted against what is closest, which represents the greatest threat.'[78] The constant assertion of difference between things in the *Treatise* is nothing more nor less than an assertion of the difference between people as consumers of things.

This attempt to situate difference at the point of consumption is a break with earlier schemes of classification in Chinese culture, such

as the fourfold scheme, dating back to the Bronze age, of Scholar/
Farmer/Artisan/Merchant where the focus is on the relationship to
production, principally agricultural production. Although I have
deliberately left it for consideration until after an analysis of the
contents of the *Treatise*, there is explicit confirmation of this social
reading of the work in its preface, which is not the work of Wen
Zhenheng but of his close associate Shen Chunze:

> Recently the sons of the rich and one or two dullards and per-
> sons of mean status have abrogated to themselves the status of
> 'aficionados'. At each attempt at connoisseurship they utter some
> vulgarity, besmirching anything which comes into their hands with
> their wanton fumbling and grabbing, to an utter pitch of vileness.
> A gentleman of true tastes, talents and sentiment thus takes vows
> not to even mention 'elegance'. Ah, it has already gone too far![79]

This eschewal of the aim of distinction, of course, stands at the head
of a lengthy work which is precisely all about how to distinguish
'elegance' from 'vulgarity'. There can be little doubt about the basi-
cally social aims of Wen Zhenheng's project, and little doubt, too, that
the prominence given to material culture and to consumption behaviour in the literature of the late Ming period reflects a generalized
intuition, if not an explicit awareness, of the part which things could
play in a hierarchically structured but highly stressed society. Things
were social actors, and texts about things were not untouched external
observers of their action but further players in their own right.

3

Words about things

The language of Ming connoisseurship

A complete survey of the language used to categorize, discuss, praise and criticize objects in the Ming period would be highly desirable but is difficult to achieve for a number of reasons. Some of these are inherent in the nature of the Chinese written language and in the tools currently available to study it. The Chinese script forms have been remarkably stable over a very long period of time, giving an aura of continuity and of essentially unchanged meaning over thousands of years. Although a lot of work has gone into recovering shifts in the pronunciation of Chinese through history, much less attention has been paid to mapping out the equally great shifts in meaning which seem likely to have occurred over the same period. And while some of the dictionaries available cite the earliest, or at least a very early, usage of a character or string of characters, none of them as yet supplies enough in the way of differentiated contexts to allow a word's progress to be followed through time.

This can lead us into some quite basic mis-comprehensions. For example, the term *hua* is now rendered as 'painting', though it is easy to demonstrate that its Ming usage is more like 'picturing', in that it includes representations in various textile techniques, such as embroidery and silk tapestry (*kesi*), which now have a different and much lower status in the practice of museums and of the art market. We need even in a basic case like this to pay more attention to when we are using 'emic' categories (that is, those recognized by the actual participants in a cultural practice), and when we are using 'etic' ones (those which may be discerned by observers, and not necessarily accepted by participants).

This attention to language is important enough when dealing with substantives, but it is even more so when looking at the terminology of aesthetics. It seems inconceivable that a character like that now pronounced *ya*, and conventionally translated as 'elegant', which first appears in the Bronze Age and which is still very much part of Chinese vocabulary today, has not in its long passage through time acquired vast new areas of meaning while losing many of those which it had in its original context. However, we are at a loss to trace these in their full ramifications.

Another problem lies in those kinds of records which survive from the Ming period, the vast majority of them being sources composed by or under the supervision of the dominant, educated section of society. As is well known, written 'classical' Chinese has always been far removed from what we can surmise of actual speech patterns, even of the speech patterns of the elite. This remained the case in the Ming period, despite the development of certain kinds of dramatic and fictional narrative which have long been accepted as embodying much closer approximations to the way people talked. These are themselves written texts and cannot be accepted as unembellished raw data for the study of the vernacular. So we cannot know how people in the Ming period talked about things; we can only know how they wrote about them, and this has to be viewed as a severe limitation.

All the authors of the works to be analysed were men, for a start, and we cannot therefore know how, if at all, Ming women, the submerged and largely illiterate section of the empire's population, thought about the material goods which they handled in their daily lives. Certainly a novel like *The Golden Lotus* includes many scenes of women commenting, sometimes in great detail, on the artefacts which surround them, particularly those relating to dress and personal adornment, but here again they are mediated through an anonymous but undoubtedly male author. Women, even the women of the upper class, are largely silenced in the Ming record, as is that vastly greater majority of the Chinese male population which lived lives of hard physical work and cultural impoverishment. The way farmers and artisans thought and talked about their tools and their products would form the cornerstone of any really complete study of attitudes to material culture in the Ming, but the evidence is as yet largely lacking.

Even within the copious written records of the dominant class, there are problems of interpretation of the sources. Written Chinese may be restricted to recording just a part of the world of Ming China as it was actually lived and experienced, but it is still a very various part. There are many different registers of written Ming Chinese, from those deemed suitable for exposition of classical Confucian texts, through those used for poetry, for political debate, for drama and fiction and for a whole range of other types of subject matter. There are the very specialized discourses of Buddhist and Taoist religion, which influenced and were influenced by writing on more secular subjects. There are any number of highly technical areas, each with their own specialized vocabulary, from the language of the texts on *qin* zither playing[1] to those on agricultural technology.

All these different 'Chineses' interpenetrate one another, yet no Western scholar (and certainly not the present author) is master of them all. The language used in talking about objects did not exist in a vacuum, and many of the key terms to be discussed below existed in other contexts as well, contexts which might well have been familiar to the authors of or audience for the texts on connoisseurship and luxury consumption. For instance, *ya* as well as meaning 'elegant' had quite precise technical connotations in the language of *qin*-playing, a skill cultivated at least nominally by most members of the elite. Similarly, its opposite *su*, usually 'vulgar' in the context of connoisseurship, also had the important meaning in Buddhist discourses of 'lay, secular' as opposed to 'clerical, religious'. Even such a simple-seeming opposition as *zhen* 'true' and *wei* 'false' extended into the area of poetic criticism, where it was particularly linked to the theories of one prominent group of poets, the Gong'an school centred on the brothers Yuan, one of whom we have already encountered as the author of the *History of Vases*.[2] We cannot know now the extent to which shades of meaning from other semantic fields are at work in the texts about things and will certainly miss much of the range of allusion and reference which created their richness for the original reader.

Even if we restrict ourselves to terminology within the broadly defined area of aesthetics, there exist problems in simply taking over wholesale the work, excellent as much of it is, which has been done on assembling the language of poetic or of painting criticism and applying it to other areas such as the discourse surrounding the material culture of the elite interior.[3] Shifts of emphasis, subtle changes of meaning and even the exercise of hard-to-identify rhetorical strategies like irony make it unwise simply to accept a term like *jia*, 'lovely, fine', as being 'the same word' when applied to a well-turned couplet, the overall appearance of a painting or the material from which a specific type of desk accoutrement is to be made. Again, the problem lies in the fact that no Western student has read a large enough quantity of Ming texts of a diverse enough nature to have a feeling for the full range and total implications of any given piece of vocabulary in one given period, never mind having that same feeling for the movement of words in time.[4] Chinese scholarship has not as yet addressed this question very much.

This present excursion is not an attempt to provide that equivalent, since its author is not competent to supply it. But it does, after the manner and under the influence of Michael Baxandall's and Peter Burke's expositions of some of the key terms at the intersection of cultural and social discourse in fifteenth- and sixteenth-century Italy,[5] try to map out some of the general contours of the terrain on which writers from the Ming elite were able to discuss the luxury artefacts of a culture where such artefacts were of considerable social importance. This was done crudely by using as a framework the number of times a particular quality is used in the 'Vessels and utensils' chapter of the *Treatise on Superfluous Things*. Any one of these terms merits a much more refined, subtle and far-reaching analysis than it is given here, but it is to be hoped that a general statement of the problem may encourage further studies to look once again, and to look hard, at translations which stand in danger of being accepted too easily.

THINGS: *WU* AND *QI*

At the most basic level, 'things' were *wu*, a word which carried a heavy burden of meaning in Confucian philosophical language as 'matter', the pair and opposite to *li* 'principle'. Trends in philosophy in the late sixteenth and early seventeenth centuries put an increasing emphasis on the 'matter', through such terms as *ge wu*, 'the investigation of things'.[6] This very broad category of *wu* at the same time included artefacts, both contemporary luxury artefacts and antiques. We read of visiting an antique shop to 'see all the things', and of rare agates as 'old things', *jiu wu*.[7] The word was commonly qualified by a period, such as 'a thing from the Shang or Zhou period', a 'typical thing of the Shang period' or 'Han dynasty things'.[8] 'Rare things' *qi wu* could apply equally to paintings in the style of the court Academy and to works of jade and silver in an archaizing style.[9] The cultural centre of Suzhou was famed for the production of 'precious and rare things'.[10] 'Harmonious things' *yun wu* were things possessed of a desirable degree of propriety and elegance.[11]

And of course *zhang wu*, 'superfluous things' gave the title to Wen Zhenheng's unprecedentedly complete survey of elite material culture. The term is derived from an allusion in the fifth-century AD *New Account of Tales of the World*, which has been translated as follows:

When Wang Gong returned to the capital from Kuaiji, Wang Chen went to see him. He observed that Gong was sitting on a six-foot bamboo mat, and accordingly said to him, 'You've just come from the east and of course have plenty of these things; how about letting me have one?'

Gong said nothing, but after Chen had left, he took up the one he had been sitting on and sent it along with him. Since he had no other mats, he sat thereafter on the coarse floor matting. Later Chen heard of it and in extreme astonishment said, 'I originally thought you had a lot of them, and that's the reason I asked for one.'

Gong replied, 'You don't know me very well. I'm the sort of person who has no extra [superfluous] things.'[12]

The use of the term 'superfluous things' thus actually means 'essentials' and is employed by Wen in a seemingly ironic sense, a usage which is not unique to him but is observable in at least one other author, who remarks of a wine jar which was a treasured family heirloom, 'this is an old thing of my family's, and yet a "superfluous thing" of my family's'.[13]

A term with a much more restricted set of meanings and a seemingly less elevated set of associations was *qi*, which had connotations of 'utensil', 'vessel', 'tool'. In late Ming usage it can mean 'machine', as in the 1627 work on the marvels of European mechanics, the *Yuan xi qi qi tu shuo*, *Illustrated Explanations of the Strange Implements of the Far West*. One of Confucius' most celebrated statements in the classics was the dictum, 'The superior man (*junzi*) is not a utensil (*qi*)', his implication being that men of superior moral qualities were not to be viewed as interchangeable cogs in the administrative machine. The word *qi* is often combined with another character meaning 'tool' or 'utensil' and then forms part of formulae such as *wenfang qiju*, 'utensils of the studio'. It is the combination *qiju* which provides Wen Zhenheng with the title of his chapter on the moveable material culture of the Ming gentleman. What it thus includes are essentially all items which are luxurious refinements to, rather than necessities of, living. It includes both antique and contemporary material and objects with a continuing function, such as the necessary tools for writing and painting, together with those which are more involved in stating their possessor's cultural eminence through display. The preamble to Wen's discussion of individual types of artefact reveals some of the implications of his use of the category:

Vessels and Utensils: In making utensils the men of old valued utility without sparing expense; thus, their manufactures were extremely well prepared, unlike the slapdash attitude of the men of later times. From bells, tripods, knives, swords, dishes and ewers down to ink and paper, they delighted in a refined excellence. They did not vainly add inscriptions and value only signatures. Today, people lack experience and are accustomed to seeing that which the world values, so that they cannot discriminate between elegance and vulgarity. Some are slaves to prettiness with no eyes for the antique, so that their surroundings show no objects of harmoniousness, and yet they talk extravagantly of 'dispositions' [i.e. interior decoration]. I have not dared to allow this lightly.[14]

The term *qi* was subject to various types of qualification, but these are usually more blandly descriptive than the types of attribute attached to *wu*. Thus, it is standard to have *jin qi* and *yin qi* for 'gold vessels' and 'silver vessels', also *tong qi* for 'bronze vessels' and *yu qi* for 'jade vessels' (*tong wu* or *yu wu* seems not to be possible). These are the terms found in the bald, bureaucratic language of the Yan Song inventory and also in the less elevated style of the Ming householder's manual.[15] This last source also frequently uses what may be the more colloquial term *cheng qi*, literally 'to become a utensil' to mean something like 'serviceable' or 'useful', as when making the point that jade cups are of no use if their ring handles are too narrow to admit the drinker's finger. This criterion of suitability for use, though explicitly stressed in the passage from Wen Zhenheng quoted above, is in fact otherwise rarely seen in the connoisseurship literature, and its prominence here only serves to underline the distance between those texts and the more prosaic world of the household manuals, aimed at a humbler fraction of the dominant class.

ANTIQUE AND OLD: *GU* AND *JIU*

The character *gu*, 'ancient', antique' has a very wide semantic spread at the period with which we are concerned. A *gu ju* is a 'former dwelling', somewhere you used to live, while a *gu you* is an 'old friend', in the sense of an intimate of long standing. The distinction between *gu* and *jin*, 'modern' dominated Ming theorizing in the field of poetry and of the most prestigious genres of prose.[16] But even in this literary context the concept was a relative one, with the 'antiquity' preferred as a model for prose being the Qin and Han dynasties (221 BC – AD 220) and that for verse being the high Tang dynasty (eighth century AD). These early periods were also those from which official Ming ideology drew much of its legitimation.

For Wen Zhenheng and his contemporaries, artefacts were an integral part of a continuum of moral and aesthetic discourse, where *gu* does not simply mean 'chronologically old', but implies 'morally ennobling'. The evidence of numerous entries in the *Treatise on Super-fluous Things* is that an object made the previous day could be deemed 'antique' if it met certain criteria in a fitting manner. To mix one or two ceramic or gourd vessels with precious metal tableware would, for example, give a dinner party an 'antique feel'.[17] As with the better studied category of 'luxury' in the West, and like several of the other terms discussed here (particularly *ya* below), *gu* is essentially not a category of artefact but a means of categorizing artefacts. Like luxuries, *gu* objects are, in the words of Arjun Appadurai, 'goods whose principal use is rhetorical and social . . . a special "register" of consumption (by analogy to the linguistic model) . . . [rather than] a special class of thing'.[18] The wider context of the deployment of these antique goods in the late Ming period is the subject of chapter 4 below.

What could be *gu*, and in which circumstances? One of the more tightly circumscribed uses of the term is that found in the inventory of the possessions of the Grand Secretary Yan Song, made by the state on the occasion of his fall from power in 1562. Of the thirty categories into which the bureaucrats responsible divided his vast wealth, the word *gu* appears in the headings of only four, and it does not appear as a description of individual artefacts in the other categories. It appears twice in the formula *gu jin* 'ancient and modern', as in 'Ancient and modern famous *qin* zithers' and 'Ancient and modern famous paintings, handscrolls and album leaves'. In neither of these two cases is ancient an absolute term. It is defined solely by opposition to 'modern' and in practice here means no more than 'prior to the reigning dynasty'. Only two categories are given over to objects generically defined as 'ancient'. They are *gu yan* 'Ancient inkstones' (a relatively short entry) and *gu tong qi* 'Ancient bronzes', a relatively long one with 1,127 items, including inlaid pieces.[19]

A broader usage of the term *gu* to categorize objects can be seen in the writings of Gao Lian and Wen Zhenheng, where it could be applied to almost any type of material, though the two dominant categories of 'ancient' artefact here are still bronzes and jades. Once more, the actual definitions are fluid but tend to coalesce around the first three dynasties of traditional historiography, the Xia, Shang and Zhou, and the Han dynasty. Gao Lian, for example, talks about the 'antique use' of jade being lost after the Han period.[20]

'Antique' could be combined with several other characters to give binomes such as, most frequently, *gu ya* 'antique elegance' or *jing gu* 'refinedly antique'. Here, the nature of Chinese grammar makes it particularly difficult to tell if the two characters are to be read as one distinct 'word' or if the two terms retain their separate identities. If the latter, there is still the problem of knowing how much relative weight to give to word order (*gu ya* is quite common but *ya gu* is not seen) and to the two, possibly unequal, parts of the term.

There was another word for 'old' in Ming Chinese, *jiu*, which carried all of the less exalted areas of meaning, for example 'old clothes', but which seems in usage to have been occasionally employed as a synonym for *gu* in the connoisseurly context. We get *jiu hua* 'old paintings' and *jiu shu* 'old books', where the context makes it clear we are talking of antiquarian rare editions, and even occasionally *jiu tong qi* 'old bronzes'.[21] The possibility may exist of a slightly ironic, tongue-in-cheek feel to the language here, just one of the kinds of nuances now lost to us.

ELEGANT AND VULGAR: *YA* AND *SU*

As a crucial polarity in the way the Ming elite regarded the manufactured world about them, 'ancient/modern', was paralleled by one of even greater importance, that between *ya* 'elegant' and *su* 'vulgar'. The individual words had their Ming meanings at least by the late Bronze Age and were in use as a pair of complementary opposites by the later Han dynasty. In the case of *ya*, however, this was a late meaning, following on from its use as a name for one of the genres in the earliest collection of verse, the *Book of Songs*.[22] The grammarians of the Han gloss the word as equivalent to *zheng*, 'regular', 'proper'. At the same time as it was used with regard to physical things, *ya* continued to have a role in the description of personal conduct and as a technical term in music criticism, standing for 'the discipline, individual and social, necessary to resist new trends and foreign influence'.[23]

It is primarily a term which operates in the realm of the social, not of the visual, and is, for example, rarely used with regard to the appearance of a painting, though it might well be applied to the subject matter, like the famous 'Elegant Gathering in the Western Garden',[24] or the social act of connoisseurship: 'The appreciation of calligraphy and painting is an elegant affair (*ya shi*).'[25] 'Men of elegance', *ya ren*, appear in one text as the small group who initiate the fashions which are then taken up by the wider world, but the formula is rather unusual, and again it might be suspected that a degree of irony is at work.[26] A close analysis of Wen Zhenheng's chapter on 'Vessels and utensils' reveals that *ya*, here including its combinations like *gu ya* 'antique elegance', *jing ya* 'refined elegance' and *qing ya* 'light elegance', is his second most favoured term of approbation, while its negatives, such as 'not elegant', 'not an elegant thing', etc., are among his more common ways of disapproving of an object. That this should be so is one measure of the essentially social criteria at work in this text, since an object's *ya* is as much a function of how and in what context it is used as it is of its materials, configuration or decorative schemes.

The statement in Shen Chunze's preface to the *Treatise on Superfluous Things*, to the effect that, 'A gentleman of true tastes, talents and sentiment thus takes vows not to even mention "elegance"'[27] should alert us to the possibility that *ya* was a quality easily overdone. In this context, there is something a little disquieting about the name of Gao Lian's studio (and by extension the full title of his *Eight Discourses*) being *Ya shang zhai*, 'The Studio where Elegance is Valued'. A cursory survey of any of the standard reference books on studio names shows that the thumping obviousness of this is unusual and that names with *ya* in them are actually rather uncommon, presumably for the very reason Shen Chunze gives.

A word which seems to be a close synonym of *ya*, though not so ubiquitous, is *yun*, originally 'harmonious' but extending into meanings like 'elegant' or 'sensibility'. A love of antiquity is 'the elegant affair of a man of learning' *wen ren yun shi*, while the 'gentleman of sensibility' *yun shi* is used as a term for the ideal figure to whom the *Treatise on Superfluous Things* is addressed.[28]

Wen Zhenheng's favourite term of condemnation is precisely the opposite of *ya*, that is *su* 'vulgar', which in some ways has a more straightforward etymology, with a cluster of meanings which all operate in the area of social classification and which are analogous to the descendants in the Romance languages of the latin *vulgus*. It also means something like 'custom', 'habit' and hence 'popular', 'of the common people'. It is generally enough on its own to damn but is occasionally combined into a formula like *e su* 'ugly and vulgar'. His other ways of disapproving of something are, similarly, at least as social as they are aesthetic; *bu ke yong* 'cannot be used', *bu ru pin* 'not worth considering', and *ji* 'it is tabooed'. By contrast, *bu jia* 'not lovely' and *bu mei guan* 'not of an attractive appearance' are rare.

LOVELY AND REFINED: *JIA* AND *JING*

Despite the importance of this underlying structure of social values, the most common term of approval in Wen Zhenheng's discussion of objects is, in fact, one where the intrinsic appearance of the item discussed is more to the fore. This is *jia* 'lovely' or 'fine', another word which seems to stand alone and not combine into binomes. Its range is largely, but not exclusively visual. The very widespread and long-lasting *jia ren* 'fair lady', 'beautiful woman' is seen as early as the late Bronze-age *Elegies of Chu*. In addition to its common application to objects, it was, albeit rarely, used as a desirable attribute of Ming painting.[29] A *jia ju* was a 'fine phrase' in poetry, and *jia* was part of the distinctive technical vocabulary of the Gong'an school of poets. Its use by one of the Gong'an theorists reveals its surface nature, when he states that a poem can be 'lovely', even if has its origins in 'falseness'.[30] It is, thus, a suspect quality, capable of deceiving those whose social qualities and qualities of character are deficient. Wen Zhenheng says of jade desk water-pots from the workshop of the famous Lu Zigang, in the shapes of archaic bronzes, 'Although they are lovely vessels, they are not worth considering.'[31]

Jing is a much more complex quality, and much harder to render in English, its core meanings being things like 'essence', 'spirit', 'finest part of' and, hence, 'fine' as opposed to 'coarse'. It had a broad range of usage, extending through metaphysics, medicine and literary theory, as well as other areas. In contrast to *jia* it is rarely used alone, but generally in combination with other terms to give, for example, *jing ya* 'refined elegance' or *jing gu* 'refined and antique'. It can be used in combinations which refer essentially not to the aesthetic but to the technical dimensions of workmanship, as in *jing qiao* 'refined and skillful', or *jing gong* 'refined workmanship'.[32]

USE AND PLEASURE: *YONG* AND *WAN*

'Utility' *yong* and *wan* 'pleasure' are an important pair of oppositions in the writing of Wen Zhenheng. This opposition appears prominently in the discussion heading his chapter on 'Vessels and utensils' (see pp. 79–80) and is followed through in the text where *ke yong* 'can be used' is one of his most frequent terms of approval, and its opposite *bu ke yong* is even more regularly used. There is, of course, a moral dimension here, with roots in the very earliest classical discussions of issues like luxury and frivolity versus simplicity and integrity. Several times classes of artefacts, particularly antique artefacts, are described as 'only fit for enjoyment, they cannot be used/are not suitable for use/cannot be used everyday'.[33]

However, *wan* 'pleasure' is not a term of denigration but a cherished value of the Ming elite. To know how to amuse oneself and one's peers was a central part of being a gentleman, and correspondingly, the word is used in a self-deprecating fashion to maintain distance from the less esteemed values of craftsmanship and professionalism. 'I did this for amusement' is one of the archetypal clichés of painting colophons, a studied unstudiedness. Consequently, paintings themselves could even on occasion be described as *wan ju* 'objects for amusement', as if taking them too seriously was risky (Shen Defu, p. 653). More common are things like *gu wan* (*wan gu* is a verb + object compound, meaning 'to enjoy oneself with antiquity' and common as the title of a genre of paintings showing gentlemen engaged in the connoisseurly discussion of paintings or antique objects) 'antique bibelots', *shi wan* 'contemporary bibelots', *bao wan* 'precious bibelots'[34] as synonyms for all the kinds of luxurious product with which this book is concerned.

RARITY AND SKILL: *QI* AND *QIAO*

'Rare' *qi* has connotations of 'marvellous' or 'rich and strange', whether in material or in workmanship. We have seen *qi wu* 'rare items' used to describe court academic paintings, but generally Wen Zhenheng reserves it for objects which partake of the nature of curiosities: old lamps of the Yuan dynasty, imported Japanese folding fans and Korean writing paper.[35] It is commonly found in combinations like *qi zhen* 'rare and treasured'[36] or *qi qiao* 'rare and intricate'. The notion of *qiao* is intricately bound up with operational skill, as in the proverb 'Even a skillful housewife cannot make porridge without any millet', or in the ceremony where women, 'begged for skill', beseeching the Weaving Girl, a deity connected with women's domestic labour, for dexterity at needlework. *Qiao* is a value of women and artisans and, as such, not to be too much noticed, even when it is being marvelled at. It is bound up with the whole area of elite attitudes to makers, which is discussed elsewhere. It shades off into a whole range of often onomatopoetic words, originally applied to the tinkling of jade ornaments, which came to mean 'intricate', 'finely wrought': *lin lang*, *ling long* are two of the most common.[37] Also linked is the concept of *gui gong* 'devil's work' for workmanship so fiendishly intricate that no mortal hand could have executed it. The archetype of this is the ball of concentric ivory spheres, a staple of the Chinese export trade in artefacts but actually attested as early as the fourteenth century.[38] 'Devilish strange' *gui yi* is another way of referring to these intriguing but ultimately aesthetically value-less curiosities.[39] 'Workmanship' *gong* is an often-encountered value in its own right or in combinations like *jing gong* 'refined workmanship', but it is not unambiguously desirable; 'although the workmanship reaches perfection, they (jade seal pads) are not worth considering'.[40]

CONNOISSEURS AND DILETTANTI: *SHANG JIAN* AND *HAO SHI*

Here we arrive at one of the truly crucial distinctions made in Ming writing about cultural appreciation, that between true connoisseurship, dependent on a combination of deep scholarship with lofty moral qualities, and shallow dilettantism, an essentially frivolous and ignorant attitude to what should be matters of the greatest earnestness. Although *shang jian* as a word meaning 'discrimination', often in the choosing of personnel, was in use from the Tang period, it is the major Song artist and artistic theorist Mi Fu (1052–1107) who is generally credited with formulating the distinction between it and *hao shi*, which was to reverberate through all writing about the visual arts for centuries.[41]

The two elements of *shang jian* can very occasionally appear reversed as *jian shang*, a usage more common today than it was in the Ming.[42] They were glossed in 1616 by Zhang Chou as *shang* 'to discriminate on the grounds of quality' and *jian* 'to tell genuine from false'.[43] It was not simply an innate quality, since we read of someone who 'gradually refined his connoisseurship', and it can just as easily appear as a verb, with another person being 'very capable at exercising connoisseurship'.[44] It usually appears with a suffix to turn it into the concrete noun *shang jian jia* 'a connoisseur', people who were possessed not only of *muli* 'power of eye' but of *xinli* 'power of mind', as well.[45] The term *jian shang* has an existence in modern Chinese, but its derogatory opposite *hao shi* seems no longer to be in use. It is in many ways the more complex and interesting term.

Hao shi means literally 'fondness for things/affairs', and *hao shi zhe* are by the Ming dynasty 'those who take an interest', in the sense of the French *amateur*, but with much of the denigratory force of the English 'amateur'. There is a parallel with the Renaissance Italian category *amorevolissimi della professione*. A rare example of its colloquial use in a Ming novel suggests that in everyday language it meant something like 'busybody'.[46] It was a term with a distinguished past behind it, however, appearing in Tang texts as something like 'art lover'. This positive, or at least neutral, sense was still occasionally used in Ming and early Qing writing. Shen Defu uses it as synonymous with 'collectors', and Yuan Hongdao uses it as the title of the tenth chapter of his *History of Vases*.[47] In broad terms, however, it is a cutting put-down, something no one would apply to themselves of their friends. It, too, is as much a social as an aesthetic category. To Zhang Dai, the *hao shi zhe* are '*flâneurs*', young men of fashion whose boats jam the Qinhuai River in the brothel quarter of Nanjing.[48] In artistic terms, the 'dilettanti', the 'others', exist to legitimize ourselves as the true connoisseurs, those who not only know what we are looking at, in the sense of not being taken in by fakes, but who appreciate what it is in its widest cultural context.

The 'dilettanti' are, however, not the bottom of the heap of distinction. In place of the dualism of 'connoisseurs' and 'dilettanti', Shen Defu erects a threefold ladder of taste, from the 'men of elegance' at the top, through the 'art loving (*hao shi*) gentry of Jiangnan, to the 'gullible' merchants of Xin'an.[49] The word for 'gullible' *er shi* means literally 'to eat with the ears', another word of ancient pedigree and a vivid metaphor for what Shen saw as the slavish, uncomprehending and uncreative following of trends set by one's social and cultural betters. It was for them that the fakers of fabulously rare antique ceramics, for example, plied their nefarious arts.[50]

OBJECTS AS COMMODITIES: *GU DONG*

Although the actual mechanisms of the market will be looked at elsewhere, there is a distinctive vocabulary of the market which ought to be considered in the present context. Wen Zhenheng frequently employs the word *gui*, playing on its ambiguity, at once 'valued' and 'valuable in a financial sense'. Above all, there is the word *gu dong*, which is now the everyday Chinese word for 'antique' (as in 'antique shop') but which was at once wider and more restricted in its Ming usage. As it is written now, the first element is the character *gu* 'ancient/antique' as discussed above, but this seems to be a later rationalization. At its first appearance in the early twelfth century, it was written with characters which are simply there to represent the sound of a word generated in the vernacular speech of the day. Originally meaning 'broken things', almost 'rags and bones', the first citation showing it applied to precious items of some age is in the verse of Han Ju (d. 1135).

The vivid descriptions of the Southern Song capital at Hangzhou, captured in its last thirteenth-century flourishing before the Mongol conquest, already speak of a *gu dong hang*, with the words, 'those who buy and sell the "seven treasures" are called the *gu dong* trade'.[51] Here, the use was not restricted to ancient objects but referred to contemporary luxuries, as well, particularly those made of rare or precious materials. Elite connoisseurship texts of the late Ming continue to write the word with its original two characters, but at the more vernacular level it was now acceptable to use the character 'ancient' for its first half, as in chapter 66 of the sixteenth-century novel *Shuihu zhuan, The Water Margin*: 'On all sides were hung painting and calligraphy by famous men, with rare and strange antiques (*gu dong*) and bibelots (*wan qi*).'[52]

The distinction made here between paintings and things is not, in fact, sustained by the general Ming usage, where it is quite clear that a painting could just as easily be a *gu dong*, if only under specific circumstances. Those circumstances were those of the market-place, and it thus becomes clear that *gu dong* is a special sort of word used generally to refer to an item when it is in its 'commodity phase', subject to the conditions of the market. It is much less usual to speak of *owning gu dong*, but we do get *mai gu dong zhe* 'those who sell gudong', *lao gu dong* 'an old dealer' and *gu dong pu* or *gu dong dian* 'a *gu dong* shop'.[53] We get objects of all types, and in particular paintings, called by this name, but only when they are potentially or actually available for sale. No one ever refers to paintings in their possession, or which are the subject of aesthetic appreciation, by this name. It is as if this were a way of reinforcing the specialness of painting, calligraphy, bronzes and jades, by 'denaturing' them during their potentially dangerous and degrading passage through the sphere of commerce. This restricted term was a means of turning cultural products into commodities while side-stepping some of the more blatant implications of so doing.

THE WORD THAT ISN'T THERE: *QU*

As James Watt has pointed out in a masterly evocation of some of the aesthetic ideals of the Ming elite:

> Another concept central to late Ming literary criticism is that of *qu* (a word with many shades of meaning: delectation, delight, interest, taste, essential meaning, expression, tendency, inclination). For the literati of this period it combines the state of or the ability to delight with the sense of taste or tendency.[54]

This almost untranslatable concept was, as Watt goes on to demonstrate, a key value in the discussion of painting, of poetry and of personal conduct. It appears in the writing of Mi Fu in the Song period and had been revived as an idea in the early Ming, but by the late sixteenth century it was particularly associated with the Gong'an school of poets, and with the major poet whose birthplace gave the school its name, Yuan Hongdao (1568–1610).[55]

However, the importance of *qu* in these contexts, which are mostly contexts of activity, seems not to have spilled over into the world of things, and in many ways what is significant is that it is rather rarely seen in those connoisseurship texts which address themselves to a precise definition and categorizing of objects. Wen Zhenheng uses it in a manner almost impossible to translate; apropos of snuffers used for extinguishing the fire in an incense burner, he says, 'Burners should be continuously alight to provide warmth even when incense is not being burned; only thus do you have a tasteful intent (*yi qu*)'. In his general discussion of interior arrangements he does talk about how in a gentleman's (*yun shi*) studio, 'as soon as one enters the door there is a lofty and elegant taste (*qu*) which shuts out vulgarity.' And a painting can lose its *qu* by being treated as a commodity in the market-place.[56] But the word is never applied directly to a type of artefact, as is done with *ya* 'elegant' or *jia* 'lovely'. There is, after all, a differential attitude, rather than a totally integrative and holistic one, to things as opposed to other areas of cultural value and aesthetic concern for the elite, at least on the level of the vocabulary used. Yuan Hongdao may use the word (it was almost 'his' word) in his *History of Vases*, but other examples are relatively rare. One such is the use of *tian qu* 'natural *qu*' in 1595 to refer to something like the 'naive charm' of very ancient jades, lost in later, more sophisticated ages, but this is far from common.[57]

DISTINCTIONS AND DIFFERENCES

It is not simply the vocabulary discussed in very sketchy terms above but the broader use of language which is of some help as a way in to the mentalities surrounding the use of luxury objects. In this regard, one of the most telling examples is Wen Zhenheng's pervasive use of formulae like, 'X is best/most elegant/loveliest, then comes Y, then again comes Z'. What is happening here is that a judgement on an object is seldom made in the abstract, but only by distinction, by opposition to other possibilities within the total world of goods. This habit is by no means an innovation of the Ming period. The whole concept of *pin* 'classifying' can be related back to the necessity to classify men on the basis of their suitability to hold office in the bureaucracy. Men were ranked before things. However, the practice had spilled over as early as the Tang period, when one of its first occurrences in this way is in the eighth-century *Tea Classic* of Lu Yu, where a ranking is made of the desirable types of tea bowl.[58]

The whole area of ranking and grading is one which dominates early writing on painting, or more accurately on painters, with considerable mental energy going into increasingly refined subdivisions, where no artist appears on his own but only by reference to those above or below him on the ladder of quality.[59] The prevalence of this mode of expression in the *Treatise on Superfluous Things* must owe something to the influence of the classic texts on painting, texts with which Wen Zhenheng would have been intimately familiar. It owes something too, however, to the degree of sophistication reached by the Ming cultural market, and in this sense it is a powerful expression of Pierre Bourdieu's ideas about 'distinction', about the role of difference in maintaining social and cultural hierarchies. Everybody has to be allowed to be better than somebody, in order to justify those at the top of the hierarchy being better than everybody.

The language of elite writers such as those just discussed by no means covers all types of Ming discourse about objects. We can dimly divine very different priorities expressed in different vocabularies, in writings aimed at a less exalted market. For example, the householder's manual regularly calls things *shiyang*, literally the 'pattern of the day', clearly meaning 'fashionable' or 'à la mode'.[60] This is a word not seen in writings like those of Wen Zhenheng, though of course it is impossible to say whether or not it formed part of his everyday, spoken language. In fiction, too, there are hints not only of different attitudes to things but of different ways of talking about them, as in *The Golden Lotus* where the most frequently remarked on attribute of an object is its material, followed by its provenance, as in the case of 'Nanjing beds' or tiles 'from the imperial kilns'.[61] These different languages of objects cannot, with the imperfect evidence available, be reconstructed in anything like their full degree of complexity, and what remains is only enough to show us how much we have lost, and how consequently monochrome must be our view of the undoubtedly polychrome reality.

4

Things of the past

Uses of the antique in Ming material culture

The idea is with us still that an all-pervasive reverence for and deference to 'the past' is the very stuff of the forms of Chinese culture. Although owing its most forceful expression, if not its earliest formulation, to the views on 'Asiatic Society' expressed in *The Philosophy of History* by Hegel, this perception has been developed over the past two hundred years as a central part of orientalist discourse about China. So a collection of essays emanating from Princeton in 1976 could confidently state as its 'basic hypothesis . . . that interaction with the past is one of the distinctive modes of intellectual and imaginative endeavour in traditional Chinese culture', posing as its central problem the way in which Western value-laden concepts such as 'originality, creativity and orthodoxy' are to be understood in the Chinese context.[1] Titles like *In Pursuit of Antiquity* or *Wen Chengming: The Ming Artist and Antiquity*[2] serve powerfully to reinforce the view of interaction with the past as being the determinant of many types of Chinese cultural production, to a degree unparalleled in Europe.

However, a quantity of recent work on cultural practice in the post-medieval Western world, much of it in response to the stimulus of David Lowenthal's *The Past is a Foreign Country*,[3] leads towards the conclusion that interaction with the past is one of the distinctive modes of intellectual and imaginative endeavour in *all* societies, or at least in those where the ways of structuring time admit of a concept of 'the past' at all. Despite the great quantity of distinguished scholarship which has tended to cast doubt on the very notion of a 'renaissance', in the sense of a radical break with the culture of preceding centuries, it would still be generally admitted that the surviving literary and physical remains of the Greek and Roman worlds exercised a fascination over the minds of early modern European intellectuals, and enjoyed a prestige every bit as great as did 'High Antiquity' with their contemporaries in China. There can be little or no justification for seeing what was happening in Europe as a dynamic 'rebirth', while what was happening in Suzhou at the same time is considered so radically different that concepts such as 'originality, creativity and orthodoxy' might well need a major redefinition.

Having said that, the intention here is not to claim that no significant differences can be discerned between the Western and Chinese engagements with their respective pasts, only to assert that the structural importance of the engagement was broadly equivalent. Many concrete differences stand out. One of the most significant (in that it may ultimately be the source of the Hegelian position) is the lack of any sense of disjunction between 'antiquity' and 'the present', such as was perceived by the European elite at least from Flavio Biondo's development of the idea of a *media aetas* in the 1430s. The point is not whether this 'middle age' supervening between the Roman empire and the Florence of the Medici actually existed but that its reality was believed in by significant thinkers at the time. In this respect, the European experience of the Christian Revelation as a crucial barrier between the present and the ancient world was particularly significant.[4] At least as many radical disjunctions in society and culture may have taken place between the China of the Han dynasty (220 BC – AD 200) and that of the Ming, but they were not felt by the majority of the elite to involve a rupture of the connections between themselves and their equivalents, as bearers of a continuous cultural tradition. The lack of any large-scale physical testimony to the actual reality of ancient times in China, with no Roman remains, no medieval castles, may in fact have served to strengthen this sense of continuity, by removing from people's gaze the most powerful proofs of the past's differentness.

This chapter will look at some of the ways in which those artefacts of the past which did survive were actually deployed in the context of sixteenth- and seventeenth-century China, to give concrete social form to that sense of continuity. Throughout the discussion, I wish to hold on to David Lowenthal's concept of 'the uses of the past', leading to the conclusion that, for all its explicitness about 'antiquity' and 'the antique', the focus of attention in Ming China was firmly on the present. I certainly, too, want to disclaim any validity for this discussion as regards other periods of Chinese history, when very different uses were being made of different pasts. I have argued throughout that the late Ming was a period when the multiplicity of things had a central role in Chinese culture which they had not previously enjoyed and when the categorization of things, the listing of them, ranking of them, feeling uneasy about them, praising them and blaming them became an issue of some intellectual concern. Within this world of goods, things of the past, things believed to be of the past and things believed to invoke the past by their sheer physical configuration, occupied a special role. The literature of connoisseurship, and the related *biji* writings, offer insights into this role.

What of the past was available to be used in the late Ming period? And out of that, what was the present culturally able to deploy? The two categories are not synonymous. To take one example, it is inconceivable that the natural progress of agriculture and grave building, together with the organized grave-robbing and more genteel proto-archaeology that was going on, did not from time to time turn up examples of the glazed earthenware tomb figures (often of horses or camels) of the early imperial period. They dated in the main from the Tang dynasty (618–906), an era whose cultural stock was on the rise for much of the sixteenth century, particularly as the favoured model for prose and poetry styles advanced by the so-called 'antique prose' school of Ming literature. Yet, there is not a single piece of evidence for one of these figures, so much admired in twentieth-century writing on Chinese art, being collected, displayed, bought, sold or otherwise entering the world of Ming material culture. Wen Zhenheng makes explicit this taboo against the reintroduction into the world of the living of certain types of burial object, chiefly those of more recent centuries, in a discussion of ceramic pillows, a type of object with an eerie reputation in imaginative literature as potential gateways to a disturbingly real experience of the people of the past, the dead:

Old kiln pillows: those which are 2ft 5in long and 6in broad can be used. Those which are a foot broad are called 'corpse pillows'. They are items from ancient tombs and must not be used.[5]

The categories of objects from the more or less remote past which could find a place were largely limited to bronzes and jades from the period up to the Han dynasty, certain types of ceramics from the Song period, and the special category of calligraphy and paintings from any era. It would be hard to put it more succinctly than was done by the contemporary Italian Jesuit observer of the late Ming world, Matteo Ricci, whose remarks, here as elsewhere, show his great degree of perception based on decades of interaction with the upper reaches of Ming society:

In this kingdom they make much of antique things; and yet they have no statues nor medals, but rather many vases of bronze which are highly valued, and they desire them with a certain particular corrosion. Without it, they are worth nothing. Other antique vases of clay or of jasper stone (i.e. jade) are valuable. But more than all these things are valued paintings by famous persons, without colour, but in ink alone; or letters by ancient writers on paper or on cloth, with their seals to confirm that they are genuine. For they are greatly given to forging antique things, with great artifice and ingenuity, so that those who do not know enough can spend great sums of money on things which then are worth nothing.[6]

The rest of the discussion in this chapter can to an extent be seen as an expansion of and commentary on Ricci's comments. Like any educated European of his day, he would expect the category of 'antiquities' to be made up primarily of coins and medals and antique marbles. Hence, his remarks on their absence in China.

His contemporaries in early modern Europe would further have concurred that the categories of 'antiquity' and of 'fake' were similarly intertwined. Enea Vico, writing in 1555, spends a considerable amount of space on the discussion of fakes and their avoidance, while in 1697 John Evelyn was still complaining that:

And now after all this Travel and Diligence, Cost and Caution in this (as in most things else) one is perpetually in danger of being deceiv'd, and imposed on by Cheats, Falsaries and Mercenary Fourbs: I do not mean our ordinary *Coiners* of False Money by Mixtures, or *Alchymical* Sophistications only . . . but by such as make a common Trade of Imposing upon the unexperienc'd in this particular of *Medals.*[7]

Ricci's emphasis on the place of antiques as market commodities, on their very great financial values and the dangers of forgery which these engendered will also be looked at in more detail in the next chapter.

The sense that objects could provide a link of great immediacy with the remote past preceded the Ming period by some centuries. The period involved stretched loosely through the Xia (conventionally dated 2205–1767 BC), Shang (1766–1123 BC), Zhou (1122–249 BC), and down to the Han dynasty (220 BC – AD 200). The Xia (the historical status of which remains a matter of debate), Shang and Zhou periods were collectively known as *san dai* 'the Three Ages' or *shang gu* 'High Antiquity', and retained great, though not total, pre-eminence as sources of political, cultural and social examples. The bronze vessels of antiquity in particular had long been objects of study.[8] They were objects of wonderment, the embodiment of fabulous cultural power and magical import to the early unifying empire of the Han period. But it was in the Song period (960–1279) that a culture driven by a revivified and systematized Confucianism elevated ancient bronzes to a pinnacle of esteem from which they were never to descend.

The earliest extant work to be devoted to archaic bronzes is the *Kao gu tu, Researches on Archaeology Illustrated* of 1092, containing 211 vessels from both the palace collections and the collections of some thirty private individuals. The catalogue entries for each piece show a rubbing and deciphering of the inscription, together with its shape, weight and provenance. It further set up the system of classification of bronzes by period which was to be used by the majority of post-Song compilers. The *Chong xiu Xuan he bo gu tu lu, Drawings and Lists of all the Antiquities stored in the Xuan he Palace* is often known by its abbreviated title of *Bo gu tu lu, Drawings and Lists of Antiquities*. Although it has rather confused origins, the work claims to have been completed in 1123 and catalogues the forms and inscriptions of 840 or so bronzes in the imperial collection. Given this focus on provenance, and by contrast with the *Researches on Archaeology Illustrated*, it includes objects without inscriptions. The compilers used the same system as the earlier work, however, in describing the bronzes and assigning them to different periods. It was more accurate as far as the names of the vessels (derived from the unillustrated classic texts of Confucian ritual) were concerned. However, a far greater advance in the field of what European antiquarians would later call studies of *realia* was achieved in the closing years of the Northern Song dynasty by the great scholar and politician Ouyang Xiu (1007–1072), with his *Ji gu lu, Records on Collecting Antiques*, a collection of 400 rubbings of inscriptions on bronze and stone objects. As the first book to be devoted to this subject, its subsequent influence was immense.

Among the immediate followers of Ouyang Xiu was the private scholar Zhao Mingcheng and his wife, the eminent poet Li Qingzhao. Their *Jin shi lu, Collection of Texts on Metal and Stone* was compiled between 1119 and 1125, containing some 2,000 rubbings of inscriptions, with added explanations of when the objects on which they are found were made, and other relevant details. In the preface, Zhao tackles the problem of discrepancies between the textually transmitted historical account and the evidence of actual objects:

When archaeological materials are used to examine these things, thirty to forty per cent of the data is in conflict. That is because historical writings are produced by latter-day writers and cannot fail to contain errors. But the inscriptions on stone and bronze are made at the time the events take place and can be trusted without reservation.[9]

It must be stressed that Zhao's work was a collection of texts, albeit one made by taking rubbings from actual vessels. It was not a book about things but about the writing on things and stands at the head of an impressive apparatus of studying these archaic inscriptions, which was sustained by collections of rubbings circulating for centuries in the learned world without reference to the objects on which they appear. The approach is, to an extent, parallel to that of some of the *realia* scholars of the Italian quattrocento, such as that seen in Biondo's great *Roma Instaurata*, and of the scholars of the subsequent humanist tradition across Europe, using coins and graffiti to solve the cruces in Thucydides or Livy. The focus remains essentially bound to the text, with the object as a support, while the uninscribed object is merely a mute witness to the past, of little use to serious antiquarian study.

The study of ancient objects, however, could supply deficiencies in the record in other ways, by bringing to light actual examples of objects mentioned in the classics. Wen Zhenheng's English contemporary Peacham, in his *Compleat Gentleman* of 1622, is eloquent on the possibilities for a recovery of the world of the Romans through the study of the objects (or the contemporary representation of objects) coming down from their material world. This approach, too, can be seen in Chinese writers of the middle Ming period. Tian Yiheng (1524–?1574; DMB, 1287) in his *biji* of 1573 entitled *Liuqing ri zha, Daily Jottings of Liuqing* investigates in minute detail but again without recourse to the aid of illustration the different types of scholar's head-cloth to be found in early texts and the various shapes of ritual jade object mentioned in the systematizing ritual handbooks which, though purporting to date from the early Zhou period, were in fact probably compiled in the Han dynasty. (Interestingly, given what archaeology has revealed about the degree of illustration in Han manuscripts, it now seems highly likely that the earliest versions of these texts were accompanied by drawings, but no one in the Ming could have known this for certain.) This is a very different world of things from that seen in the writings of Wen Zhenheng, a milieu of scholarly detachment from objects' current meanings, where it is their value as testimony to the past that is at issue. It is a world of things which is less and less in evidence as the sixteenth century turns into the seventeenth and issues relating to the social meaning of consumption come to the fore.

The great texts of Song-dynasty archaeology continued to circulate and to be objects of admiration throughout the late Ming period. He Liangjun, in a *biji* published in 1569, praised the *Drawings and Lists of Antiquities* in effusive terms: 'The transmission of the forms and patterns of the Three Ages down to our own day has depended on the survival of this book.'[10] The commercially sophisticated Ming printing industry answered to the demand for copies of this and other desirable antiquarian works with a flood of reprints in the decades just before and after 1600. Robert Poor has calculated that there were reprint editions of *Drawings and Lists of Antiquities* in 1588, 1596, 1599, 1600 and 1603, and of *Researches on Archaeology Illustrated* in 1600 and 1601. (Plate 3).[11] This gives a total of seven printings of these two works in the fifteen years between 1588 and 1603, as against only six editions over the preceding 496 years since the first publication of the *Researches* in 1092.

There was, however, no sense that the achievements of these two milestones could be extended by further research (as there would be in the eighteenth century), and in fact the late Ming is notable as a period when there was almost no serious work being published in the key antiquarian discipline of epigraphy. The discipline did not, in fact,revive until the middle of the eighteenth century, when large compendia of bronzes and jades in the imperial collections were published as part of the cultural policy of the ruling house.[12] Was it simply reverence for Song antiquarianism which prevented members of the Ming elite from extending the scope of their interests into the areas it had mapped out so effectively 500 years before? Or was it rather that an overwhelming concern with the social implications of the symbolic value of antique objects, as giving entry to full participation in the highest levels of elite culture, temporarily replaced the scholastic mode as a way of using the past?

As has been seen in chapter 3 above, in a discussion of the range of reference of the term *gu* 'antique' in late Ming texts, it could have a very wide spread, covering objects which were not chronologically old at all. Throughout the literature, however, the dominant categories of antique artefacts are bronzes and jades, categorized with reference to the earliest dynasties. The definition of 'High Antiquity' had not been a constant; the eighth-century painting theorist Zhang Yanyuan used the term to refer to the relatively much more recent period of the Han dynasty and the Three Kingdoms, down to the third century AD.[13] This was simply because there was no painting surviving from any earlier period, but it show the essential fluidity of the term, with the 'antiquity' of the object being relative to the date from which the oldest examples were still extant.

As with more contemporary objects, the principal way Wen Zhenheng has of treating the body of ancient bronzes is to rank them, grouping them on the grounds of the desirability of owning them. The stress is on the possessor, and any sign of interest in the objects as intrinsically important testimonies to ancient times is missing. Indeed, the only evidence of intersection between Wen's 'consumerist' approach to bronzes and that of the antiquarians is that he employs the highly specialist names for the various bronze shapes which are found in the antiquarian texts, one of the most enduring achievements of which is to fix a relationship between extant objects and the terminology of the unillustrated ritual manuals. The precise names for each shape are not possible to translate into separate English equivalents:[14]

> Regarding bronzes, the most valued are *ding, yi, zun li* and *dui*; then come *yi, you lei* and *zhen*; then come *fu, qui, zhong, zhu*, 'blood-oath basins', *lian hua nang* and such things. The difference between the Three Ages is that Shang pieces are plain and have no inscriptions, Zhou pieces have fine and dense inscriptions in seal-script, and Xia pieces are inlaid with gold and silver of a hair-like fineness . . .[15]

He goes on to make statements about the style of script involved at various times and to defend uninscribed pieces against the common charge of spuriousness on the grounds that they were 'pieces used amongst the common people, who had no merits to record'. Wen is here alluding to a famous passage from the Han-dynasty ritual compilation *Li ji, Record of Rites*, where the types of inscription to be found on bronze vessels are correctly summarized.[16] This passage would have been familiar to all members of the Ming elite, even to those who could not decipher actual inscriptions on bronzes. Thus, it seems that the fact of an object's being inscribed was of importance to its value, even if the content of the inscription went generally unread. The 1,127 'Antique bronzes' in the inventory of Yan Song's property in no case have their inscriptions recorded by the cataloguers. It seems possible that even quite learned members of the Ming elite could not, in fact, read the archaic script of the bronze inscriptions. Though aware of their general import, they certainly chose not to read them.

An entry from the *biji* of a mid-Ming writer from the same Suzhou region named Wang Qi (1433–499) is typical in the way in which it describes a single object, here singularized by its association with Chen Youliang (1320–1363), one of several unsuccessful warlords

contending for power with the first Ming emperor around the time
of the collapse of the Mongol Yuan dynasty:

> The descendants of the false ruler Chen Youliang were scattered
> throughout Huang and were all menial people. One family owned
> a *you* [a bronze shape rather like a bucket with a domed lid] of very
> ancient manufacture, which my friend Wu Yuanbi obtained for one
> bolt of brocaded satin, when magistrate of the district. The bronze
> was big enough to contain a *dou* [10.31 litres] of millet, with a
> colour of yellow earth both inside and out, and flecks of vermilion
> and azure in it, and was inlaid with gold, silver and copper. It had
> corroded and bore an inscription all in rectangular characters. It
> was a genuine Shang object.[17]

There is little trace here of any curiosity as to what the inscription
might actually say, a position which would seem unacceptably obtuse
by the eighteenth century. From this time objects were actually identified from their inscriptions (e.g. the famous 'Marquis of Kang gui'
in the British Museum), not by the more ephemeral connection of an
owner, like the failed warlord Chen Youliang.

It should be said right at the beginning that the value of a passage
like this, which could be duplicated from a number of contemporary
authors, for the study of these bronze vessels in their original context
of manufacture is nil. Wen Zhenheng and Wang Qi, along with the
great majority of their contemporaries, are simply wrong about all the
points of distinction they choose to draw out. One of the most widespread and striking of these mistaken beliefs is the universal Ming
conviction, seen in both authors, that the earliest, and particularly the
Xia dynasty, bronzes were inlaid with gold and silver. Whatever the
outcome of the current ferment over the mythical status or otherwise
of this most venerable of Chinese state formations, inlaid bronzes are
out of the question. The objects believed to be Xia must therefore be
from the Warring States era of the late Bronze age at the very earliest,
and at the latest they were of the Yuan and Ming periods, several
thousand years closer to Wen's own time. The very large number of
surviving inlaid bronzes for which this later date now looks plausible
goes some way towards dimly suggesting the vast market for these
supposedly most venerable traces of High Antiquity.[18]

In the passage from Wen Zhenheng quoted above, he is the carrier
of a clear Ming consensus about which forms of bronze vessel were
most desirable, the clear favourite being the *ding*, a deep bowl shape
on three legs (Plate 3). These tripods are listed first in the Yan Song
inventory, but are also ranked first by Wang Qi and Zhang Dai.[19]

The phrase 'tripod ritual vessels (*ding yi*) could stand in for the whole category of 'bronzes', or even for 'antiquities' generally. Their prominence may be due in part to statements in early imperial ritual texts, which give the tripod forms a particularly heavy symbolic load as talismans of the state or as miraculous tokens of Heaven's favour to a just ruler.[20] Another point of note is the use of the term *gui* 'valued', ambiguous in Ming Chinese as in modern English. This was not a purely disinterested aesthetic ordering, as we shall see.

We can approach 'antique' objects, and antique bronzes, in the Ming context from another angle, by looking at some of the contexts in which they were deployed. One of the most striking facts which emerges from texts about elegant interior design at the period is that ancient objects were more than occasionally 'used' in a functional as well as a rhetorical or social sense. Zhang Dai tells the story of the chance excavation of the tomb of the Bronze-age magnate Duke Jing of Qi, which yielded three plain bronze platters and two great decorated vases, which he describes as 'archetypal pieces of the Three Ages'. He concludes, 'I hear they are now in someone's ancestral temple in Anhui province.'[21] Archaic bronzes were used as incense burners or as vases, the belief being prevalent that their long interment in the soil gave them miraculous properties of preserving the life of cut flowers and plants.[22] There is plenty of textual and pictorial evidence that this was done, in spite of Wen Zhenheng's dictum that: 'The bronzes of the Three Ages, Qin and Han dynasties, and incense burners of Guan, Ge, Ding or Longquan ware, are fit objects of connoisseurly enjoyment (*jian shang*). They are not suitable for everyday use.'[23]

Jades were employed in various ways on the writing table. Gao Lian describes an antique jade, the original function of which he claims not to know, in use as a water dropper, a square pad (original use also unknown) used as a pad for seal vermilion, and sword slides and shroud weights in the shape of pigs used as paperweights.[24] Of course, this functional deployment of objects seems likely to have had its 'sociotechnic' as well as its 'technomic' side,[25] by suggesting a full symbolic possession of the values embodied in the concept of 'antiquity', in addition to the message of wealth and prestige being conveyed by the simple fact of their possession. This 'manner of possessing' would be likely to assume even greater significance in a context where the desired treasures were available to all those possessed of sufficient economic power, through the workings of the well-developed art and antiques market.

One context in which 'antique' objects seem not to have been too frequently deployed in the Ming period was that of burial. It was customary at the time to include in the tombs of all those who could afford them either actual examples or simulacra, in the form of wood or ceramic models, of the elements of material culture which the dead person had enjoyed in life and would enjoy after death. Food and clothing were there certainly, but so were items like writing implements, suggesting aspirations to some form of cultural life and social intercourse beyond the grave. It is relatively rare, however for any three-dimensional object subject to the varying definitions of 'antique' to be included in the complement of grave goods. One late sixteenth-century tomb has produced illustrated books published over a century previously, suggesting bibliophile tastes on the part of its occupant.[26] Men were sometimes buried with favourite items from their painting collections. The wealthy merchant Wang Zhen (d. 1496) was buried at Huai'an county, Jiangsu province with a group of twenty-five paintings, two of which purportedly dated back to the Yuan dynasty, though the majority were by artists loosely definable as 'contemporary'.[27] The tomb of Xu Yufu (d. 1613) has produced a painted fan by the famous Wen Zhengming, who had died when Xu Yufu was in his early teens. Zhang Dai records that an uncle of his turned down a large offer from the famous collector Xiang Yuanbian for three treasured pieces of Song porcelain ('a white Ding incense burner, a Ge ware vase, and a Guan ware ewer for wine'), on the grounds that he wished them to follow him into the grave.[28] This is recorded as a slightly eccentric thing to do. There is up to now only one example of a scientifically excavated tomb of Ming date which has proved to contain archaic metalwork, in the form of square *ding* of the Shang dynasty and a Warring States round *ding*. There are also in the tomb, whose occupant was buried in 1618, a Tang mirror and a Song incense burner.[29] As I will argue, the very high monetary value of the pieces may have had much to do with the desire to prevent their permanent removal from the world of circulating commodities.

Wen Zhenheng situated the 'bronzes of the Three Ages' on a continuum with the most favoured types of collected ceramics, and the approach to these ceramics, the majority of which dated from the Song period (960–1279), provides some interesting contrasts and comparisons. But the underlying principle is the same; a ranking of types of objects must be established. In the case of bronzes, it was the shape which provided the determining criterion of desirability over period or place of manufacture (this last would in any case have been unknown). In the case of ceramics, on the other hand, it was the various 'wares' (the Chinese word is *yao*, meaning literally a 'kiln') which provided the necessary labels. Most of these, which remain the main classificatory tool in the study of these ceramics and in the contemporary art market, are geographical names, generally of broad areas where the ceramics were made in the Song.[30] So 'Ding ware' is named for Dingzhou, quite a large administrative region in the northern province of Hebei which included a number of kiln complexes of different sizes. 'Cizhou ware', 'Longquan ware' and several others are named on the same principle. Some of the names of ceramic types have other sources; 'Guan ware' is literally 'Official ware', supposedly manufactured in kilns under direct imperial control at the Southern Song capital of Hangzhou in Zhejiang province. There are more fanciful ones, like 'Ge ware', literally 'Elder brother ware', from a picturesque anecdote about a family of potters, and the fabulous 'Chai ware', as ephemeral as the tenth-century kinglet after whom it is called. The ceramics of the early Ming period, which were in the process of becoming raised from the status of mere luxury tableware to that of 'antiques', were identified by the 'reign period' of the emperor in whose time they were manufactured; hence 'Xuande ware' (made between 1426 and 1435, 'Chenghua ware' (1465–87) and so on. The proliferation of these names in the writings of Ming and later collectors testifies less to the degree of development of the ceramic industry (for we have little idea of how the producers of these bulk commodities may have chosen to categorize them) than it does to the development of a collector's market, for which above all a suitable degree of differentiation and an agreed terminology is essential.

The consensus among Ming writers as to how the various wares should be ranked largely follows the listing in *Essential Criteria of Antiquities* of 1388, where the order is: Chai ware, Ru ware, Guan ware, Dong ware, Ge ware, Xiang ware (these are all types of crackle-glazed stoneware), ancient Korean ware, ancient Ding ware, Jizhou ware, ancient Cizhou ware, Fujian ware, Longquan ware, ancient Raozhou ware and Hezhou ware.[31] The classification of some types as 'ancient' may be to distinguish them from the contemporary products of kilns which were still in full production. In the 1490s, Wang Qi's description of his brother's art collection could include 'Guan ware' as a shorthand for all forms of fine ceramic, and to an extent this remained the practice through into the seventeenth century. The list in *Treatise on Superfluous Things* some 250 years later does not at first sight appear to be very different: Chai ware (which Wen admits he has never actually seen, only heard about), Guan, Ge, Ru, Ding, Jun, Longquan, Xuande ware, *shufu* ware (a type of white glazed ceramic associated with the court in the Yuan dynasty), Yongle ware (1403–25) and Chenghua ware (1465–87).[32] The latter two are described as 'extremely expensive, but not very elegant'.

A list like this is to a large extent traditional, not the result of independent judgement, and it may not represent actual practice, but it has misled some modern students of Chinese ceramics into the generalization that the crackle-glazed stonewares of the Song period enjoyed an unchallenged pre-eminence in the eyes of Ming connoisseurs. A more detailed analysis of Wen's statements about actual ceramic types in the course of his chapter on 'Vessels and utensils' shows that the type most often mentioned in a positive context is the white porcelain of Dingzhou, which has ten mentions, as against six for Guan ware, five each for Xuande and Ge wares and four for the celadons of Longquan. However, it will not do on the strength of this to substitute one generalization for another and say that 'Ding ware' was preferred by Ming connoisseurs. It also leads the list of ceramic types which are *un*desirable in certain contexts, with more negative mentions than any of the alternatives. For example, paperweights of Guan, Ge or Ding ware 'are not objects of elegance', ceramic seals 'definitely cannot be used' no matter what they are made of, and brush-testers of Ding ware or Longquan ware just 'are not elegant'.[33]

This observed contradiction between Wen Zhenheng's ordering of ceramic types in his general discussion on collecting them and his entries on actual shapes of ceramic object may well be attributable to the tension apparent in a work like *Treatise on Superfluous Things* between the textually founded consensus in aesthetic rankings and the necessity to rank and prescribe in relation to the actual situation prevailing in the market-place at the time of writing. It may also reflect changing tastes (since tastes *have* to change, in order for the mechanisms which are central to the use of goods as social markers to work at all in a mobile society). Another *biji* of 1573 shows Ding ware rising up the ladder of ceramic ranks, coming ahead of the crackle-glazed stonewares,[34] while it was Ding ware which was the focus of most of the faking of antique ceramics in the sixteenth and early seventeenth centuries, a sure sign of its importance.

The major shift in taste observable at this period, however, is the growing desirability as the Ming period went on of more contemporary work in all forms of artistic production. In ceramic terms this meant the porcelain from the early Ming reigns, above all those of Xuande and Chenghua. These reign periods began to shift from being merely definitions of chronology to being labels which might identify an object in the round of commodities, guarantors of aesthetic meaning, in much the same way that, for the British antiques trade, 'Queen Anne' or 'Elizabethan' became necessary to the operation of their work of authorizing statements about value, though at a very much later date.[35]

This enlargement of the boundaries of the desired which is observable in the late Ming was a process that contemporaries were well aware of, and it was not, in fact, restricted to ceramics. One of the classic statements of the way this shift was perceived is that by Wang Shizhen quoted in chapter 2 (p. 61). Another version of the same passage with very similar wording can be found in the *biji* of Shen Defu, one of the honorary editors of Wen's *Treatise*, writing in 1606:

> In objects for amusement and enjoyment it is the antique which is valuable, but in the present dynasty this has ceased to be so. Thus, the prices of Yongle carved red lacquer, Xuande bronzes and Chenghua porcelain vie with those of antiques. The Song dynasty is famous for carved lacquers, which are now extinct and can hardly be obtained. The bronze vessels and ritual objects of the Three Ages are fewer day by day. From the Five Dynasties and the Song period the so-called Chai, Ru, Guan, Ge and Ding wares [note again the traditional list] are particularly thin, brittle and easily destroyed, so they are replaced with recently produced pieces. This began with one or two men of elegance, got its first strength among the fashion-conscious gentry of Jiangnan, and spread to the easily persuadable great merchants of Anhui.[36]

It does not seem too far-fetched to argue that this broadening of the category of 'antique' to include material which, though it might not be sanctified by association with the revered dynasties of former times, was yet rare enough and expensive enough to be difficult of access did owe something to the expansion of the numbers of those anxious to deploy culturally prestigious goods to make social statements about themselves. The supply was enlarged to meet increased demand by altering the definition of what constituted culturally prestigious goods. We see this in *Ranking of Antique Objects* (remembering that 'antique' does not have to mean chronologically old) by the famous Li Rihua (1565–1635; DMB, 826–30) as translated by Chu-tsing Li:

1 Calligraphic pieces of the Jin and Tang dynasties
2 Paintings of the Five Dynasties, Tang and early Song
3 Calligraphic writings and rubbings of the Sui, Tang and Song
4 Handwritings by Su Shi, Huang Tingjian, Cai Xiang and Mi Fu
5 Paintings of Yuan artists
6 Handwritings by Xianyu Shu, Yu Ji and Zhao Mengfu

7 Paintings by Ma Yuan and Xia Gui of the Southern Song
8 Various marvelous paintings by Shen Zhou and Wen Zhengming of Ming dynasty
9 The running and cursive style calligraphy of Zhu Yunming
10 Assorted handwritings by other famous literati
11 Brilliant examples of bronze vessels and red jades before the Qin and Han
12 Ancient jades of the *xun* and *lin* types
13 Tang inkstones
14 Ancient *qin* zithers and famous swords
15 Finely printed books of the Five Dynasties and Song
16 Strange rocks of a rugged and picturesque type
17 A combination of some old, elegant pines and small needle-like rushes in a fine pot
18 Plum trees and bamboos that are fit for poetry
19 Imported spice of a subtle kind
20 Foreign treasures of a rare and beautiful kind
21 Excellent tea well prepared
22 Rare and delicious food from overseas
23 Shiny white fine porcelain and mysterious coloured pottery, old and new

In addition to these, white rice and green dishes, and cotton robes and rattan cane are exquisite objects for the literati to use. They should be aware of the ranking of these objects, like the ranking of scholars in the Lingyan Hall of the Han dynasty, which was arranged by the wisdom of a just ruler. If a vulgar merchant marks some fragile pieces from the Xuande and Chenghua reigns with exorbitant prices, it will be an error . . .'[37]

In this passage, the explicitness of the process of ranking is matched by the largely conventional nature of the judgements expressed. Even the most 'vulgar' of merchants would be likely to know at this period that Jin and Tang calligraphy was at the very acme of the criteria of desirability. This is very much a prescriptive list, rather than being in any sense a description of actual consumption behaviour, even within the very limited register of consumption encompassed by the concept of 'the antique'.

There is evidence that 'collections' of antiquities tended to be quite small and that the vast numbers of these objects seen in the Yan Song inventory were quite exceptional. An account entitled *My Family's Calligraphy and Pictures* from the very end of the fifteenth century, when the much smaller size of the class which was in competition for them allowed a more generous distribution of luxury goods, gives a good general picture of what a 'collection' worth boasting about might be expected to contain at that date:

> My family formerly possessed the 'Hall of 10,000 Volumes', with a very extensive collection of writings. They were all collated and comparative government editions of the Song and Yuan periods, half of which had manuscript inscriptions and colophons in famous hands. There was a manuscript of the *Epitome of the Mirror of Government* by Zhu Xi, in mint condition, and a collection of Tang and Song autographs by famous men in several tens of boxes, and some hundred or more scrolls of famous paintings; all of these belonged to Yujian. There was a 'Studio for the Congregation of Antiquities', expressly for the collection of ancient bronze *ding, yi,* bells and *you,* and for ancient jades in the shapes *huan, jue, zhi, dou, fang xiang* and *fou qing;* all of these were inscribed. There were several antique *qin* zithers, the pick of them being, 'One day in autumn', 'Three generations of thunder', 'Jade frosting the heavens', 'Night-wearying crane', and 'Frost-rimed pine'. As for the other things gathered there, such as woven silk tapestry pictures, carved lacquer, vessels of Guan ware, they all belonged to my elder brother Tanzhai. The two gentlemen [the author's two brothers, Wang Yujian and Wang Tanzhai] were most capable connoisseurs, with an extremely fine eye, and there was not a single fake. When guests arrived, they would display them for their amusement . . .[38]

In the third month of the fourth year of the Longqing reign (equivalent to 1570), the 'Four Great Families' of Suzhou (who are not further identified but who almost certainly included the family of Wen Zhenheng himself) held a joint showing of their art treasures, which appears to have been a semi-public affair open to anybody of acceptable social standing who wished to attend. The event was recorded by Zhang Yingwen in his *Pure and Arcane Collecting.*[39] Between them, the four most prominent families in one of the richest and most culturally dedicated cities of the empire could produce forty 'ancient bronzes', including the sub-category of mirrors, and forty-two 'ancient jades'. Leaving aside the actual age of the objects involved, this does not seem a particularly impressive total. There is other evidence that an individual member of the elite might own only a relatively small number of 'antiques'; one thinks of Gu Yuanqing's 'ten friends'.

To possess such objects was clearly of value to any claim to elite status, but Western art-historical writing may have mistaken its centrality in the period preceding the later sixteenth century. Some of it gives the impression that a passionate involvement with the

production and consumption of works of art, meaning here calligraphy and painting, was a standard accomplishment of the Chinese
'scholar gentry' (as already noted, there were 300 *jinshi* degree grad-
uates every year, but how many of them have survived as figures in
the history of art?) and that art collecting was a universal pastime
through the late imperial period. This is not how it seemed to contemporaries, who were once more aware that something had happened
in the decades before 1600 to expand greatly the number of those
choosing to involve themselves in the art market. Shen Defu is, again,
a characteristically acute witness:

> At the end of the Jiajing reign (1522–66) the empire was at peace,
> and prosperous members of the official classes, in intervals between
> the construction of gardens and pavilions and the training of singing
> and dancing girls, turned to the enjoyment of antiquities.[40]

He goes on to name seven officials of very high rank who were
distinguished as prominent collectors, who 'did not grudge spending
large sums on their collections. They were renowned throughout the
Jiangnan region.' He names two in particular, who were famous for
this, who held positions in the Ming 'shadow government' at the
southern capital of Nanjing. He adds significantly that 'At court, this
fashion was not so pronounced.' The Ming emperors were in no sense
'art collectors', and the very idea of an imperial collection languished
under them.[41] A typical anecdote regarding the imperial attitude to
painting is likely to be a tale of 'de-accessioning', as when the famous
scroll 'Going up the River at the Qingming Festival' left the palace in
the reign of the Jiajing emperor (r. 1522–66).[42] The higher ranks of
the Peking bureaucracy were similarly not noted as connoisseurs of
the arts.

The exceptions were Yan Song and his sons, owners as we have seen
of a fabulous number of treasures. Their collection, like that of their
contemporary also named by Shen Defu, the prominent official Zhu
Chenggong, was dispersed by confiscation and subsequent sale. At the
beginning of the Wanli reign (1573–1620), Shen continues, the Grand
Secretary Zhang Juzheng (1525–1582; DMB, 53–61) 'also had
this passion', but his collection shared the same fate, much of it
passing to Han Shineng (*jinshi* of 1568) or the merchant-collector
Xiang Yuanbian 'at high prices'. Then, along came Wang Shizhen
(1526–1590) and his brothers, who set the seal on the collecting of art
and antiquities as a necessary part of the elite persona, 'and the
frivolous of Jiangsu and Zhejiang provinces all rose up and called
themselves great connoisseurs'. The role of leading collector in the

empire was at the time of writing, in the first decade of the seventeenth century, disputed between Dong Qichang and a man who is now completely obscured by Dong's great posthumous reputation as an artist, one Zhu Jingxun, a son of the high official Zhu Gen (MRZJ, 143). This fashion had by then been taken up by the merchants from Anhui, who were the prey of the dealers from Suzhou.

What Shen Defu's statement suggests is that it was only from the middle of the sixteenth century that the 'enjoyment of antiquities' shifted its role from being a personal predilection, one of a number of potential types of privileged cultural activity, to being an essential form of consumption which was central to the maintenance of elite status. In the late Ming and Qing periods it was no longer acceptable not to be a 'lover of antiquity'. Shen tells us nothing of the works of art or individual pieces owned by these 'great collectors' of the later sixteenth century (contrast this with the loving naming of individual zithers in the family holdings of Wang Qi); he simply tells us that they spent a very great deal of money. He Liangjun writes in 1579 of his passion for the collecting of 'genuine traces' (i.e. of famous masters of painting and calligraphy) with the statement, 'I would at once buy them at a high price, not grudging the possibility of bankruptcy.'[43] This has become the necessary salient part of the activity. My aim here is not to engage in some naively reductionist analysis of Ming culture, where everything is 'about' money, but to argue that, by concentrating on a very small number of active aesthetic players like Dong Qichang and his close circle, we have mislaid the role played by the very much broader body of cultural consumers in sustaining the Ming discourse about 'art' or 'collecting'.

There were attempts made in the period to increase the supply of antiquities to an expanded body of consumers, both by returning to the commodity market genuine early items which had been withdrawn from it through burial and by the creation of fraudulent antiquities. As regards the first strategy, part of the problem lay with the very unequal geographical distribution in the late Ming of the three-dimensional types of antiquity, particularly bronze vessels, and of the demand for them. The economic and cultural heart of the empire had long since shifted to the lower Yangtze Valley, from where almost all of our evidence for consumption behaviour comes, while the centres of the Bronze-age states had been situated much further to the north and west, in what was by the late sixteenth century a region of severe comparative underdevelopment. It was recognized at the time quite correctly that the province of Henan, site of the Shang capital, was the major source of bronzes for the antique trade.

Zhang Dai tells of one gentleman-dealer from there with a

collection (or stock, the source is typically ambiguous) of sixteen bronze wine goblets of the particularly slim and elegant form known as *mei ren gu*, 'beautiful lady beakers.'[44] These were much in demand as flower vases, and someone further away from the source of the supply would have been very unlikely to possess so many. Such a number could only have been built up by systematic digging, differing from the age-old practice of grave robbing in that the search was not for instrinsically precious materials like gold and silver, but for antiquities. The despoliation of graves was held in general abhorrence, but one early seventeenth-century writer complained that it was becoming common, as dealers and their peasant agents searched for, 'the bronze vessels of the Three Ages, and the jades, ceramics and paintings of the Tang and Song dynasties.'[45] The ritual bronzes of Duke Jing of Qi, the same ones which ended up on an ancestral altar in Anhui, came to light when someone excavated (the word used is *fa jue*, still the modern Chinese term for an archaeological excavation) his tomb.

Chance finds did continue to play a part, and one example can stand in for many. In 1639, while digging was going on in the ramparts at Shangzhou in the remote north-western province of Shaanxi, a grave was accidentally brought to light which contained a sword, scales of golden armour and a jade jar decorated with nine fabulous beasts.[46] The latter was 'speckled with blood,' stained from long burial in a manner which made it even more attractive to connoisseurs of jades, among whom the erroneous belief was universal that contact with a corpse could impart this patina to the stone.

Evidence for excavation and for chance finds of antiquities is scattered through the *biji* of the period. The evidence for systematic forgery is, if anything, even richer. Faking came to occupy such a prominent place in certain sections of the luxury handicraft trades that it has seriously distorted our understanding of what was going on in these industries until very recently. The chief areas affected were the 'high' arts of calligraphy and painting, metal working, jade working and, to a lesser extent, ceramics. The notion of forgery is intimately connected with the notion of a market, either a real or a symbolic one, in the types of objects concerned, and the history of forgery in China can be written as a history of the development of a commodity market in luxury goods, the scope of forgery expanding in keeping with the expansion of that market-place, as more and more types of cultural products came to be viewed as having the potential to be commodities.[47]

Calligraphy and painting were bought and sold first, and so forged first, from as early as the fourth century AD.[48] The Song period saw

the development of a commodity market in archaic bronzes, and so
the beginnings of the manufacture of fraudulent versions of the real
thing.[49] By the late Ming period, any painting and almost anything
broadly susceptible to categorization as an 'antiquity' (and remember
that this now included ceramics of just 100 years old) could potentially
have a value as a commodity and so could fall within the ambit of
the forger's activity. Not the least forged of artefacts were literary
texts, often claiming to be of very great antiquity and, hence, of
immense cultural significance. These 'pious frauds' had been part of
Chinese cultural at least since the Han dynasty. Leading Ming
manufacturers of such texts, like Feng Fang (*jinshi* of 1523; DMB,
448-9) and Wang Wenlu (1503-1586; DMB, 1448-51) often seem to
have found it remarkably easy to have recently manufactured work
accepted as genuine, a probable reflection on the low state of
philological and textual studies during the period, paralleling the lack
of interest in the texts of bronze inscriptions. In the eighteenth century
both disciplines were held in much higher esteem, and forgers had a
much harder time.

The literature on material culture itself is, as we have seen, the site
of several very successful frauds, either of complete fabrication, like
the *Nine Records from a Banana-shaded Window*, attributed to Xiang
Yuanbian but actually formed by cannibalizing the *Random Notes of
a Scholar in Seclusion* of Tu Long, or by attaching famous names as
'editors' or 'collators' to texts with which they may have had no
connection. This last practice was very prevalent in Ming publishing,
and it is doubtful if a famous writer like Chen Jiru was in fact associated with more than a very small proportion of the numerous books
on all sorts of subjects which now carry his illustrious name.[50] Book
production in general was a field where forgery was rife. At least one
publisher even produced and distributed a flyer denouncing a specific
edition of a competitor as pirated, something we know from the unique
copy of this document pasted some time before 1596 into the *Album
Amicorum* of the Dutch scholar Bernardus Paludanus (Plate 4).[51]

We can get some sense of the expansion of the scale of forgery in
the luxury and art markets, though sticking to the same basic categories of material, by comparing those categories where it is warned
of as a possibility in the fourteenth-century *Essential Criteria of
Antiquities* with that found in a delightful poem on 'Bogus Antiques'
by Shao Changheng (1637-1704), brought to light and translated by
Wai-kam Ho. The earlier text lists: bronzes, paintings (by implication),
works of calligraphy, *qin* zithers, a particular type of brick used to
make resonating tables for playing the zithers on, inkstones made of
ancient roof tiles, Islamic steel blades and ceramics of Guan ware (the

only ceramic type out of a total to be so noted). Now here is Shao Changheng, in Wai-kam Ho's version, warning of the dangers of the Suzhou marketplace:

> In old Suzhou, at Changmen the city gate,
> Many shops stand neatly in rows like fish scales.
> Among the most numerous are antique stores.
> Let's see what works of calligraphy and painting are in store.
> Wang Xizhi is represented by look-alike 'iron-stones',
> Zhu You is called Wu Daozi.
> Previously, fakes were mixed with the genuine;
> Now it has become cleverer in recent years.
> The good artists do not create their own works,
> They copy and take pride in their close-likenesses.
> Buffalo and horses are invariably signed Dai Song and Han Gan,
> Landscapes are always called the Elder and Younger Li.
> From Dong Yuan and Juran to Tang Yin and Qiu Ying,
> Every master is subject to all manner of imitation.
> Calligraphy by Su Shi and Huang Tingjian were copied by filling
> out the shapes delineated with double outline.
> Tang and Song stelae are ground and cleaned.
> Sutra papers are made to look old by smoking,
> Xuanhe collection is documented by 'imperial seals'.
> The bigger the name, the easier the sale;
> A thousand pieces of gold is nothing uncommon.
> The current trends have been dominated by Dong Qichang;
> Labels boasting his name can be found in every village.
> How amazing that the world of brush and ink could be so commer-
> cialized by a few unethical merchants!
> When it comes to the authenticity of bronze *yi* and *ding*,
> Be wary of the Qin and Han archaic scripts.
> Patination can be made by chemicals;
> How pleasing are their colours in rich red and green.
> Ceramic wares of Chai, Ru, Guan, Ge and Ding:
> Their prices are comparable to fine jade pieces.
> People in high places are so proud of their connoisseurship,
> They will keep on buying with all the money they have.
> How many authentic antiques can there be?
> No wonder the market is filled with forgeries.
> Trust your ears and ignore what you see –
> All sad things in the world are just like this.[52]

Clearly the area in which concern about fraudulent manufacture was most concentrated was that of calligraphy and painting. This was partly a matter of the technology involved. Although, as I have said, the degree of elite participation in the creation of paintings as works of art may be exaggerated by the art-historical literature, every member of the educated classes was trained to handle a brush and learned to write by imitating the hands of famous early writers. There were, thus, no technical barriers to the production of fakes. Even decent facsimiles of early types of paper and silk could be made, to give an authentic appearance of age to recent work.[53] There has been a considerable degree of attention to these problems of authenticity in the connoisseurship of painting.[54] More recently Joan Stanley-Baker has cast a rigorously sceptical eye on the whole question of how the authenticity of a Chinese painting has been historically negotiated, through the whole elaborate process of colophons, copies and collectors' catalogues. She has made a study of the *Bao hui lu, Records of Precious Painting* of 1633, written by the upper-degree holder Zhang Taijie, and demonstrates the essentially inverse nature of the relationship between fame and genuineness in the fabulous treasures it purports to record.[55]

Zhang Taijie's subsequent reputation is that of a dealer in bad faith, but we know other instances of the participation of respected members of the elite in the production of faked calligraphy and paintings, with no opprobrium seeming to attach to them for this ostensibly subversive activity. Shen Defu comments:

> Antiques have long been the subject of many cases of faking, and this is particularly so in Suzhou. Scholars all depend on it to make a living. In recent generations, no one was as refined and pure as Zhang Fengyi, yet he could not avoid being involved in it for his livelihood. Wang Zhideng was totally dependent on these stratagems for his income . . . the *aficionados* came daily to Wang Zhideng's house to negotiate.[56]

Zhang Fengyi (1527–1613; DMB, 63–4) was an extremely famous literary figure, renowned for some of the most popular dramas of the day, while Wang Zhideng is none other than Wen Zhenheng's wife's grandfather (see Appendix I). The fact that Wang Zhideng's immense wealth, sufficient to make him the owner of the fabulous calligraphic treasure, the 'Clearing Weather after Sudden Snowfall Letter,' came from forged art works is almost less surprising than the fact that one of his peer group could mention this in print without any sense of disapproval.

It seems simply to have been the case that this sort of contempt for 'vulgar authenticity' was an important strategy of the highest sector of the elite in distancing themselves from the much broader group who could both afford works of art and were aware of which works of art carried high status but were not themselves active participants in the world of art. In the same spirit, avant-garde artists of the twentieth century have 'forged' their own work, or the work of others, as a signalled distance from the disciplines of the market. Far from subverting the market, of course, such activities were only likely to reinforce the importance of 'authenticity' as a value and strengthen the mechanisms of authority by which the market operated. These mechanisms tended not to be so much related to the actual pictorial representation, or sample of calligraphy, in question as to the apparatus surrounding it. This involved signatures of artists (since by this period only workshop productions of low social status went unsigned) and seals and inscriptions of the artist, of owners and of friends of both who were invited to view the work and append their comments to it.

On many, though not all, of the occasions when a painting went from being a commodity to being singularized as the possession of an individual, the fact of the singularization was permanently marked by the affixing of a seal. Although this was not unknown in Europe, where Lorenzo de' Medici was accustomed to have his name inscribed on antique vases and cameos in his possession,[57] and drawings and prints have since the seventeenth century carried owner's stamps, it was certainly not the case that paintings, once they became the subject of an art market, carried with them intrinsic evidence of their pedigree. The pedigree was just as important, but the evidence for it remained in the main extrinsic to the work. A possible explanation for this may lie in the very much larger size of the Ming market, where social contacts between a numerically very large elite spread over an immense empire could not of themselves be relied upon to carry the history of a given art work. Hence, the necessary support of seals and inscriptions.

It was, therefore, understandably around this apparatus that much of the ingenuity of forgers was focused. A common strategy was to separate the authenticating apparatus from the picture itself and then use the former to support the claims of a second, forged picture.[58] A typical late Ming 'fake' painting (Plate 5) produced from scratch will expend very little effort on a simulacrum of the stylistic mannerisms of the supposed artist, compared to that put into the seals and inscriptions.[59] However implausible these (which as pieces of writing were by far the easiest to produce) may look now, they were what sold the work. The lustre of a famous owner made for a considerable part of an object's market value, as I shall try and demonstrate in the next chapter.

The ease with which paintings could be forged, and the size of the demand for art works at the period, led to the vast scale on which it was done. One late sixteenth-century estimate gloomily suggested that no more than one in ten of the paintings to be found in the hands of collectors was genuine.[60] Recently, the Chinese scholar Yang Xin, in an article entitled, 'The Commodity Economy, the Spirit of the Age and the Forgery of Calligraphy and Painting' has chosen to identify the late Ming, along with the late Northern Song (eleventh – early twelfth centuries) and late Qing (nineteenth century) as the three 'high tides' of art forging, in each case being intimately linked with further development of an art market.[61] With the other kinds of antiquity in which 'authenticity' was an issue, the fact that the techniques of manufacture were more or less in the hands of artisans, rather than of members of the consuming class, only increased the degree of anxiety which the latter felt about the possibilities of being deceived.

Bronzes were a borderline case in this respect. Just as bronze vessels were the first class of antique item to enjoy a developed market, so they were the first class of item to be subject to falsification. This appears to have happened from the twelfth century, when the first warnings against forgers and the first recipes allowing for the reproduction of antique patina on bronzes of recent vintage appear side by side in a text like *Records on Metal and Stone*. By the sixteenth century these recipes are ubiquitous; there is a particularly hair-raising example in the householder's manual. This involves boiling the object three times in a liquid for which the formula is given and then burying it for a day in a pit full of vinegar lees, after which 'it will then have all the colours no different from an antique bronze.[62] However, much more sophisticated and technically demanding work was also being undertaken, as Gao Lian in particular testifies. He talks, for example, about the creation of pastiche bronzes from sections of genuine early pieces and lists several centres in which such things were done.[63]

In the case of jades and ceramics, the technology involved restricted the manufacture of fakes to the professional, with the main centre for the former once again being Suzhou. It has until recently been standard practice to ascribe many of the surviving, potentially Ming-dynasty jades with decoration which imitates or alludes to that of Bronze-age vessels to a current of 'archaism' sweeping through the visual arts. This current certainly existed, and the notion of *fang gu*, 'imitation of the 'antique', like *all'antica*, did not necessarily carry connotations of bad faith. Its influence, however, may well have been exaggerated, allowing the notion of 'archaism' to envelop what were originally attempts to capitalize on the ever-expanding antiques market.[64] The same seems true to a lesser extent in the case of ceramics.

The single most desirable type of ceramic object to Ming collectors, as regards material and form, was the incense burner in white Ding ware, according to one early Qing source 'the finest of all Song ceramics'.[65] This same source tells the tale of one of these coveted items, the property of a member of the high bureaucracy called Tang Houzheng (1538–1619). Tang became friendly with a remarkable character named Zhou Danquan, 'potter, fabricator of imitation antiques, all-round artisan, restorer, curio dealer, wily trickster, erstwhile Taoist, later-day Buddhist and, on occasion, painter,[66] to whom he showed the incense burner. On the pretext of examining it carefully Zhou measured the vessel and copied its design on paper (incidentally a very rare piece of evidence for the use of drawn designs in a Ming craft industry), returning six months later with an identical piece. Tang paid to have the fake put out of circulation and preserve the value of his own genuine piece, though his less scrupulous grandson after his death sold it to a vulgar but wealthy collector for an immense sum. The length of time taken to procure the copy clearly suggests a trip to the ceramic-producing centre of Jingdezhen, relatively remote from the lower Yangtze heart of the art market.

Here, the distance, geographical and symbolic, between the anonymous artisan producers of ceramics and their consumers was at its greatest, and reliable information was hardest to obtain. For it is the case that *there is no such thing* as a 'Ding ware incense burner,' at least not in the terms in which such things are described in the Ming collectors' literature. The shape simply was not manufactured in the Song period. However, there are in existence today a number of ceramics like those described, which are clearly of late Ming date and of Jingdezhen manufacture (Plate 6). They seem on balance highly likely to be the (literally) fabulous treasures which the Ming market in antique ceramics had erected at the pinnacle of its subtle system of differentiated rankings. The consensus that such things *could* be genuine, sustained by the connoisseurship literature, was sufficient to sustain the operation of the market, regardless of the objective truth about the commodities which that market existed to circulate.

5

Things in motion

Ming luxury objects as commodities

Karl Marx's formulation of the concept of a 'commodity economy' has been one of the central terms of the debate between historians in the People's Republic of China, and to a lesser extent in Japan, over the 'sprouts of capitalism' question and the extent to which 'late feudal' China was tending of itself to develop towards the higher and necessary stage of capitalism. To those working within this Marxist framework, the two entities of 'commodity', as very broadly a particular kind of manufactured goods intended principally for exchange, and 'capitalism' are indissolubly linked. The existence of the first is a necessity for the generation of the second. Thus, any evidence found in the Ming period for commodity production is brought forward as part of the proof that a capitalist mode of production was, indeed, tending to develop spontaneously in China.

More recent work, however, has tended to query the nature of the linkage between the two, arguing instead that a highly commoditized economy can exist independently of capitalism in any one of a number of sophisticated pre-modern societies, of which the pre-modern societies of Asia are perhaps the classic example. This work achieves its most forceful expression in a volume of essays edited by the anthropologist Arjun Appadurai, who himself formulates it in this way:

> Let us characterize commodities as things in a certain situation, a situation that can characterize many different kinds of thing, at different points in their social lives. This means looking at the commodity potential of all things, rather than searching fruitlessly for the magic distinction between commodities and other sorts of thing. It also means breaking significantly with the production-dominated

Marxian view of the commodity and focusing on its *total* trajectory from production, through exchange/distribution to consumption.[1]

If this work is correct, and I would be among those who say that it is, then the effort put into the investigations of the 'capitalist sprouts' has been misdirected. Not wasted, in that it has brought to light and subjected to fierce, often partisan, discussion a body of extremely valuable material on the Ming economy and society. However, that material clusters around questions of the organization of production and pays relatively little attention to questions of consumption, or even to the crucial stage of an object's social life during which its status as a commodity is most exposed, the moment of sale. We know something about Ming workshops, particularly in those industries, like textiles and ceramics, where the 'sprouts' were deemed to be most prominent, but very little about Ming shops and retailers. We know something about the accumulation of capital, but relatively little as yet about spending patterns, even among the best documented sections of the elite.

If we are to accept the much broader definition of a commodity situation proposed by Arjun Appadurai, with its triple division into the commodity phase (allowing thereby for the possibility of a thing moving in and out of the state of being a commodity), commodity candidacy (the cultural framework which determines which things can be exchanged) and commodity context (the social or geographical arenas in which the possibilities for the exchange of things can be concretely realized), then how can we use this model to approach the Ming world of goods?

To begin with, the attribute that logically comes first is that of commodity candidacy, 'the standards and criteria (symbolic, classificatory and moral) that define the exchangeability of things in any particular social and historical context'.[2] What could and could not be a commodity in Ming terms? The answer seems to be that there was very little which was not at least potentially a commodity; in addition to the manufactured artefacts under consideration here, agricultural land, entertainment, sexual services, religious and ritual services (all of them things which are or have been rigorously excluded from the commodity sphere in some other cultures) were susceptible to this definition.

Rights in people, too, were included. Although full slavery was not a part of Ming social relations, various types of servile and semi-servile tenant status existed in the countryside, and personal servants, too, were often indentured under terms which severely limited their personal freedom to seek another master.[3] Their status as at least temporary commodities could be marked by their names; it is fairly easy in reading a Ming novel to tell who the servants are from the distinctive nature of their names, which often link them to their functions and to the objects for which they were responsible. It could even be argued that women in Ming society, particularly those whose status was that of secondary wives or concubines, were in effect commodities, exchanged between families for very large sums of ready cash. They also often have the names of things. When in the early 1640s the scholar bureaucrat Gong Dingzi exchanged 1,000 ounces of silver for the celebrated courtesan Gu Mei, he was not simply living out one manifestation of Ming romanticism, where affairs between men of the elite class and women who lived on the sale of sexual and cultural services were generally acceptable to the former.[4] The fact that the woman's price should survive as a matter of record is powerfully suggestive of the kind of relationship of which it was just a particularly spectacular example.

Another kind of commodity, and one which was new in the late Ming period, was knowledge, transmitted personally or through the medium of published books. The almanacs and encyclopaedias, the route books of Ming merchants, the collections of model essays for the civil service examinations and the very guides to elegant living themselves are commodities which make a commodity out of kinds of knowledge which had existed in earlier centuries but which had not been bought and sold. Then, the merchant had learned the route from Nanjing to Suzhou by experience, the son of an elite family had learned the approved style for examination essays from his tutor, and the rules of taste in things had been learned through social intercourse with a peer group. By 1580 all of this knowledge, or a version of it at least, could be bought.

Certainly, none of the types of artefact included in the twelve chapters of the *Treatise on Superfluous Things* stood outside the commodity sphere, the products of the arts of calligraphy and painting not excepted. It has been suggested that it was not until the eighteenth century, in the merchant-dominated ethos of the city of Yangzhou that 'the taboo against speaking of a painting as a commodity within a transaction' broke down.[5] Certainly, there is no Ming evidence for the posting of a blatant price list of one's works, as the retired official Zheng Xie (1693–1765; ECCP, 112) did in 1759. Xu Zhengji has shown how Zheng Xie's action was in effect a protest against the age-old, subtler forms of treating a picture as a commodity, which could enmesh an artist in a whole network of reciprocal social obligations.[6] I will argue, however, that to see the eighteenth century as the first age in which it was socially permitted to talk about a painting as a commodity puts the turning point too late.

A great deal of the discourse of Ming art history, both in writings of the time and in more modern scholarship, relates to the supposed difference between the work of 'professional' and 'amateur' painters, the latter not only being fully within the social elite while the former only potentially enjoyed that status as a by-product of elite patronage. It is quite clear that in the sixteenth and seventeenth centuries this perceived difference was of very great importance. However, there may be a gain to us now in being less bound by the emic categories of the time and looking at all types of picture-making as potentially providing objects of exchange, whether they were made to the order of a patron and paid for at the time of execution, or whether they were made as part of some more insubstantial social transaction between members of the elite, since inscriptions suggest that hardly any paintings were made for the painter's own amusement or for his own continued possession. Every painting was for something.

In a crucial paper, Celia Carrington Riely has demonstrated how Dong Qichang used his own painting as a tool of great strategic importance in the creation and maintenance of a network of connections, *guanxi*, which were the indispensable condition for a successful bureaucratic career.[7] Paintings by those with regional or national reputations were valuable from the minute they were painted and could enter the commodity market at any time after they had left the possession of the original recipient. This was true even of the work of the classic exemplars of the 'scholar-amateur' model in art, such as Shen Zhou (1427–1509; DMB, 1173–7) and the family of Wen Zhenheng himself, chiefly represented in this context by his great-grandfather, Wen Zhengming, and his grandfather and great-uncle, Wen Peng (1498–1573) and Wen Jia (1501–1583).

Their work was particularly prized by the art market, paradoxically for its associations with a denial of the possibility of treating a work of art like a commodity. James Cahill has written: 'learning and a high level of culture theoretically placed one outside the marketplace, where one's creations were not for sale; but in a strictly practical sense, the fruits of learning were objects of value, marketable commodities just as were the productions of the artisan'.[8] This ambivalence applied equally to calligraphy and literary skills. Wen Zhengming was himself well aware of this ambivalence, and the multitude of anecdotes surrounding his life include the claim that, at the same time as he refused to paint to order for politicians, foreigners or merchants, he would give works to needy friends or relations as a form of subsidy, in the knowledge that they would be sold immediately.

Wen's work was definitely being forged in his own lifetime, a sure sign of its commodity status. A handscroll like 'Herb Mountain Cottage', now in the Shanghai Museum, done in 1540 collaboratively by Wen Jia and two fellows students of Wen Zhengming, was circulating in a number of forged versions less than a hundred years later, when it was seen by Li Rihua (1665–1635) in the possession of a man named Xu Renqing in Jiaxing.[9] As far as is known, Xu Renqing was no relation of any of the executants of the painting, and Jiaxing, though close enough to the Wen family's base in Suzhou in terms of modern transport, had its own elite circles which were not necessarily connected to those of the larger centre. Li Rihua talks about having seen three forged versions of this testimony of intra-elite intimacy, something which it is hard to imagine having come to pass if the work had remained within the families of those men for whom it had its original, social meaning.

The fan with the painting and calligraphy by Wen Zhengming himself which was excavated from the tomb of Xu Yufu, who died in 1613 and who again had no recorded connection with the painter's family, is another material testimony to the fact that the market-place could provide goods whose explicit meaning lay in an attempt to negate the market-place as a model of the way society ought to be structured. This very powerful tension in the late Ming between the facts of art as a commodity and an accepted ideology which said that it was wrong to make a commodity out of artistic production for which the artists had received no financial remuneration has, it seems to me, been the source of much confusion down to the present. If, instead of puzzling over whether the categories 'professional' and 'amateur' (or their grander manifestations 'Zhe school' and 'Wu school') have any real meaning or any basis in observable stylistic features, we simply accept Bourdieu's formulation that 'art is one of the major sites of denial of the social', then we may shed more light on how the market in Ming painting appeared to the larger body of consumers.

It is a curious fact that the smallest quantity of surviving information on how Ming paintings or earlier paintings circulating in the Ming dynasty (and I will treat the two together from here on, though aware of some of the unsatisfactory consequences of doing so) existed as commodities relates to the transactions between indubitably 'professional' painters and their patrons. Mette Siggstedt's meticulous study of the mid-Ming professional painter Zhou Chen (*c.* 1470–*c.* 1535) is yet unable to produce any firm evidence as to how the patron – client relationship operated. The lack of dedicatory inscriptions on a quantity of his work suggests that he may have worked directly for the market, although we do know that at one stage he lived, under duress, in the home of Yan Song, the inventory of whose confiscated property contains a number of Zhou Chen's works, possibly destined as presents.[10] There is, of course, practically none of the archival material such as illuminates the patron-artist relationship in Italy, and we have to rely on chance records in the *biji* literature.

It is this which gives us the story of how Zhou Fenglai (1523–1555), from the town of Kunshan, paid the most renowned of professional artists Qiu Ying the very large sum (quite how large will emerge below) of 100 ounces of silver for a handscroll of the Zixu and Shanglin hunting parks, fabulous gardens celebrated in the literature of the early imperial period. This took Qiu several years to complete (one source gives the scarcely credible figure of six years) and formed the centrepiece of the lavish celebrations staged by Zhou for the eightieth birthday of his mother, celebrations on which he spent in all a fortune of 1,000 ounces of silver.[11] Following Zhou 's early death, the painting found its way into the collection of Yan Song, to be confiscated with his entire possessions in 1562. What seems particularly significant about this episode is that the painting's price (something which can originally only have been known to the painter, the patron and intimate members of their households) was transmitted along with it, long enough to be recorded in a late Ming source. The size of the price became part of the object's meaning, ultimately to become separated from the actual painting (which does not survive).

Another piece of information on the working practices of the same artist, Qiu Ying, survives in the form of a letter to a patron, delivered along with a completed painting for which the patron's brother has already paid, in silver. Qiu asks that any future commissions should be addressed to him directly and not via the intermediary employed in this instance, a relative he does not get on with. He finishes with the statement that he has paid 1/10 of a silver ounce to the patron's messenger who has collected the completed scroll, a quite reasonable sum of money which suggests that the commision itself was quite an expensive one.[12] The tone is neutral and businesslike, with none of the elaborate self-deprecation found in the colophons recording gifts of paintings between members of the elite, and there is no sense that it is utterly unseemly to speak of a picture in this way.

The fact that relatively such a small amount of material survives regarding the commissioning of works of art should not be over-interpreted to mean that discussion of the subject was totally taboo; there is very little primary material surviving on any of the other areas of commodity transaction in which the elite were involved, for example, the sale of land.[13] The fault lies more with the general loss of primary documentation in China, as against the survival of edited and published sources which filtered out all material not thought suitable for a permanent record. If we had to rely on contemporary *printed* materials for a study of art patronage or of the prices paid for works of art in fifteenth-century Florence, we would be equally bereft.

Much more survives from towards the end of the sixteenth century on the market in 'antique' painting, or paintings from earlier in the Ming period. Here, we can document to an extent prices and types of transaction, and even follow individual works of art as they move socially, carrying prestige and prominence from one owner to another. Some evidence is scattered in *biji*, but some of it exists in a more concentrated form. The subject is even discussed in quite open terms by Wen Zhenheng:

> *The cost of calligraphy and pictures:* For calligraphy prices, the standard is set by regular script. One hundred characters in drafting script by Wang Xizhi are worth one line of running script, and three lines of running script are worth one line of regular script. When it comes to works of his like the *Yueyi lun, Huangtingjing, Huaxiang zan* and *Shimu wen*, then their value cannot be calculated by the number of characters. It is the same with painting prices: landscapes, bamboos and rocks, and the portraits of famous ancient worthies are worth as much as works in regular script. Human figures, flowers and birds are, if small, worth as much as running hand. Large figure paintings, Buddhist images, palaces and pavilions, beasts, insects and fish are worth as much as drafting script.[14]

Wen goes on to talk of the palace portraits of the meritorious officials of the Song dynasty as being 'national treasures beyond price'. His use of a fairly crude 'rate of exchange', based purely on number of characters, between works of calligraphy in the three most widely used forms of the Chinese script does not have to be read too literally. This convertibility, however, is a powerful metaphor for the status of works of art as commodities. There remains, beside this general stock of exchangeable goods, a reserved realm of ancient 'national treasures', literally priceless and literally fabulous, in that they are as likely as not to be works no longer actually in existence, marvels on which no living person has set eyes. Their position beyond the reach of the market-place only strengthens the hegemony of the market-place over lesser treasures.

A contemporary of Wen Zhenheng named Tang Zhixie (1579–1651), in a work on painting of about 1640, provides a further rationale for the distinction between the prices of contemporary work and those of 'antique pictures' in a chapter entitled 'Antique pictures have no fixed prices':

> Pictures have their prices; that of a contemporary picture depends on the fineness or coarseness of the work, that for a contemporary name depends on the size of the reputation. They do not vary that much, being based on no more than whether people esteem them or don't esteem them. But as for famous pictures by men of ancient times, how can they have set prices? Once, there was a man who owned a Jing Hao landscape scroll which he wanted to sell, amd the Song dynasty Court Servitor Yue Zhengxuan bought it from him for 100,000 copper cash. This was later seen by Wang Boluan, who obtained it by adding 300,000 to the price and considered himself fortunate thereby. Boluan at that time was a Painter-in-Attendance in the Hanlin Academy, charged with determining the quality of all court painting, and all the painters of the age looked on Master Wang's likes and dislikes as the standard, as his connoisseurship was very capable.
>
> Then again, Wang Guxiang (1501–1568; MRZJ, 69) obtained a set of pictures in four scrolls by Shen Zhou, of a marvelous quality. A vulgar official of Suzhou heard of their beauty and entered into negotiations with him, offering 200 ounces of silver, but Wang was unwilling in the end to sell. Later, Wang Xianchen (*jinshi* of 1493; MRZJ, 80) spent two days sitting or reclining in front of this picture. Its owner, Guxiang, said that the painting had met its true friend and went on to tell the story of the 200 ounces. Wang Xianchen then exchanged an estate worth 1,000 ounces for it.
>
> Then again Li Xianggong of Xinghua once lost a scroll by Xie Shichen (1487–after 1567; DMB, 558–9) and posted a notice, rewarding its recoverer with 50 ounces of silver, from which the value of the painting can be known. Stories like this are unending, so blind men mustn't keep asking the price of paintings.[15]

The value of works of art, as we see here, was a slightly mysterious thing, more unpredictable than the price of rice or land, but there is no suggestion that the fact of being able to buy and sell them is strange or untoward. It is the actual prices which astonish.

One productive source for these prices in the late Ming period is the cataloque of paintings seen by an otherwise not particularly famous member of the elite named Zhan Jingfeng, whose precise dates remain unknown but who passed the second level *juren* degree in 1567. His *Dongtu xuan lan bian, Compiled Hermetic Connoisseurship of Dongtu*, which has a preface dated 1591, is similar to a number of Ming painting catalogues in the lack of any discernible formal arrangement to its 400 or so accounts, of various lengths, of works of art seen either in the hands of friends and acquaintances or in the market-place.[16] What makes the work particularly valuable for present purposes is that a number of the entries (although still a tiny minority) contain anecdotes about the cost of art works or the circumstances in which they changed hands. A close reading of the text suggests that Zhan Jingfeng may well have worked as an agent for the much more wealthy and prominent members of the elite such as Wang Shizhen, his brother Wang Shimou (1536–1588) and another high official from Suzhou, Han Shineng (*jinshi* of 1568), on whose behalf he describes seeing works or visiting dealers and collectors. He may well have derived income, as well as patronage, from his role as a negotiator between the elite, of which he formed a part, and the art market. His *Compiled Hermetic Connoisseurship* appeared posthumously and shows little sign of editing or tidying up by his heirs. Hence, the survival of material on the prices of art works may betray its origins in some sort of diary or account book, maintained as a necessary professional reference.

A skillful piece of textual recovery has reassembled what may once have been the catalogue cum collector's notebook belonging to the famous merchant magnate Xiang Yuanbian (1525–1590). Xiang seems to have arranged his art collection by assigning each object a character from the *Thousand Character Essay*, a piece of continuous prose used in teaching children to read and also as a sort of ABC. Weng Tongwen has recently tracked down in later collector's catalogues sixty-six pieces of painting and calligraphy bearing these distinguishing marks.[17] Some of these entries also record inscriptions on the paintings in which Xiang records the prices he paid for the work. This seems to have been a unique practice of his, and it is hard to avoid the temptation of attributing it to his mercantile background and to his willingness to be explicit about what everyone knew but no-one cared to record. In more than one instance he employs a slightly curious formula to record the fact of paying money for a picture without recording the actual price. His inscription on a painting of 'Plum Blossoms' by the Yuan dynasty artist Yansou, now in the Freer Gallery in Washington, reads:'Ink plum blossoms by Yansou, in the collection of the Dweller in the Forest of Ink, Xiang Yuanbian. Obtained for a price of [ ] ounces from Mr An of Wuxi. Recorded on the first day of the eighth month of the Third year of the Longqing reign [= 1569].'[18] There is simply a blank where the figure ought to be, a blank which is scarcely big enough for one character and would certainly not take two. The price was therefore either under ten ounces of silver or a round hundred. Why did Xiang do this? As the inscription stands it is a record of the fact that hard cash was paid and, thus, a blatant infringement on any taboo against speaking of a painting as a commodity, without a record of the sum. It forces our attention to the painting as a commodity, while continuing with the sort of mystification more applicable to reserved goods, held back from full participation in exchange.

We cannot tell, either, why Xiang chose sometimes to foreground the price of a work in his collection by mentioning it in his inscription and sometimes omitted it. Was he boasting about bargains? Boasting about his wealth? The latter explanation is attractive but unlikely, since, as we shall see, some of the prices recorded are not huge by the standards of the art market. Appendix II contains a brief note on each of the priced works found in Zhan Jingfeng's *Compiled Hermetic Connoisseurship* and in Weng Tongwen's reconstruction of the Xiang Yuanbian catalogue, together with one or two other works once belonging to Xiang Yuanbian recorded in other sources, and a selection of prices for bronze vessels and ceramics which survive in the *biji* literature. These mostly come from the period 1560–1620. I have arranged the prices in the appendix in ascending order, the unit being the ounce of silver, or *liang*, equivalent to 37.5 g.

Of course, it is impossible at this distance to say anything about the genuineness or otherwise of the objects I have listed, and for the present purposes it does not really matter. What is recorded is simply that a given item fetched a given price on the assumption of the purchaser that it was genuine and, hence, worth so much. It is similarly impossible to 'do' any sort of economic history from this scattered and anecdotal data, but it does seem plausible that some of the relative values at work in the art market can be discerned even from such a small sample. Further data, which doubtless exists though in a scattered form, would confirm or undermine what I am suggesting here as some of the broad principles governing the prices of these particularly privileged classes of objects in the years between about 1560 and the fall of the dynasty in 1644.

Firstly, and this is not particularly surprising, the dearest pieces of calligraphy were considerably more expensive than the dearest paintings. Only four paintings reach or surpass the figure of 200 ounces of silver (disregarding the album of sixty leaves for 300 ounces). Significantly, two of those reached these very high prices following the intervention in their favour of the arbiter Dong Qichang. By contrast, we have a record of eight sales of works of calligraphy making these very high prices, including three four-figure sums, and the Ming record price for work of art, the 2,000 ounces paid for Wang Xizhi's *Zhan jin tie*, 'Gazing Nearby Letter'. The particular place accorded to works of calligraphy in the Chinese cultural system has long been acknowledged by western scholars, even if its full implications have been rather submerged in the low profile given to such work in museum displays and in general histories of Chinese art.

Esteemed calligraphy was rarely anonymous, or at least only the very earliest samples were, and the immediacy of the production of a piece of writing meant that owning it provided the most intense degree of identification with a famous owner. This identification was one of the driving forces behind Ming collecting, as has been argued above in Chapter 2. In a study of the interplay of aesthetics and social values in Chinese calligraphy, Lothar Ledderose has even gone as far as suggesting that 'whether there ever have been independent aesthetic values in Chinese calligraphy is a question deserving further study'.[19] The huge sums paid for a very particular treasure such as the 'Gazing Nearby Letter', carrying with it down through the centuries from its creation a very heavy freight of personal and social associations, are therefore a reasonable expression, in an age when most things could be commodities, of the importance put on association. Xiang Yuanbian was buying the past, not a personal past like that embodied in the portraits of possibly bogus ancestors coveted by European *nouveaux riches*, but a past of universally acknowledged value.

If one would expect calligraphy to be on the whole dearer than painting, it is perhaps rather more unexpected to discover that the major categories of three-dimensional antiquity, bronzes, jades and ceramics, were also very high in price relative to pictures. Five individual objects appear at prices in excess of 200 ounces, and if we set an arbitrary borderline at 100 ounces, then the figures are even plainer, with the number of items in each class recorded as fetching this or a larger sum being: six for pictures, ten for pieces of calligraphy and fourteen for bronzes, ceramics and jades. The very scarcity of supply of the right kinds of objects alluded to in the previous chapter is here reflected in the prices. Of course, it could be objected that the only object prices to be recorded at all were super-prices, noteworthy for their unusual size and unrepresentative of the mass of transactions. It is impossible to disprove this, but it can be advanced that the tone in which these figures are discussed (and across a somewhat broader sample of sources than that providing the data on calligraphy and pictures) is not one of astonishment but rather of an acceptance that such things cost such amounts of money. The same relative disposition of prices obtained in the Italy of the high Renaissance, where the nineteenth-century French scholar Eugène Müntz was able to demonstrate that, in Lorenzo de' Medici's inventory, antique cameos, medals and vessels were considerably more valuable than any

小滿四月中坐功圖
運主少陽三氣、
時配手厥陰心胞絡風
木

坐功
舜日寅卯時正坐一手
舉托一手拄按左右各
三五度叩齒吐納嚥液

治病
肺腑蘊滯邪毒脇支
滿心中憺憺大動面赤
鼻赤目黃心煩作痛掌
中熱諸痛

Exercises appropriate to the fourth month, one of the illustrations to the 'Discourse on being in harmony with the four seasons', one of Gao Lian's *Eight Discourses on the Art of Living*, 1591.

Table of *huali* wood, about 1600, with openwork panels carved in the shape of dragons between the legs. By Courtesy of the Trustees of the Victoria and Albert Museum, FE. 18–1980.

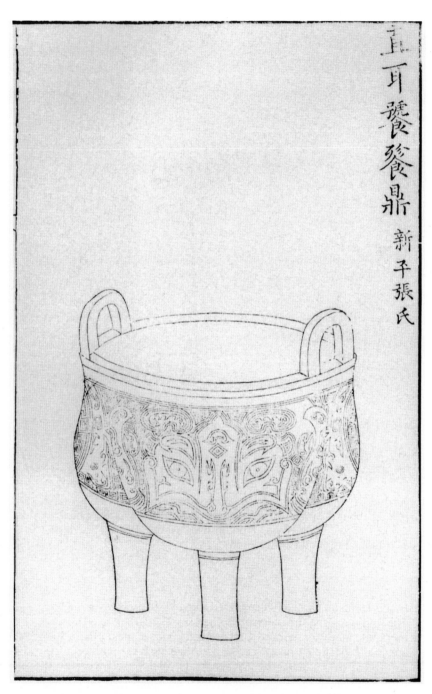

直耳饕餮鼎 新平張氏

An archaic bronze vessel of the tripod form known as *ding*, from a 1601 reprint edition of *Researches on Archaeology Illustrated* of 1092, *juan* 1, p. 17.

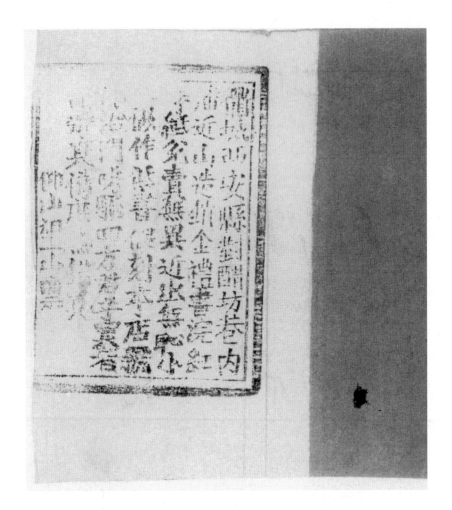

(above) A handbill issued by the publishing house of Zi Yibin, complaining about the piracy of an edition of an unidentified text called the *Golden Ritual*, by a rival, Pan Jinshan. About 1590. The Hague, Koninklijke Bibliotheek, 133 M 63.

(right) Hanging scroll on silk, painted about 1550, probably in Suzhou. The spurious signature is that of Li Zhaodao (fl. first half of eighth century), and there are spurious seals and colophons of the northern Song imperial collection (eleventh century), Ma Zhi (fourteenth century), Ke Jiusi (1312–65) and Wen Zhengming (1470–1559). By courtesy of the Trustees of the Victoria and Albert Museum, E.422–1953, Sharples Bequest.

(above) Incense burner of white porcelain imitating Ding ware, made about 1550–1600. By courtesy of the Trustees of the Victoria and Albert Museum, Circ. 130–1935.

(right) An illustration to the drama *Ideal Love Matches* by Li Yu, showing an antique shop. After Fu Xihua (1980), no. 633.

The opening passage of the handscroll 'Dwelling in the Fuchun Mountains', painted between 1347 and 1350 by Huang Gongwang, showing the colophon by Dong Qichang and the seals of the Qing dynasty imperial collection. Collection of the National Palace Museum, Taiwan, Republic of China.

painting. The reversal of these relative positions to that obtaining nowadays comes at a later date.[20]

It is rather harder, but not totally impossible, to say anything about the relative values of individual types of items within the class of paintings. The evidence is just not rich enough to support generalizations such as, 'Yuan painting was more valuable than Song', and so correlate prices with the aesthetic debate raging at the period about the merits of the two periods. The price instability was felt by contemporaries, as expressed in the quotations from Wen Zhenheng and Tang Zhixie above, with their frank admission that no rules can be set for the possible value of a given picture. Four of the pictures recorded are ostensibly of Tang date (618–906), four are Five Dynasties or Song (907–1279), nine are Yuan (1280–1367) and a mere three for which we have prices are from the period of the then-ruling dynasty, the Ming. There is, however, no discernible pattern to the distribution of the different dynasties across the range of prices.

There is, as I will argue, a connection between the intervention of Dong Qichang, as leading proponent of the supremacy of Yuan painting, and the record 1,000 ounces for which he pawned Huang Gongwang's 'Dwelling in the Fuchun Mountains' in about 1630, but other Yuan paintings by equally illustrious names seem relatively 'cheap', and certainly far less than the 200 ounces paid for 'Spring Night in the Han Palace' by Qiu Ying, whose death in *c.* 1552 makes him a near contemporary of the purchaser Xiang Yuanbian, born in 1525. Not only that, but Qiu as a 'professional' painter could have been expected to see his work relatively discounted. It is certainly not the case, however, that what was true in late sixteenth-century Italy, where 'the age of an object renders it more valuable', was true of the market for paintings in the Ming period.[21] Wen Zhenheng was explicit:

> Calligraphy is arranged by period, the Six Dynasties not being up to that of the Wei or Jin, the Song and Yuan not being up to the Six Dynasties or Tang. This is not true of painting. In Buddhist and Taoist subjects, ladies, and oxen and horse, the modern is not up to the ancient. In landscape, forests and rocks, flowers and bamboos, and birds and fish, the ancients are not up to the moderns.[22]

With painting, not simply subject matter but also association and 'biography' were equal, if not more important, determinants of price.

Despite the difficulties of doing so, and with all possible caveats about the provisional nature of any conclusions, it is necessary to

make some linkage between the prices paid for these categories and
the rest of the Ming world of commodities. I have talked of art works
as 'expensive', and the reader is entitled to demand 'How expensive?
Expensive by comparison with what?' Even the crudest answer to this
demands some consideration of what we can know about the Ming
economy at the time, in particular those aspects impinging on what
in Arjun Appadurai's terms could be defined as the 'commodity
context'. Several factors can be taken into consideration.

Firstly, there is the two-tier Chinese currency system, where copper
coins minted under state auspices at a number of centres and theoretically weighing 1/10 of a Chinese ounce (the *liang* of 37.5 g) were used
for small-scale transactions, while larger transactions were made
possible by the use of silver, which was not minted into coin but which
circulated by weight. The unit was the *liang* itself, or fractions of it.
The silver ingots thus had to be re-weighed at each transaction and
could be freely mutilated and modified to produce the required
weight. The two systems, of copper and silver, operated independently of each other in theory, but clearly, the ratio of exchange
between these two forms of money was not stable, and the fluctua-
tions in it provide one of the continuous themes of Chinese economic
history in the later imperial period.[23]

Another constant was the shortage of money and credit in the traditional economy, with the low level of production of indigenous mines
acting as a constant brake on economic development. This situation
was to be dramatically altered in the later sixteenth century by the
immense influx of silver, firstly from increased mining in Japan after
at least the 1540s, and then from the Spanish empire in America,
brought to East Asia by European merchants to purchase both raw
materials and the luxury manufactures, such as silk and porcelain, of
China. This trade boomed in particular after the end of the prohibi-
tion on overseas trade, lifted in 1567. The silver came in the form both
of ingots, which were immediately remelted into the Chinese format,
and of Spanish coins, which were also remelted or else circulated
by weight, their face value being ignored. These coins are occasionally recovered through archaeology, marked with the stamps of
the Chinese money-changers through whose hands they must have
passed.[24]

The trade in silver and its implications for the larger Chinese
economy has been noted by a number of historians and studied in
some detail by William Atwell, from whom the following simplified
account is derived.[25] The scale of the silver imports was considerable, and it accelerated at great speed after the establishment of a
centre for trans-shipment at Manila in the Philippines in 1571, to

decline only in the 1630s and 1640s, with stricter controls on the export of precious metals from Peru. One contemporary Mexican source asserted that in 1597 the quantity of silver carried from Acapulco to Manila had reached 345,000 kilograms, falling back in 1602 to 143,750 kilograms. These quantities can be seen reflected in the figures for the silver entering the Taicang Vaults, the main central state agency for the collection of government revenues, where a dramatic rise is registered for the years after 1571, continuing on to the end of the dynasty.

This was also partly due to the fact that government tax and other revenues were now increasingly collected in silver, rather than in kind as had been the practice earlier in the dynasty. Such a development was closely allied to a growing monetarization of the economy generally, with all forms of barter tending to go out of use and prices increasingly expressed in cash equivalents. We have seen above Wang Yuanqi's story from the very late fifteenth century of the purchase of an antique bronze by means of silk cloth (see p. 99). This sort of transaction does not appear in the sources relevant to the period 100 years later, when the flood of silver had transformed the economy, particularly of the prosperous south-eastern coastal provinces. It is just worth reminding ourselves yet again of the degree to which all our Ming evidence is skewed in favour of this most culturally and economically developed region of the empire and to accept that generalizations made about it may have much less validity for the inland northern provinces.

Generalizations about the movement of prices through the Ming period are particularly hard to make with any confidence. Some price sequences for the basic agricultural commodities, principally rice, have been established tentatively by the Chinese historian Peng Xinwei,[26] and these have been used by a member of the French school of socio-economic historians in the Braudelian tradition to produce a rough scheme of periodization.[27] Taking as his bench mark the price of a *jin* (596.82 g) of rice expressed in silver, he defines the following periods:

1 1368–1450 Relative stability
2 1450–1510 Almost a doubling of the price of rice
3 1510–1580 Relative stability
4 1580–1660 Very sharp price rises

The effect was that rice was twice as dear in the decade 1641–50 as it had seen 100 years earlier. This was exacerbated by the economic decline of the 1630s and 1640s, a number of bad harvests and the consequent tax and rent resistance movements of an overburdened peasantry, who sold their produce for copper coins which were fast devaluing against the silver in which they were required to pay their taxes. There was a steep rise in the price of foodstuffs and other necessities and, it has been posited, a decline in the price of non-essential goods. Wages too rose, the annual remuneration of a mercenary soldier being around six ounces in the 1550s, as against eighteen ounces by the beginning of the seventeenth century.[28] China was experiencing a 'price revolution' every bit as dramatic as that on the other side of the world. The trans-oceanic linkage of the Americas, Asia and Europe had brought into being that 'world system' which henceforward would mean that no one area would develop in total isolation, unaffected by changes to its trading partners.

The information available to us on the prices paid for items of non-essential consumption, against which we might measure the prices of the art works recorded above, is very scattered and in any case sparse. So, too, is any material on the income of the Ming elite which might enable us to gauge what proportion of capital an art collection might represent. The salaries of Ming officials were pegged at a very low level; the President of one of the Six Ministries in theory received 152 ounces of silver a year, but the actual income of such a figure was vastly magnified by presents, customary fees and bribes, all of which are unrecorded. It was not his official salary which allowed the Grand Secretary Zhang Juzheng to build a mansion in Peking valued, on its confiscation, at 10,000 ounces of silver.[29] There is, however, a considerable body of prices embedded in the inventory of Yan Song's possessions from the early 1560s, and although this predates the very steep rise in prices of the latter part of the century, it is of some value in the creation of a very broad-brush picture. It has to be borne in mind that the most valuable items in each category are not expressed in the inventory in cash equivalents, as they were simply absorbed wholesale by the treasuries of the imperial household.

One of the categories there which shows the greatest differentiation of types of products is that of silk textiles, clearly not only a very important part of luxury consumption but also the product by this time of a highly commercialized industry. The most expensive items recorded are bolts[30] of a patterned silk called *gaiji*, a novelty in the early part of the sixteenth century. These were valued at 2 ounces of silver each. Gauzes (*sha*) were the same price. The next most expensive kind of silk was valued at 1.5 ounces per bolt, and so on variously down to the cheapest type of silk at 0.3 ounces per bolt. The garments for which money prices are available (remembering that these were not the grandest items in Yan Song's wardrobe) varied between 1.3

ounces and 0.5 ounces each.[31] The impression that silk textiles were relatively expensive is born out by the prices seen in the late Ming novel of *nouveau riche* life, *The Golden Lotus*. This book, likely to have been written somewhere between 1582 and 1596, contains a wealth of 'realistic' social detail, but it has to be used with caution as a source of 'facts' about the Ming period, due allowance being made for comic exaggeration, authorial irony and other distorting rhetorical devices. The material on prices which the novel contains has been conveniently gathered together and can perhaps be used with caution as a cross-check on the data in other sources.[32] For example, in chapter 56 of the novel, one character pays 6.5 ounces for seven women's silk garments, a figure roughly in line with the inventory prices, and elsewhere a bolt of fine silk appears valued at 2 ounces.

The novel also takes us into areas of consumption we would very much like to know more about in estimating the relative weight to be given to different areas of expenditure, where a good meal for two with wine in a restaurant costs 0.13 ounces (chapter 96), and 0.1 ounce is a reasonable contribution per head towards a good picnic on an excursion (chapter 52). It even takes us into transactions of an artistic nature, as when the central character, Ximen Qing, pays a holder of the *juren* degree with 0.5 ounces and a pair of fine handkerchiefs for executing a calligraphic inscription for display (chapter 77). Here, we see the skills of the scholar elite reduced quite plainly and openly to commodities with a reckonable money value.

Again Ximen Qing pays a professional painter 10 ounces of silver and a bolt of silk worth 2 ounces for painting the funerary portrait of a deceased favourite concubine (chapter 63). This looks like a very large sum by comparison with some of the antique works of art whose prices are tabulated in Appendix II, but the point here may be to underline the inappropriate extravagance of Ximen Qing's grief, expressed through lavish funerary display and reckless spending. The same may be true of the 50 ounces paid for a lacquer screen in chapter 45 and the 60-ounce valuation put on a lacquered bed inlaid with mother of pearl in chapter 96. The most expensive piece of furniture recorded in the inventory of Yan Song's non-fictional furniture is 8 ounces for a decorated lacquer bed, while the average value of a table was only 0.22 ounces and of a chair 0.2 ounces. Ordinary ceramic table wares work out at an average of 0.13 ounces per time in the same source.[33]

Another anecdote exists with data on the prices of new ceramics, for when the important writer and artist Li Rihua (1565–1635) was serving as an official at the porcelain production centre of Jingdezhen, he ordered a set of fifty cups from a man called 'Hao the Nineteenth', and paid 3 ounces of silver (0.06 ounces per cup) for them.[34] One early Qing source records that:

> In the early Chongzhen period (1628–44), the kilns produced no fine pieces, the price of the best not surpassing 0.3 to 0.5 ounces of silver per item, with the ugly ones at 0.5 ounces for ten pieces. In the early Shunzhi reign, Jiangxi had only just been pacified, and the ravages of the soldiery had not ceased, so that the ugliness of the ceramics was even greater than previously, though their price was tenfold. The ugliest sold for 0.4 or 0.5 ounces each, while those with even any degree of glossiness sold for several times this, even though vastly inferior to Jiajing wares.[35]

The most expensive contemporary ceramics would appear to have been the red stoneware teapots of Yixing, produced by individually named and ranked artisans in a situation of close elite patronage. Zhang Dai has a teapot by one of the three top names of Yixing as costing between 5 and 6 ounces.[36]

With regard to what might be termed another area of cultural consumption, the Japanese scholar Isobe Akira has found three references to the cost of books in the late sixteenth and early seventeenth centuries, with a luxury illustrated edition of a novel at 2 ounces and two other literary collections at 0.8 ounces and 0.12 ounces respectively.[37]

What these figures cumulatively tell us is that the prices for the most expensive antique works of art, the three- and four-figure sums paid for great historic calligraphic masterpieces, for inscribed bronze vessels and for the finest Song ceramics, were very great indeed. These things were accessible only to the very wealthiest and were comparable to the prices they paid for their mansions and for the large estates which sustained their wealth, like the vast chief eunuch's palace mentioned in *The Golden Lotus*, chapter 14, as changing hands for 700 ounces. Agricultural land clearly varied greatly in price according to quality, but one estimate has prime land at anything between 28 and 40 ounces per hectare in the late Ming.[38] Clearly a four-figure sum paid for a piece of calligraphy could potentially represent a large proportion of its owner's capital, tied up in an extremely mobile form.

If we now attempt to say something about the 'commodity context' of Ming luxuries, the social and geographical arenas in which luxury objects were exchanged, we are even more bereft of hard information than that on which the preceding unsatisfying and inevitably anecdotal discussion of prices is founded. There is clearly a reluctance in the sources to discuss this in any detail, and we certainly find implicit or explicit distaste for the notion of speaking openly of a work of art as a commodity (though this hardly squares with Xiang Yuanbian's gleeful inscription of prices paid on the art works themselves). A certain studied vagueness of language is used to cloud the fact of trade in culturally prestigious items and even a rather specialized vocabulary. The word I have been translating as 'ounce' is in standard Chinese *liang*, but in the context of art works and antiques the sources almost always prefer the synonym *jin*, which literally means 'gold' or 'gold piece'. Gold pieces had not been minted for millennia, and gold itself was not used as a medium of exchange, but the word seems to have had elegant and archaic references, separating out the special things for which it was the appropriate currency from those ordinary things which could be paid for in more prosaic *liang*. The bland bureaucratic language of the Yan Song inventory always prefers the bald *liang* to the slightly more poetic *jin*.

Unwillingness to articulate the workings of the market, however, clearly does not contradict the existence of a vigorous market and of a variety of forms of market transaction in which works of art could be involved. It is currently the general practice for museums to occlude the prices paid for their acquisitions, even when these have passed through the art market with a blaze of publicity, and the cost of items recently added to the collections is generally held back even from professional colleagues, as much from a perception that it is unseemly to emphasize such concerns as from any regard for operational secrecy. Similarly in the late Ming, we find our material as often as not in the interstices of accounts whose main concern is elsewhere, and what follows leans rather more heavily than is comfortable on the testimony of Zhan Jingfeng, who at least has the value of recording a wide variety of different types of context for art market transactions. He is the source of tantalizing details like the information that the market for works of art was partly subject to differences of regional taste, horse paintings being very popular in the north.[39] Works of art could be sold individually or as complete family collections. Towards the very end of the fifteenth century, two eunuchs shared the immense purchase price of 40,000 ounces of silver for the collection of Mu Zong, descendant of one of the Ming founder's favourite generals and practically autonomous ruler of the southwestern frontier province of Yunnan. The share of one of these eunuchs (who, of course, had no direct progeny) passed to á nephew, who was himself also probably a eunuch, and then to his younger brother, before being broken up piecemeal at the close of the sixteenth century.[40]

Inheritance was, of course, an important method of transfer, as we shall see, but it was also known for sales to take place within a family, for example from an uncle to a nephew, the price then obviously remaining a secret between the two parties. The same is true of sales directly from one owner to another.[41] But there were also specialist dealers in all the types of commodity we have been considering, who in some cases came from families which had made a hereditary speciality of the art business over several generations; 'A friend's family had for generations been major dealers in antiques, and one day he brought a large hanging scroll to me . . .', writes Shen Defu, revealing that there existed no insuperable barrier to friendly social intercourse between a member of the landed elite like Shen and an art dealer and also that the latter were in the habit of visiting the homes of the former to show them their latest wares.[42] The shared discourse of dealers and elite customers is seen powerfully in the case of Zhang Taijie, discussed by Joan Stanley-Baker. Zhang was the author of a catalogue of his collection/stock, entitled simply *Bao hui lu*, *Catalogue of Painting Treasures*, published in 1633 and listing an impressive series of wholly fictitious masterpieces. Utterly implausible as they all seem now and have done since subjected to the more rigorous standards of eighteenth-century connoisseurship, there is no question that he was not taken seriously by his contemporaries. This must have a great deal to do with the fact that he was himself a holder of the *jinshi* degree and, hence, a social equal of his customers. With taste and connoisseurship being socially conditioned, Zhang could hardly fail to enjoy general success and esteem.

But conviviality had its limits. It was an unnamed 'dealer from Nanjing' who visited Zhan Jingfeng in 1590 with a landscape by the Song politician Wang Anshi, and another member of the art trade is referred to by a nickname, as the 'old Muslim from Yangzhou'.[43] Dealers could also visit the homes of prospective vendors, and it seems that Zhan is casting himself in this former role when he talks about how he saw Wang Wei's 'Wangquan Villa under the Snow' at the home of one Hu Bianxiu of Nanjing who 'wished to sell it' or tells of how he 'managed to see' a Buddhist figure painting by the Tang artist Zhang Sengyu 'at the home of a member of the Hangzhou gentry who wished to sell it'.[44] It was also possible to visit the homes of the grander dealers, which functioned as shops and where purchase was likely to again be veiled by social forms imitating those in use among the elite, in a strategy similar to that still employed at the top end of the art market, where stock is displayed 'by appointment only' in an environment imitating that of the wealthy domestic interior, and prices are certainly not overtly visible. Zhan Jingfeng gives several examples of this in Suzhou, Hangzhou and in Peking.[45]

Pawnshops, too, acted as places where art could be acquired, and some of them may even have specialized in these high-value goods.[46] A woodcut illustration to the seventeenth-century drama *Ideal Love Matches* shows a much more modest antiques shop (Plate 7), with shop front exposed to the street in a manner similar to those of establishments selling textiles, medicines or grain, and the same author, Li Yu (1611–1680; ECCP, 495–7), is responsible for another fictional but much grander antique dealer's place of business, the 'House of Gathered Refinements' in his short story collection *The Twelve Towers*.[47] Li adds the antique business to the 'three elegances in the midst of vulgarity', being the selling of books, flowers and incense. He tells of three young men who open adjacent shops in Peking, dealing in books, incense and flowers and antiques. They knock down the interconnecting walls to make one large emporium, and business flourishes until the most handsome of the youths receives the unwelcome attentions of Yan Shifan, the notorious son of Grand Secretary Yan Song. The boy is kidnapped, castrated and passed on to a wealthy eunuch as a sort of private curator of his collection. The incidents may be melodramatic, but the details of the background carry conviction. The antique dealer will, for example, not buy three classes of goods; things that are too cheap (they lower the tone), fakes (which destroy customer confidence) and objects of uncertain provenance (for fear of lawsuits over stolen goods). Plausible, too, are the difficulties of trying to get payment out of a politically untouchable member of the high bureaucracy, who takes objects home on approval and then proves unwilling to part with their price.

Shops were in any case closely associated with dwellings, even of the grandest sort. In *Jin ping mei*, the central character's silk shop and pawnshop are in the front of residential premises, and when in the 1640s a Grand Secretary was recorded as having installed a jewellery shop in the street frontage of his Peking mansion, it was not the fact itself that was worthy of note but the scandal that the shop was simply used as a front for the reception of bribes.[48] In antique shops of the smaller kind the goods were fully available as commodities on a 'first come – first served basis', with no attempt at the more cushioning types of social obligation. This is made clear by a couple of stories in Zhan Jingfeng on the well-worn collectors' theme of 'the one that got away', as when he encountered in Peking a great bargain in the form of a small landscape scroll by the Tang artist Li Sixun, offered for sale at a mere 7 ounces. Unfortunately, he had come out browsing without any money, and by the time he had rushed home for his purse and returned, the piece had been snatched up by someone named Wang from Shanxi. The incident clearly rankled.[49]

Luxury shops and businesses associated with the antiques trade clustered together, as in the famous Zhuanzhu Lane in Suzhou and along the banks of the canal linking Suzhou to the nearby beauty spot of Tiger Hill to the north-west, a popular resort of the well-to-do. A trip round the antique dealers could be a pleasant recreational outing, as when Feng Mengzhen, then residing on Hangzhou's West Lake, made such an outing 'to see all the things'. Feng also made the purchase of 'rare books, old works of calligraphy and paintings', a task he set himself to accomplish once every six months, giving some idea of the rate at which the collection of a wealthy man might grow.[50] The most important thing from a dealer's point of view was to be near a steady supply of such well-off customers as he. Thus, we hear about a Taoist monk who operated an antiques business from his monastery on the island of Jiaoshan, in the middle of the Yangtze near the city of Zhenjiang, perfectly placed to intercept prospective customers en route along the river, travelling from south to north China, or simply making one of the short excursions which were such a feature of upper-class male life.[51] Zhou Danquan (encountered in the previous chapter as a forger of Ding ware incense burners) was also a Taoist monk, at least during one stage of his colourful career, and he, too, seems to have operated a business from within the cloister walls.[52] A third Taoist dealer was Wang Fuyuan, once a disciple of Wen Zhengming himself, whose base of operations was the small but wealthy city of Jiaxing.[53] Shops catering to the elite could just as well be situated outside the city walls in some scenic spot, and Zhang Dai recalls one such parade of shops specializing in luxury ceramics, including Yixing teapots, set in attractive scenery at Mingshan, a couple of miles outside the city of Wuxi.[54]

A number of periodic markets provided specialized contexts for the sale of art works and antiques. In Hangzhou, such a market was held every day at the Zhaoqing Temple,[55] while in the capital there were three such periodic markets. That at the Lamp Market was held once a year from the first to the tenth of the first month, and Zhan Jingfeng seems to have found this one of his most fruitful hunting grounds for bargains.[56] The market at the Temple of the City God was held each month from the fifteenth to the twenty-fifth day. Here, according to Shen Defu:

Calligraphy, antiques and paintings, both genuine and false, are displayed. The northerners cannot tell them apart, and they are often acquired cheaply by the merchants of Suzhou. Carved lacquers and incised lacquers from the Palace have recently increased their prices tenfold. In ceramics the dearest are those of the

Chenghua reign, then those from the Xuande reign. A cup used to count only several ounces, and when I was a child [Shen was born in 1578] I did not think of them as valuable treasures. A pair of Chenghua wine cups now fetches 100 ounces, and a Xuande incense burner almost as much. It is all due to the leaders of fashion from Suzhou making these things the subject of their 'elegant discussions', which the imperial relatives and big merchants blindly and frivolously imitate, that the flood of rising prices has reached this point.[57]

A slightly later text, *Di jing jing wu lüe, Résumé of the Sights and Goods of the Imperial Capital* of 1635, confirms that this site could still show three *li* of stalls of:

ancient and modern books, Shang and Zhou bronzes, Qin and Han dishes and mirrors, Tang and Song paintings and calligraphy, as well as pearls, ivory, jade curiosities and silks from Yunnan, Guangdong, Fujian, Hunan, Jiangsu and Zhejiang. Now, the sages did not value things because they were strange and did not order curious things to be made. Rather, things were forceful but refined, their workmanship was solid and good.[58]

The authors go on to give detailed accounts of the types of goods available in this market, which mixed antiques with contemporary luxuries, like silk textiles and decorated writing papers, and with imported curiosities like Tibetan bronze Buddhas, images of Jesus from the 'Western Ocean', Sanskrit scriptures and Japanese fans.

There was also in Peking the market at the rear gate of the palace, held on the fourth day of every month and notorious for the selling of items smuggled (or legitimately removed, the Ming emperors were great dissipators of their art holdings) from the imperial collection:

Any curious precious objects or rare treasures presented to the Household would all be gathered together at this Inner Market. Even palace manufactures like Xuande bronzes, Chenghua porcelain, Yongle lacquers from the Orchard Factory and Jingtai enamels of the imperial workshops, their curiousness and craft surpassing that of antiquity, were bought for high prices at the Inner Market by the *aficionados* (*hao shi zhe*) of the whole empire.[59]

Here, some of the operators could be very small, not to say distinctly shady, and we read of precious items being taken out of the seller's bag to show to customers, as when one collector encountered the lid of a jade jar long in his possession, brought out of the sack of a dealer from Henan encountered in the capital.[60]

If we come down from the general level of the context in which works of art as commodities changed hands, we are fortunate in that the types and quantities of documentation attached in particular to the most prestigious paintings mean that we are able to deploy in this context Igor Kopytoff's fruitful concept of an object 'biography', to trace these objects' movements through society. The cumulative effect of a number of such studies would be of immense value in exposing lines of cultural as well as economic power in imperial China, but nothing of this scope is attempted here. Instead, advantage will be taken of two exemplary studies of the pedigrees of individual paintings, or at least of those segments of their total biographies relating to the late Ming. These are Riely's study of the ownership of Huang Gongwang's masterpiece from the Yuan dynasty, 'Dwelling in the Fuchun Mountains' (Plate 8), and Wen Fong's equally detailed account of 'Rivers and Mountains after Snow', another handscroll believed in the Ming at least to be by the great Tang poet and painter Wang Wei.[61]

The 'Fuchun Mountains' scroll is recorded by the Ming artist Shen Zhou in 1488 as having at some earlier stage been in his collection, but we are then ignorant of its whereabouts for nearly a hundred years, until a colophon by Wen Peng (also a famous artist in his own right, and ancestor of our Wen Zhenheng) records it in 1570 as being in the collection of someone named Tan Zhiyi in the southern capital of Nanjing. From then on, the density of documentation increases. In the early 1590s the painting was in the hands of another official in Peking, surnamed Zhou. It must have changed hands, and moved all the way across China, shortly after that, for in 1596 its most illustrious Ming owner, Dong Qichang, wrote on it: 'Recently, I was sent as an imperial envoy to the Sanxiang region in Hunan, and passed through Jingli, where my friend the Secretary to the Grand Secretariat Hua arranged for me to buy this painting . . .'[62] Dong still owned the painting in 1627, but by 1634 it belonged to a Wu Zhengzhi, resident in Yixing, who in turn bequeathed it at some stage to his son, Wu Hongyu. In 1651, at the very beginning of the Qing dynasty, a colophon by Shen Hao reminisces about seeing it 'twenty years earlier' in the hands of Wu Hongyu, who told him how Dong Qichang had pawned the scroll to his father for 1,000 ounces of silver. Further colophons from 1652, 1657 and 1669 record two further owners.

What this tangled history reveals is that the painting, in the century from 1570 to 1669, changed hands eight times, an average of once every twelve and a half years, much more frequently than once a generation, even in a situation of youthful marriages. Only two of those transmissions were definitely by inheritance rather than sale, though the most significant transfer was, in fact, an act of pawning between close friends (Dong Qichang to Wu Zhengzhi), for the weight of 375 kilograms of silver, a considerable fortune. The painting's mobility across time is paralleled by its geographical mobility, from Nanjing to Peking to Hunan, then with Dong Qichang at his home in Songjiang from 1602 to 1622 and probably accompanying him to Peking and Nanjing again before his colophon of 1627 back in Songjiang, before its move to Yixing. A painting like this was concentrated capital, not just in monetary terms but in terms of cultural prestige. Its owner was guaranteed the type of connections essential to a successful bureaucratic career.

The same degree of volatility is reflected in the history of 'Rivers and Mountains after Snow'. Between 1595 and 1642 the painting changed hands, not counting occasions on which it was borrowed, five times (or once every 9.4 years), only one of those transfers being by inheritance. Again, it passed through the hands of Dong Qichang, being borrowed by him from Gao Lian's friend Feng Mengzhen in Hangzhou in 1595. In a colophon written on the scroll in 1642 by the politician and poet Qian Qianyi, we see very explicitly the notion of an 'unworthy purchaser', in a metaphor vivid with the unease felt by some at the reduction of an art work to an item of trade:

> After Feng Mengzhen died, the scroll was purchased by a rich man from Xin'an. Thus, a fine work of mist and clouds fell into being a heap of copper cash for more than thirty years, but finally I was able to rescue it.[63]

Qian might have 'rescued' Wang Wei's masterpiece from its distasteful commodity state temporarily, but no one was able to ensure that such things did not have to descend into the soiled world of commerce again. The market was a powerful force in Ming society, a powerful metaphor for new kinds of interaction between people, as well as between things. By the time Dong Qichang pawned 'Dwelling in the Fuchun Mountains' for 1,000 ounces, he had himself created a very large part of that value through the very fact of his ownership, manifested through colophons and seals. He had also done it through his fundamental rearrangement and systematization of the canons of quality in the history of Chinese painting, where he had vigorously championed Huang Gongwang and his Yuan contemporaries as the most accomplished of all masters from the past.[64] I am far here from aiming to suggest a crude manipulation of the market on Dong's part but am, rather, positing that in our reading of the aesthetic debates surrounding Dong Qichang we keep in mind an awareness of the nature as commodities of the art works being discussed. In particular, we should be aware of the competing tug between the desire to avoid commoditization, through singularizing devices like owner's seals and colophons, and the need periodically to 'test the market', particularly in the sense of testing the degree of acceptance of revised canons of quality, through a more or less grudging acceptance of an art work's commodity potential.

6

Anxieties about things

Consumption and class in Ming China

A distrust of, and even a distaste for, the social role of artisans and their products has deep roots in traditional Chinese political economy. The wealth of the empire was based on agricultural production, from the single-minded pursuit of which the manufacture of anything other than essential tools of production or necessities for survival was seen as a potentially unsettling distraction. This feeling is encapsulated in the concept, first formulated in the writings of several thinkers of the late Bronze age (sixth – fifth century BC), of the distinction between the 'roots' (*ben*) of the state and its 'branches' or 'extremities' (*mo*). The roots were to be defined as agriculture, the extremities as craft or industrial production, and trade or commerce. Overlaid on this idea was the division of society into four classes, ranked hierarchically from the 'officers' (*shi*; in the later imperial period the term had the connotation of 'scholars', but it originally referred to a hereditary ruling class with as much a military as a civil ethos), the farmers (*nong*), the artisans (*gong*) and the merchants (*shang*). The first two classes were seen as the necessary roots, the latter two as the essentially redundant extremities, or even as parasitical excrescences on the labour of the peasantry.

To the sixth-century BC thinker Han Fei, later characterized as a founder of the 'Legalist' school, craftsmen and merchants were to be listed among the 'Five Vermin of the State':

An enlightened ruler will administer his state in such a way as to decrease the number of merchants, artisans and other men who make their living by wandering from place to place, and will see to it that such men are looked down upon. In this way he lessens the number of people who abandon primary pursuits [i.e *ben*] to take up secondary occupations [i.e *mo*] . . . When offices and titles can be bought, you may be sure that merchants and artisans will not remain despised for long; and when wealth and money, no matter how dishonestly gotten, can buy what is in the market, you may be sure that the number of merchants will not remain small for long . . . These are the customs of a disordered state: . . . Its merchants and artisans spend their time making articles of no practical use and gathering stores of luxury goods, accumulating riches, waiting for the best time to sell and exploit the farmers.[1]

Although definitions of the 'roots' and the 'extremities' were subject to fluctuation through the subsequent centuries of the imperial period, this underlying mistrust remained as a constant. The state, after all, derived its wealth overwhelmingly from the taxation of agriculture, and the ruling class as individuals derived their wealth from the same source. Hence, state attempts actually to promote manufactures or trade in them could not but be seen as potentially subversive. This is not to say that the state did not at times (and particularly in the Song dynasty) derive wealth from these sources or that there were no rich merchants or entrepreneurs even at a period well before that of the Ming. Such men most certainly existed, but at the deepest level their activities remained the object of suspicion and mistrust within the land-owning ruling class. Any politician who proposed that the state encourage trade as a source of revenue risked attack on the grounds that he was subverting very ancient and deeply ingrained notions about the ordering of society.

The notion of 'roots' and 'extremities' was used also from an early period to separate out the basic core of an activity from its inessential parts, within the four hierarchical categories into which the population was to be notionally divided. Thus, one late Han-dynasty text from the second century AD, by the writer Wang Fu (85–163) puts it: 'Among the hundred artisans, usefulness [i.e. of their products] is the root and cunning decoration the extremity. Among merchants, the transportation of goods is the root, and selling is the extremity.'[2] The idea that wasteful luxury drains the vital energy of the body politic is, of course, not exclusive to China, but there is also in some classical and pseudo-classical sources a sense that the health of that body is very intimately linked with quite precise details of the shape and decoration of certain kinds of craftsmen's products.

Although we can do no more than speculate about the attitudes of such a distant historical period, the immense care and the considerable cost and effort put into the sacrificial vessels of the early Bronze age bespeaks a concern with the physical details of things to be used in a context of rituals crucial to the maintenance of the royal line.[3] And another Han-dynasty text well known in later dynasties, the *Shuo yuan, Garden of Tales*, compiled in the years 16–6 BC by Liu Xiang, has this telling anecdote:

> Duke Mu of Qin asked You yu, 'What were the reasons whereby the enlightened Kings and sage Emperors of ancient times obtained and lost their states?' You Yu said, 'Your servant has heard that they obtained them through frugality and lost them through extravagance.' Duke Mu said, 'I am willing to hear about the canons of frugality and extravagance.' You Yu said, 'I have heard that when Yao possessed all under heaven, he ate his food from an earthenware vessel and drank his broth from an earthenware vessel. His territory stretched south to Jiaozhi and north to Youdu, and east and west to where the sun rises and sets. None failed to submit to him. Yao resigned the empire, and Shun accepted it. When Shun ordered vessels for eating and drinking, they cut and carved wood, cast bronze and iron, worked with the knife and lacquered them black as utensils. And thirteen of the feudal lords became extravagant and failed to submit to him. Shun resigned the empire, and Yu accepted it. Yu made sacrificial vessels which were lacquered on the outside and painted in vermilion on the inside. He had painted silks for his cushions. His goblets and ladles were coloured, of increasingly extravagant decoration. And thirty-two states did not submit to him. The Xia dynasty of the Hou Clan collapsed, and the Yin and Zhou succeeded them. They made great vessels and established the Nine Tripods. Their vessels for feasting were decorated and worked, their goblets and ladles carved and intricate. The four jade disks and four curtains, the cushions and mats were decorated and patterned. Thus was great extravagance, and the states which did not submit numbered fifty-two. If you, my lord, are over-fond of decoration and pattern, then your vassals will be boundlessly extravagant. Thus it is said, "The Way is frugality".[4]

Despite (or to an extent because of) the immense antiquity of these ideas, in particular the distinction between *ben* and *mo*, they had lost nothing of their potency as the central terms of economic debate in the Ming period.

A good example of this from within the relevant period can be found in the writings of Zhang Han (1511–1593; DMB,72–4). Himself from an artisan background, his distant ancestors having been silk weavers, he rose to the highly influential position of President of the Board of Civil Office, in effect Minister of Personnel. In one of his works, bearing a preface dated 1593, he adheres without any sense

of inappropriateness to the archaic four-fold classification system for
the population of the empire. His *Treatise on Merchants*, in which he
shows only a limited degree of sympathy for a mercantile point of view
(despite having served in some of the most commercially developed
regions of China), has been translated in full by Timothy Brook.[5]
His *Treatise on the Hundred Artisans*[6] is similarly closely bound
to traditional Confucian distrust of the potential for social chaos
involved in the inappropriate transformation of the morally 'good'
products of agriculture. Zhang Han begins with an account of the
frugality of the ancient sage kings, their concern above all for
agriculture:

> The customs of the present age have reached an extreme of extrava-
> gance, they are 'different every month and dissimilar every season'
> . . . Nowadays, the wealth and goods of the empire are concen-
> trated in the capital, yet half of them are produced in the south-east.
> Thus, those possessing the skills of the hundred artisans similarly
> mostly come from the south-east, particularly from the Jiangyou
> (modern Jiangsu) region, with Zhejiang and Zhili coming next, and
> Fujian and Guangdong after that.

He goes on to explain how at the beginning of the Ming dynasty those
people who were registered as artisans were mostly criminals of some
sort, compelled to labour for the state in a system of service obligations. However, the population has grown and the number of artisans
stayed the same, allowing them to escape their service obligations and
work for themselves, pandering to the outrageous extravagance of the
hereditary nobility of the capital: 'From ancient times, the capitals of
kings and emperors have easily fallen prey to extravagance and
luxury.' Peking has suffered from this ever since becoming the capital.
Goods from everywhere are clustered there, and prices are high, 'so
that the people of the south-east are happy to converge there, with
no thought for the long journey'. A luxurious style of living emanates
from the court outwards. Mindful perhaps of his own background,
Zhang then argues that artisans are still necessary for the essential
transformations of natural products:

> However the sage kings and imperial rulers did not treasure rarities
> or value goods which were difficult to obtain, fearing lest the
> hundred artisans flaunt rarities and peddle their skills, rushing into
> licentiousness, making the useless and harming the useful, aban-
> doning basic tasks and pursuing secondary occupations in an
> unsuitable manner.

He argues that ancient artisans made only essential things and were, thus, an aid to the farmers, not a parasitical hindrance to them, and continues with an updated version of the anecdote from the *Garden of Tales*. In this story the political fate of an unsuccessful warlord, one of the original rivals of the Ming dynasty's founder, is foretold by the luxury of the artefacts with which he surrounded himself:

> Our Great Progenitor August Emperor swept out the barbarian Mongol Yuan dynasty and took possession of the empire. It happened that the officers garrisoning Jiangxi province presented the carved and gilded couch which had belonged to Chen Youliang. The Emperor said to his attendants, 'What is the difference between this and the seven-treasures urinal of Meng Chang? If his very couch was of such intricate workmanship, the rest of his possessions can be imagined. Both father and son of the Chen family were limitlessly greedy and covetous, how could they avoid extinction!' And he ordered the couch destroyed.

The implications in Zhang's following passage are that subsequent Ming emperors were far from upholding the virtuous frugality of their great ancestor. He goes on then to a comparison of the different regions of the empire, in terms which would have commanded almost universal acceptance:

> As for the customs of the populace, in general those south of the Yangtze are more extravagant than those north of it, and no extravagance south of the Yangtze surpasses that of Suzhou. From of old the customs of Suzhou have been habituated to excess and splendour and a delight in the rare and strange, to which the sentiments of the people there are invariably drawn. The clothes of Suzhou people are splendid, as if to be otherwise were to be without culture. The vessels of the people of Suzhou are beautified, as if to be otherwise were to be without value. The whole world appreciates the clothes of Suzhou, and Suzhou gives clothes still more craftsmanship. The whole world values Suzhou vessels, and Suzhou gives vessels still more craftsmanship. In this way the extravagance of Suzhou customs becomes even more extravagant, so how can the desire of the world for the things of Suzhou be stifled and turned to moderation? To turn people's inclinations from moderation to excess is easy, but to return them from excess to moderation is difficult.

Zhang Han concludes by focusing his disapproval on unseemly and unnecessary decoration, on 'carving and inlaying' as a source of damage to the needs of agriculture and sericulture, twin pillars of state and society. He tell how, as a conscientious local magistrate, he had forbidden the manufacture of elaborate festival lanterns, made at great cost only to be set alight and destroyed in minutes. Yet, ironically, in his home province of Zhejiang it is the official families who take the lead in making and enjoying these wasteful luxuries, a typical example of failure of moral leadership on the part of the natural rulers of the social order.

There can be doubt that, whatever standards prevailed in terms of actual consumption behaviour, and despite the undoubted growth in commercial prosperity in at least the wealthier parts of the empire at this time, the views of Zhang Han were the 'official' line of the ruling elite. The Ming unease about things may have been pronounced, but it was very ancient, sanctioned by the most authoritative type of classical text, and to a certain extent conventional. There is at least one striking piece of evidence of a more 'modern' attitude to consumption, in the form of a remarkable essay by Lu Ji (1515–1552; DMB, 1003), which has again fortunately been translated in total by Lien-Sheng Yang, whose translation is quoted below.[7] Lu Ji was a son of that same Lu Shen who had written the *Record of Curious Ancient Vessels* mentioned in chapter 1 above and who came from a wealthy office-and land-holding family based on the lower Yangtze Valley city of Songjiang. Yang traces back to the Warring States period a submerged yet tenacious tradition of thought in China which runs counter to the conventional preference for saving and frugality over spending and lavishness. This tradition surfaces very explicitly in Lu Ji, who opens uncompromisingly;

> Those who discourse on government as a rule wish to prohibit extravagance, assuming that restricting spending will enrich the people. However, as an early worthy has observed, as to the wealth produced by Heaven and Earth there is a fixed amount. One person's loss becomes the gain of another.

Lu argues that the wealth of Suzhou and Hangzhou is attributable to the lavishness of life there, with jobs being created for all sorts of 'boatmen, sedan chair carriers, singsong boys and dancing girls'. The heavy spending on food by 'rich merchants and powerful families' benefits the farmers; the heavy spending on clothes benefits the weavers. People are not extravagant because of the activities of traders, but rather trade flourishes because of the extravagant lifestyle of the population, and this is of wide benefit. These ideas strikingly anticipate, by some 150 years, Bernard Mandeville's classic formulation of 'economic rationalism and moral cynicism' in *The Fable of the Bees*, where 'private vices are public benefits'.[8]

These were attitudes which in a sense it was heretical to voice quite so blatantly, but it is unlikely that they were the product of a single eccentric. On the contrary, they may well have represented a set of views commonly held by the elite or by educated merchants, with whom they consorted as social equals, but which rarely made their way into the written record, dominated as that record was by the most conservative sections of the bureaucratic class with its roots more firmly in landholding and with a fixed hostility to commercial enterprise.

Certainly, the suspicion of artisans seen in Zhang Han continued to be a force in Ming political life, at least at the higher reaches of the bureaucracy. Despite the rise in the status of certain named 'stars' like Hu Wenming and Lu Zigang discussed above in chapter 2, the social categorization 'artisan' remained formally a menial one throughout the dynasty. This did not stop men technically of an artisan background from rising high up the ladder of bureaucratic success, but it remained a subject of note when they did so. Shen Defu recounts a number of scandalous anecdotes from the fifteenth century of the rise to power of such people under the aegis of exceptional and improper imperial favour. In the Jiajing reign (1522–66) a carpenter by the name of Xu Gao even rose to the Presidency of the Board of Works, something looked upon as totally subversive of good government.[9]

The Ming state, like previous dynasties, did not simply disapprove of consumption which was uncontrolled and socially inappropriate; it made every attempt to police and control such consumption through the operation of a system of sumptuary laws. In the perceptive analysis of Arjun Appadurai, this external method of regulating consumption stands between the status system of simpler and more stable societies, with restricted and stable sets of commodity types, and the fashion system of highly complex societies, where the types of commodity available are in constant flux and taste is, therefore, the necessary mechanism for regulating the social aspects of consumption. His definition is hard to better: 'Sumptuary laws constitute an intermediary consumption-regulating device, suited to societies devoted to stable status displays in exploding commodity contexts, such as India, China and Europe in the pre-modern period.'[10] It is the visible tension between the state's attempts to regulate consumption legally, defining who could have what in terms of the social status they already enjoyed, and the increasing lack of effect such regulations had in an 'exploding commodity context' which gives rise

to much of the distinctive late Ming attitude to the world of commodities. This attitude in turn gives rise to the manuals of taste and style,
such as *Eight Discourses on the Art of Living* and *Treatise on Superfluous Things*, with which the earlier part of this book has been
concerned.

That these more 'modern' forms of brake put on consuming should
appear in China at roughly the same time as – or even, as I have
argued, ahead of – their appearance in early modern Europe, and yet
were part of societies which after the sixteenth century were to diverge
at an ever increasing rate, suggests that the distinctively European
development of a capitalist society may well have to be explained at
a level deeper than that of a special attitude to material culture and
manufactured things. The 'sprouts of capitalism' remain as hard to
dissect in early modern Europe as they are in Ming China, even if their
ultimate flowering in the former and ultimate 'failure' in the latter part
of the world is impossible to ignore.

A comparative look at the situation in China and Europe in the
century or so from 1550 to 1650 reveals a strikingly similar picture,
with an increasing lack of regard paid by consumers to the state's
attempts to intervene in their behaviour. However, in China as elsewhere the formal legal structures of the sumptuary laws remained in
place, even if widely flouted. What did vary was the actual types of
commodity consumption with which such legislation was concerned.
Not all sumptuary legislation was concerned with material culture,
and one of the key lines of social stratification, at least in early
Chinese culture, was determined by the length and elaborateness of
mourning rites allowed to individuals. The elaborateness of graves
and funerals remained one of the major focuses of control into the
later imperial period, as well.

The bones of those parts of the Ming laws which are concerned with
things are, however, contained in the 'Monograph on Carriages and
Dress' contained in the official *Ming History* which, although not
published until the early eighteenth century under the Qing dynasty,
is based on contemporary source material, principally the Ming legal
code as embodied in the *Da Ming hui dian*,*Statutes of the Great Ming*,
particularly the revised edition of 1587. These *Statutes* are illustrated,
at least in those sections which pertain to the ceremonial dress of the
emperor and his court.[11] The 'Monograph' has four chapters and is
concerned with imperial ceremonial, as well as with the sumptuary
laws. Thus chapter 1 deals with carriages, sedan chairs, parasols
and horse trappings, chapter 2 with garments for the emperor,
empresses and princes of the blood, chapter 3 with official garments
and chapter 4 with seals, tallies, palace buildings, other types of

building and, lastly, utensils (*qiyong*).

The complete *Ming History* text of this last entry, which is identical to the wording given in the 1587 *Statutes*, is as follows:

Prohibitions on the Use of Utensils: In the twenty-sixth year of the Hongwu reign (1393) it was decreed that Dukes, Marquises and officials of the First and Second Ranks might have wine pots and wine cups of gold, and for the rest use silver. Officials of the Third to Fifth Ranks might have pots of silver and wine cups of gold, while those of the Sixth to Ninth Ranks might have pots and cups of silver, for the rest making use of porcelain or lacquer. Items of woodwork should not make use of cinnabar, gilt or painted gold decoration, or of carvings of dragons or phoenixes. The common people should have pewter wine pots, wine cups of silver, and for the rest use porcelain or lacquerware. Couches, screens and window lattices of variously coloured and decorated lacquer belonging to officials should not be carved with dragon designs or be of vermilion lacquer decorated with gold. Military officials and officers should have bows and arrows of black lacquer, while bow cases and quivers must not employ vermilion lacquer or painted gold decoration. In the fourth year of the Jianwen reign (1402) a reprimand was issued to officials and populace, forbidding the unlawful use of gold goblets (*jue*, actually an archaic bronze shape) for wine and the use of gold-decorated vermilion lacquer on woodwork. In the sixteenth year of the Zhengde reign (1521) it was decreed that officials of the First and Second Rank might not use vessels of jade, but only of gold. Merchants and practitioners of craft skills might not use vessels of silver and were in all respects to be as the common people.[12]

Although these prohibitions remained in force throughout the dynasty, it is worth nothing that there seem to have been no new types of object brought within the scope of the regulations after 1521.

This kind of ranking ultimately goes back to systematizing ritual texts such as the *Rites of Zhou* or the *Record of Rites* which, though purporting to describe the ideal institutions of the Western Zhou dynasty around 1000 BC, were actually edited or even composed in the first centuries of the unified bureaucratic Han empire after 206 BC. These early texts, which as one of the 'Thirteen Classics' and 'Five Classics' respectively enjoyed an unchallengeable canonical status in the Ming, go into even greater detail about the paraphernalia surrounding the ruler and his courtiers:

For his memorandum-tablet, the Son of Heaven used a piece of sonorous jade; the prince of state a piece of ivory; a great officer a piece of bamboo, ornamented with fishbone; ordinary officers might use bamboo, adorned with ivory at the bottom.[13]

What these texts of High Antiquity share with all subsequent sumptuary legislation, and indeed the vital feature that they share with all such regulating ordinances, whether in the ancient Mediterranean, early modern Europe or elsewhere, is that they begin with categories of person which are assumed to be immutable and then assign to those categories specific types of object. Thus, they operate in an exactly opposite manner to a manual of taste like the *Treatise on Superfluous Things*, which is just as much concerned with social control. The *Treatise* and its related texts begin invariably with types of thing, specifically described, and then relate to them essentially social categories like 'vulgar' or 'elegant'. Here can be seen rather neatly the transition from a human-centred view of the world of goods to one in which the goods, actors in a market-place which state action cannot control, enjoy albeit limited and ambiguous form of autonomy.

If Ming sumptuary legislation was structurally very similar to mechanisms operating in Europe at about the same time, there were also few visible differences in the actual types of object consumption with which the two cultures concerned themselves. The eagerness of the state to exercise control in China can be seen as decreasing along a spectrum of goods from clothes, through buildings, vessels for wine, and then at the bottom other types of artefact. The prohibitions on clothes are expressed more in the matter of which fabrics might be permitted to which ranks of society, rather than in the matter of cut. In Europe, too, clothes were the dominant focus of concern, and throughout the late fifteenth and early sixteenth centuries this had been constant across the whole of Christendom. Guazzo remarked that the lower orders should be made 'to wear such apparel as may be at least different from gentlemen; if they will needs have it as costly'.[14]

Clothes remained the worrying area uppermost in the minds of sumptuary legislators in the Catholic countries of the early modern period, as the very extensive dress regulations from the states of seventeenth-century Italy make plain. Five such laws were passed in Rome, eleven in Milan, twenty-one in Florence and over eighty in Venice, where in another parallel with China types of conveyance such as gondolas and carriages were also subject to restrictions.[15] The *Junta de Reformacion*, on which the Count-Duke of Olivares (coincidentally an exact contemporary as to the years of his birth and death of Wen Zhenheng) pinned his hopes for a regeneration of Spain's national power and prestige, placed a great deal of emphasis on the regulation of dress, and indeed, its only lasting success seems to have been the exclusion of the ruff from the fashionable dress of the Spanish court and aristocracy, and its replacement by a plain starched collar.[16]

However, the publication of the *Junta*'s Articles of Reformation in 1623, not long after the *Treatise on Superfluous Things* appeared at the other end of the globe, is perhaps indicative of a growing gulf between the 'modern' Protestant states of northern Europe and those of the Catholic south and east. The sumptuary dress laws of England, first promulgated in the middle of the fourteenth century, were actually repealed on the accession of James 1 in 1604, and attempts over the next two decades to revive them had more to do with trade protection than with social control.[17] In the Netherlands, whose consumption behaviour has been so exhaustively documented and comprehensively analyzed by Simon Schama, sumptuary laws on the consumption of artefacts were never even promulgated, let alone enforced. Despite the attempts of Calvinist divines to have such godly regulation of behaviour made part of the law of the land at the Synod of Dordrecht in 1618, they failed to have enforced measures which were so manifestly at variance with the source of the republic's commercial strength and, hence, the prop of its very existence. When national disaster threatened in 1655 and penitential resort was had to a moderation of consumption, it was the size and length of feasts which were the targets of restriction.[18]

There is then a paradox here. China's sumptuary laws in the late Ming period were unprecedentedly complex, reaching into areas of consumption with a degree of detail which was not paralleled in Europe. The prohibitions on tableware, for example, were more rarely applied in European states, two of the best documented examples being the Bohemia of the Emperor Rudolf 11 in the decade after 1600[19] and the Spain of Olivares' *Junta* in the early 1620s. These cases were both innovations, moving beyond the traditional concentration of European sumptuary laws on dress. But at the same time the Ming regulations were something which had lain on the statute books for some hundreds of years since the founding of the dynasty. The great majority of the regulations in the 1587 *Statutes* date from the reign of the founding emperor in the late fourteenth century, the only vaguely 'contemporary' reference being a regulation of 1574 forbidding the 'hat of loyalty and calm' (*zhong jing guan*) to those who were not officials.[20] There was no attempt made to alter the regulations to take account of new types of product or of the shift in terminology applied to silk textiles in the two centuries since the regulations were first promulgated. The Yan Song inventory of 1562 clearly ranks the material in a rough order of value and ranks the textile section also in order of value (this can be confirmed by looking at those textiles which were converted into sums of cash). Yet the sumptuary laws persist in 'forbidding' to the 'common people' some textiles of relatively low value, while allowing others which were ranked more highly by the compilers of the inventory. There is no mention at all in the law code of *gaiji* (literally, 'altered loom'), a sumptuous brocaded type of fabric which was only developed in Fujian province in the early part of the sixteenth century and which was one of the most expensive types in Yan Song's luxurious and extensive wardrobe.

The Ming sumptuary laws received no updating or reinforcement at a period not only when they were being most openly and consistently ignored but when some major European powers were still turning to them as a fit object of the statesman's concerns and a major weapon of economic and social policy. In very crude terms, the Chinese willingness, even if it was only a result of inertia, to let the sumptuary legislation wither through neglect thus aligns this 'feudal' (in Chinese Marxist terms) state more closely with the bourgeois, capitalist Netherlands than it does with a great land empire like that of the Spanish Habsburgs and makes Chinese consumption behaviour of the late Ming period seem rather more 'modern' than we might otherwise expect.

The seeming lack of interest on the part of the government in updating the sumptuary laws may well have been simply a recognition that they were no longer enforceable in the face of universal disregard for the sanctions they contained.[21] This disregard could go right to the very top, as when the emperors themselves by the gifts they gave to favoured individuals wreaked havoc with what was supposed to be a precisely designed system of the manifestation of official status through dress. In Ming theory, garments decorated with the *long*, the five-clawed, horned dragon, were reserved for the very highest members of the imperial clan itself. Officials were supposedly dressed in robes decorated with another mythical reptilian beast, the *mang*. Shen Defu records that *mang*-decorated robes presented by the court were highly prized and that in his time there were innumerable examples of them in commodity circulation in the Huating and Jiangling regions of the lower Yangtze. He recounts how in 1447 an edict had noted the illegal manufacture of garments with designs of *long*, *mang* and two other mythical animals supposedly reserved for the dress of high officials and had prescribed the death penalty for makers of such things. In 1488 an erudite official had pointed out that, by the earliest and soundest philological sources, a *mang* ought to be a creature without legs and complained that 'the *mang* of today are all made with the form of a dragon (*long*)'. The use of legged dragons was then prohibited, but as Shen concludes, it is the emperors themselves who have continued to contradict their own edicts by bestowing these theoretically illegal garments on their favourites.[22]

The extent to which economic and political power could override the sternest prohibitions on the unauthorized possession of official dress assigned to specific bureaucratic rankings are strikingly shown by the garments in the Yan Song inventory.[23] For Yan possessed large numbers of robes decorated in ways which did not accord with his bureaucratic rank. His ownership of a small number even decorated with 'imperial' dragons formed a substantial element in the charges of lèse-majesté and corruption which brought about his fall from power, but he also owned very large numbers of robes with designs appropriate to grades lower than his own. These may well, as presents from him to his vast network of clients at all levels of officialdom, have formed the material sinews of his *guanxi*, his 'connections', on which the political power of any successful player of the Ming political game depended. That he should have had no difficulty acquiring such theoretically restricted goods ('enclaved' is the term used by Appadurai) is a testimony to his unprecedented dominance of the bureaucratic apparatus, but there is no reason to believe that the same thing was not happening on a smaller scale right throughout the empire, as regulation crumbled in the face of an ever-expanding market-place.

From the middle of the sixteenth century in China, the level of complaint about luxury, waste and excess, the railing against contemporary falling-away from an imagined Spartan past which seems to have been a constant in any number of pre-modern societies, rose and rose to become a flood. Zhang Han's claim in 1593 that 'the customs of the present age have reached an extreme of extravagance . . .' was widely endorsed. Elsewhere, he gives specific details on the decline of respect for the dress regulations:

The dynasty has definite regulations for the dress and ornaments of women of official families. In the Hongwu reign (1368–1402) the regulations were both strict and clear, and people obeyed a uniform law. As times changed and customs became more lavish, people all set their resolve on venerating riches and excess and, as if they no longer knew there were clear prohibitions, rather set about trampling on them. For example, 'kingfisher-bead' [probably green jade] headdresses and clothes and ornaments with decoration of dragons or phoenixes were originally allowed only to empresses and princely consorts. The formal headdresses of wives of officials were allowed golden ornaments if of the Fourth Rank or above, and silver-gilt if of the Fifth Rank or below. For their large-sleeved robes, those of the Fifth Rank or above were allowed *ning si* silks, self-patterned twill and openwork silks, those of the Sixth Rank and below used self-patterned twills, openwork silks, satins and spun silk cloth, and all had their ordained limits. Nowadays men dress in brocaded and embroidered silks, and women ornament themselves with gold and pearls, in a case of boundless extravagance which flouts the regulations of the state.[24]

Tian Yiheng, in a *biji* collection with prefaces dated 1573, provides a shocked and appalled catalogue of flagrant disregard for the regulations pertaining to the decoration of private dwellings and to the dress of wealthy private women, who were now wearing both the dark colours (he specifies deep blue, green and scarlet) and the heavily brocaded and embroidered fabrics which were theoretically forbidden to them: 'Nowadays the very servant girls dress in *qi* and *luo*, and the singsong girls look down on brocaded silks and embroidered gowns.' In 1570 an attempt was made to restrict or forbid the consumption of a luxury fabric called 'Song-dynasty brocade', not a specific technical description but the market term for a brocaded silk sumptuously decorated with bold patterning of interlocking circles, often involving gold thread. The weavers simply renamed the same stuff 'Han-dynasty brocade' and went on making it.[25]

This kind of behaviour was felt to be dangerous to a very high degree. Frederick Wakeman has noted:

The association of gaudy clothing with political and social decadence has venerable antecedents in China. Xunzi (*c*. 300–237 BC) wrote: 'The signs of a disorderly age are that [men's] clothes are gaily coloured, men are made up to look like women, customs are lewd, minds are set on profit, conduct is filthy, music is deviant, and ornamentation is vile and variegated.'[26]

These, and in particular the fear of the blurring of the social division between men and women through 'deviant' types of consumption which we have already remarked on in the *Treatise on Superfluous Things*, were to become stereotypical views, and they can be paralleled from other cultures. In 1615 the Spanish Franciscan Juan de Santamaria was reaching back into his classical tradition to quote the Roman writer Sallust:

when a kingdom reaches such a point of moral corruption that men dress like women . . . that the most exquisite delicacies are imported for its tables, and men go to sleep before they are tired . . . then it can be regarded as lost, and its empire at an end.[27]

Commentator after commentator in the late Ming would have been prepared to echo these sentiments of a contemporary from an otherwise alien culture. Their complaints were often conventionalized to a tedious degree and addressed not only the traditional areas of concern such as dress (which with its propensity to camouflage the 'real' social status of its wearer is the type of consumption most likely to subvert a rigid social stratification) but also newer sources of anxiety about unrestrained hedonism. Tian Yiheng frets about the growth in gambling in the cities of Hangzhou, Suzhou and Changzhou and in spending on sexual pleasure, particularly with the handsome boy prostitutes favoured by high officials in the capital, Peking.[28] The 'growing extravagance of upper-class life' after about 1550 is charted also in longer and more lavish meals enjoyed by the wealthy and in the creation of a culture of expensive restaurants in the big cities.[29]

In particular, the aping by the lower orders of specific types of cultural consumption, access to which had been previously restricted by cultural as much as by economic barriers, upset contemporary elite commentators. The seventeenth-century gazetteer of Tongcheng county, Anhui province, a relatively less-developed, predominantly agricultural region, which has been studied in detail by Hilary Beattie, reports: 'by the Chongzhen period (1628–44), extravagance became excessive and distinctions were confused.'[30] The one was a clear consequence of the other. We have seen how texts like the householder's manuals acted to dissolve some of these cultural barriers, by providing information on types of commodities and services which would confer the appearance of a background of education.

The Chinese historian Wang Shixiang has brought to light a particularly interesting passage from the works of the Songjiang writer Fan Chao (born 1540) which documents the extension of this politer life-style through the use of one particular type of commodity, fashionable furniture from Suzhou in rare imported hardwoods. Fan writes:

When I was young I saw not a single piece of hardwood furniture, like writing tables or 'meditation chairs'. The people only had square tables of gingko wood or gilded lacquer. Then Mo Shilong (fl. 1552–1587; DMB, 1073) and the young gentlemen of the Gu and

Song families bought a few pieces of hardwood from Suzhou. In the Longqing (1567–72) and Wanli(1573–1620) reigns even servile functionaries and official's runners used hardwood pieces, and cabinetmakers from Huizhou strove to open shops in the town, making furniture and other things for weddings. The powerful and extravagant did not think southern elm wood to be sufficiently valuable, so for their beds, cupboards and tables they would use only *huali* wood, burl wood, ebony, *xiangsi* wood or boxwood. This furniture was extremely expensive and fine, costing tens of thousands of cash, an extravagant custom. The particularly strange thing is that even officials' lictors and runners who had a house would set up a small place for relaxation, with wooden panelling, goldfish and various pots of flowers in the courtyard, with a hardwood table and a flywhisk, and call it a 'study' (*shufang*). I have no idea what books officials' lictors and runners studied.[31]

The study, the highly ritualized site of all the cultural practices held most dear by the elite, was now just an optional extra in the homes of the most despised type of sub-bureaucratic functionary.

Some of the high spots of irony in the novel *The Golden Lotus* are reached in the description of the study of the central character Ximen Qing in chapter 34, with literally a full house of the trappings of high culture; the landscapes by famous hands hung on all four walls (there is an extra layer of irony here, as we know from Wen Zhenheng that hanging pictures opposite one another in this way was an extremely vulgar solecism), the antique bronze incense burners, the black lacquered *gu qin* zither, and the shelves piled high with literary works and the tools of literary creation. These last could presumably have been bought by the yard, for we know from numerous incidents in the book that Ximen Qing is effectively illiterate, relying on his son-in-law to do all his writing for him, and is never seen to pick up any sort of reading matter at all. Yet, he is still a participant in the same set of aesthetic values as the most deeply cultured, creative and innovative writer or poet, his synthetic study praised by his sycophants for its 'striking simplicity, a lesson in elegance'.

Ximen Qing's consumption, of food and drink, of commercialized entertainment and sexual services, of fine clothes and expensive furnishings, as well as of the trappings of the scholar ideal, are certainly a conspicuous part of the texture of *the Golden Lotus*. But in general, how conspicuous was consumption in the Ming empire? What attitudes were expressed towards wealth and the manifestation of wealth through material culture? Firstly, there was a strand of attachment to the idea of moderation as a desirable value in itself, a sort of

Chinese echo of the ancient Greek saw, 'Nothing in excess'. The view that too much of a good thing was bad for you is expressed by Wang Daokun, encountered in chapter 1 as the eulogist of the father of Gao Lian, who, as his own writings on the role of moderation in the maintenance of a healthy body show, would certainly have concurred:

> Dwelling in the mountains is a splendid thing, but if you become slightly over-attached to it, then it is like the market-place or the court. The connoisseurship of calligraphy or painting is an elegant thing, but let it ever so slightly become a craving, and it becomes like trade or commerce. Poetry and wine are a joyous thing, but if you become even slightly greedy for them, then they are hell. Hospitality is an untrammelled thing, but as soon as a vulgarian disturbs it, then it is a Sea of Bitterness.[32]

These sentiments are, once again, largely conventional, but there is other evidence of a more practical reason for avoiding very conspicuous display of wealth. The householder's manual puts it like this: 'Your dwelling should not be extravagant and gay, splendid and ostentatious, which will cause endless envy and covetousness and be the source of catastrophe. Let it be elegant (*ya*) and plain, pure and decorous.'[33] Not only would the flaunting of prosperity through goods bring about disruption in the social fabric and bring under strain the values of harmony, reciprocal obligation, acceptance of hierarchy and consensus which underpinned the Confucian world order; it would also bring very real danger to its perpetrators, who at the very highest levels of society might instigate imperial envy, summary and brutal confiscation, and the destruction of the family's economic and social position literally overnight. James I might have grumbled that the huge palace of Audley End was 'too large for a subject', but the relative distribution of power between the king and the great aristocrats of Jacobean England was very different from that between the Wanli emperor and his ministers, who held their goods and lives more or less at his pleasure.

The perils of over-ostentation were, therefore, both immediate and drastic. The entire thirty-fifth chapter of Tian Yiheng's *biji* collection is entirely taken up with what might be called 'biographies of the conspicuously rich and corrupt (he almost takes the two as synonymous) who came to bad ends.'[34] He begins with a semi-mythical late-Yuan character called Shen Wansan, a proverbial plutocrat of whom he observes, 'Nowadays, when people talk about a rich man, they always call him a Shen Wansan.' He then goes through a list of the notorious eunuch dictator Liu Jin (d. 1515; DMB, 941–5), the favourite and general Qian Ning (d. 1521; DMB, 1152), their co-conspirator in the riots of the unbalanced Zhengde emperor, the military officer Jiang Shan (d. 1521), and none other than the disgraced Grand Secretary Yan Song himself, whose years of power had coincided with the author's maturity. In each of these cases Tian gives a lengthy (for Yan Song it is extremely lengthy) listing of their property on its confiscation by the state, and there is inescapably present in his appalled and fascinated recounting of Yan Song's '3,185 items of pure gold vessels weighing 11,033.31 ounces, among which there were five golden wine pots decorated with five-clawed dragons, two round cups with lobed handles decorated with five-clawed dragons and three dishes decorated with five-clawed dragons . . .'[35] something of the shocked prurience with which the modern world received news of the hoarded wealth of Ferdinand and Imelda Marcos. Tian Yiheng is both appalled and interested at the same time. It is perhaps worth noting too that, in a text at least notionally intended for publication, he shares with the sumptuary laws and, indeed, with the writings of Wen Zhenheng and others what I am attempting to identify as a Chinese concern with precision of description of the physical attributes of things. He is not content to quote global figures for the ill-gotten gains of these fallen favourites; he must list the particulars.

However, if great wealth and corruption were widely suspected of being inalienably bound together, something which could only act as a brake on even the most 'rational' kinds of conspicuous consumption, then the corollary social failing of excessive meanness certainly existed, too. We have already seen He Liangjun remark on the excessively and sanctimoniously austere aspect given to a dinner table by the use of porcelain vessels alone, when items of precious metal were more appropriate to the owner's wealth.[36] When the 'eccentric model official' Hai Rui (1513–1587; DMB, 474–9), a man who ostentatiously lived (in poverty) on his official salary, took over as governor of Suzhou in 1569, he overstepped the mark with a personal sumptuary law banning luxury manufactures, limiting the amount to be spent on entertaining him, and insisting on official stationery having smaller margins. By taking the rhetoric of 'frugality' literally, he threatened the entire social stability of the region, and he was forced out of office after eight months.[37] And there is no sense in the writings of contemporary European observers of late Ming society that the propensity of the wealthy and powerful to display their status through a visible show of luxury goods operated very differently from the situation with which they were familiar in their native Spain, Portugal or Italy. The lavish entrance portals of the mansions of members of the official class are remarked on by all these Western commentators.

At the same, early modern Italy and Ming China were very different societies, and even if some of their consumption patterns can be paralleled, the objects of conspicuous consumption could be very different. The lavish spending on architecture, including the architecture of 'public' spaces such as churches chronicled by Peter Burke[38] has no exact parallel in China, although it is certainly the case that lavish gardens open to the respectable public operated as obvious markers of wealth, particularly in the case of the aristocratically owned gardens of Peking. The large gardens in which the wealthy increasingly indulged at this period were certainly a form of conspicuous consumption, especially in the densely populated lower Yangtze delta where land hunger was at its most pressing, but this consumption of expensive space was conspicuous in its full effect only to those other members of the same class who might be invited behind the walls. The commoner outside was conscious only of walls, of a denial of access, and of the privatization of space, in an experience which was clearly different from that of the Italian citizens forced daily to walk past the facades of palazzi or churches boldly displaying the arms and names of the great families who ruled over them. But, in the main, architecture, which was 'the principal means by which Italians staked out their claim to grandeur and magnificence . . . the one art form the upper classes were interested in reading about',[39] was not a focus of 'artistic' competition in China, and mansions differed from one another in size rather than in basic design or fashionability of appearance.

If Ming China lacked many of contemporary Europe's sites of public conspicuous consumption through architectural display, it was also relatively impoverished at the highest levels of society in sites of what David Cannadine has called 'consensual pageantry', public rituals which affirm and cement the social order.[40] Ming emperors were never, or hardly ever, seen in public, and they made few progresses. Religious display was not something in which the official classes participated, although there certainly were lavish and spectacular festivals which were occasions for the deployment of wealth. Tanaka Issei has described the growth in the period under consideration of regional dramatic forms, in which plays chosen to please the gods were performed either at village level, or under the patronage of groups of merchants, or even under the patronage of the powerful lineage organizations which were then consolidating themselves across the southern half of the empire.[41] He sees the late Ming as an era of the concentration of power, which brought with it the appropriation by the elite of an older popular culture and its transformation at their hands into a more acceptable, socially regulatory form. Clan spending on these events could not have been more conspicuous, but it was focused on the exaltation of the position of the group, rather than the individual. It ratified a structure of dominance which was actually created and sustained by other means. The elite also participated, to an extent, in popular cultural forms such as the display of decorated lanterns at the Lantern Festival the late Ming. Zhang Dai writes of his native Shaoxing that:

> From mansions down to the humblest alleyway, no family is without lanterns, or does not display them . . . Great and humble families sit mingled at their doors, eating melon seeds and candied beans, watching the daughters of official families coming and going.[42]

Once again, however, this is less a case of conspicuous consumption than conspicuous participation in forms of cultural practice which acted to blur, rather than make clearer, lines of class division. On the whole, it seems likely that social distinction expressed through things was as its sharpest among the different sections of the elite, where the need to emphasize distance from that which threatened to be most close was particularly acute.

We come, therefore, to the very difficult question: how was the Ming elite stratified, and what degree of mobility existed between its different segments? This question has been the subject of a considerable amount of research in China, Japan and the West, much of it revolving round the 'feudal' nature of traditional class relations (in the case of Chinese or Japanese Marxist scholars), or else around the relationship between formal markers of status, like access to potential political power expressed through the examination system, and social dominance at a more grassroots level, in the growth of the typical late-imperial Chinese 'gentry society'. Recent Western syntheses have tended to stress a growth in social stratification and in social conflict attendant on the commercialization of agriculture, the creation in Frederick Wakeman's words of a 'complex and restless social landscape'.[43] They all see the growth in absentee landlordism as a significant feature in the increase of social distance between the top and bottom of society, with the rich being more and more based in the walled cities or their immediate suburbs, which offered them more stimulating arenas for social interaction with their peers, better access to luxury manufactures and protection from any potential social violence directed at them by a peasantry for whom the old forms of patriarchal authority had less and less meaning. Wealth was becoming increasingly concentrated. In the more prosperous provinces of the

Pacific littoral, it was concentrated in the hands of families who in general could buttress their economic position through examination success and political power. These were the *shen shi*, unsatisfactorily rendered in English as the 'gentry', and better seen as a status group than a class, in Dennis Twitchett's formulation.[44]

In the northern and inland provinces a very significant factor was the concentration of fertile land in the hands of the hereditary imperial aristocracy. This is an interest group which has been little studied in recent years in the West, though Chinese historians have frequently produced their extreme rapacity as convincing evidence of 'feudal' decadence.[45] Their deliberate exclusion from any form of political influence has rendered them of less interest to Western historians preoccupied with the more distinctively Chinese meritocratic and bureaucratic official strata of society. It should be born in mind, however that to visitors to Ming China from early modern Europe these enforcedly idle aristocrats, whose claim to prominence through birthright would have seemed so natural, bulked large on the social scene. Gaspar da Cruz wrote one chapter, 'Which treats of the nobility of the houses of the kinsmen of the blood royal, and likewise of the magistrates who are in the principal cities',[46] his relative ordering of the two groups unconsciously expressing the order of precedence in his native Portugal. The hereditary aristocracy of collateral imperial relatives, descendants of the military adherents of the dynasty's founder, and the families to which they were related by marriage may have been despised by the political elite and scrupulously insulated from political influence, but they were a very prominent part of the Ming social landscape, the masters in an economic sense of millions of peasants and consumers on a lavish scale. in 1614 the Prince of Fu spent 280,000 ounces of silver on the building of a new mansion for himself in the city of Luoyang, capital of the increasingly impoverished inland province of Henan.[47] Hardly surprisingly, these princes were the target of the greatest degree of violence in the peasant uprisings which, beginning in provinces like Henan, were to topple the dynasty in 1644.

The increasing prosperity in the late sixteenth and early seventeenth centuries of the south-eastern provinces, and above all of the lower Yangtze valley, meant not only that those who were already rich become very much richer but that those who had previously enjoyed what was a modest sufficiency of essentials now began to find themselves with spare resources. Productive outlets for these resources were extremely limited. The concentration of landholding in fewer and fewer hands meant that this safest form of investment was not really open. The very primitive mechanisms of credit and of commercial investment, which in China lagged far behind those to be encountered in the Europe even of the fifteenth century, meant that investment in trade or production was similarly stultified. In a powerful critique of the whole 'sprouts of capitalism' argument, Ray Huang has argued that the immense size of the Chinese empire and its huge population (estimated at around 150 million in 1600) gave the lower Yangtze Valley the appearance of a developed economy without the substance. The priorities of the central government were economic stability, not economic growth, and any imbalance between the wealth of different areas was seen as dangerous.

Huang stresses the small-scale nature of most merchant enterprises at this time, the majority having capital in the region of only 200–300 ounces of silver. A successful merchant was by definition one who had ceased to trade, in favour of landholding or the investment of wealth in pawnbroking, a reliable but economically deadening source of income. He quotes the economic historian Peng Xinwei to the effect that there were 20,000 pawnshops in the empire in the sixteenth century, as opposed to 7,000 in the nineteenth, though these figures cannot be other than very speculative.[48] In the light of Huang's telling arguments, it seems reasonable to posit that increased wealth, and the distribution of increased wealth to a broader section at the top of society, was in fact channelled into increased consumption and new forms of consumption, of material culture, just as contemporaries described. With regard to England at this time, Lawrence Stone has stated:

> No one denies that at all times and in all countries, merchants have put some of their wealth into the purchase of land, since it was a secure, if not particularly rewarding, investment. But the issue here is how far they aspired to the trappings of gentility that went with establishment in a rural seat.[49]

The position being advanced here is that, in the richest parts of China, where landowners themselves often no longer lived on their estates but rather in the towns, the 'trappings of gentility' had become more or less entirely divorced from ownership of land. Luxury goods, and in particular those prestige-bestowing goods like antiques and paintings, were all entirely within the late Ming commodity sphere, and so the 'trappings of gentility' were potentially available to all who could afford them. Not only were they available, they were acutely competed for in a situation where demand was rising much faster than supply.

Sandi Chin and Cheng-chi Hsü, in their study of Anhui merchant culture and patronage, quote the words of one late Ming – early Qing writer which capture the gusto with which the merchants of Huizhou entered into a new world of goods:

> I remember the past splendours of the collections in our Huizhou area – there was no place that could compare with Xiuning and Shexian. Moreover, the difference between refinement and vulgarity [of a person] was thought to depend on whether or not he owns antiquities. Accordingly, people fought to acquire things, without concern for price. The antique dealers all rushed to the area. Those who were doing business outside the area collected antiques eagerly and brought them more. Thus, extensive collections came into being. This fashion started with the official Si-ma Wang and his brothers; then a certain Wu family in Xin'an and a Wang family in the Conglu Ward all followed . . .[50]

The 'Si-ma Wang' referred to here is none other than Wang Daokun (1525–1593), already encountered in this book as the author of the funeral inscription for Gao Lian's father and as a man who, in fact, lived by the sale of the cultural skills of the elite, turning his prestige as holder of the highest examination degree into a lucrative practice as a hired writer.

The transfer of forms of cultural valuation is here personalized in the extreme, but this idea that social emulation is at work in the extension of forms of consumption from the bureaucratic elite to the merely rich is seen elsewhere in Ming writing. In this vein, there is the ascription of the taste for hardwood furniture in the fashionable interior to the painter and aesthete Mo Shilong, and I have already quoted the claim of Wang Shizhen that fashions in collecting began in Suzhou, the heartland of the cultural elite, and spread to Anhui, more famous for merchants than for scholars. Shen Defu talks of how the fashion for including pieces of the early Ming period in the category of 'antiques', 'began with one or two men of elegance, got its first strength among the fashion-conscious gentry of Jiangnan, and spread to the easily persuadable great merchants of Anhui'.[51] In a passage entitled 'Things that have the names of people', Shen lists items of dress in use among the elite and concludes, 'Thus there can be no doubt at all that famous scholars set the fashions in dress.'[52]

The appearance of the concept of 'fashion' brings us back to the central Ming anxiety about objects and to a potential palliative for that anxiety. 'Elegance' can smooth away at least some of the social anxieties engendered by excess, by re-establishing the necessary distance from those whose houses may be crammed with 'paintings by famous hands', yet who hang them in a crass and vulgar manner. The writer of the preface to *Treatise on Superfluous Things*, Shen Chunze, puts into his own and the author's mouths a piece of dialogue which, while it overtly seems to suggest that trivial things are not the correct concern of the scion of such a distinguished family, actually reinforces the idea that 'taste' is not only the natural inheritance of the product of such a distinguished lineage, but something over which, in a sort of *noblesse oblige*, they are compelled to set and maintain standards:

> I said to Wen Zhenheng, 'Your late great-grandfather, the Grand Scribe Wen Zhengming was the very nonpareil in the Suzhou region of sincere antique virtue and lofty rectitude and lived to be nearly a hundred years old. The family's transmitted renown has been both fragrant and widespread. Its "paintings in poems" and "poems in paintings" have been the very high point among the ingenious minds and marvellous hands of Suzhou, who are all members of your lineage. When in days past I visited you and dallied with you for some days in your Hall of Grace and Beauty, your Studio of the Jade Bureau, both more beautiful than painting can convey, this compilation was always among your personal belongings. Is this not troubling yourself needlessly, just wielding your brush to waste your paper?' He said, 'No, it is not. My only fear is that as the minds and hands of the men of Suzhou change day by day, just as you say, so the very foundation of these small idle affairs and superfluous things may be unknown in days to come. I hope to prevent it with my writings.' This is indeed the case. The words, 'cutting away excess and doing away with extravagance' would of themselves be a sufficient preface for this book.[53]

And yet, there remains the problem of the self-subverting, almost auto-destructive nature of a text like the *Treatise on Superfluous Things*. It is, one most repeat, a guide to how to consume commodities appropriately, which is itself a commodity. Cannot anyone, therefore, vulgar or not, simply purchase a copy and avoid such solecisms as hanging paintings opposite one another? The only way out of this seeming dilemma is to accept a degree of difference between authorial intention and possible reception and to remember that, once a society has been fully penetrated by commodity exchange and a mechanism of fashion and emulation set up, it is a constant and self-sustaining system, in which those who are constantly encouraged to catch up with the makers of taste can never do so, as the desirable acts of consumption are constantly shifted. The *Treatise* is, thus, in a sense a freeze-frame from a film of a relentlessly fluid game of emulation, a type of attempt to impose order on chaos which is typical of the very early stages of establishment of a fashion mechanism. It acts less as a guide to late-Ming reality than as a pointer to the forms of social interaction in which Ming objects must be inserted if we are to comprehend them in their social aspects.

Conclusion

The things with which Gao Lian dealt in his *Eight Discourses*, and which Wen Zhenheng discussed in his *Treatise*, have continued to seem superfluous to historians of Ming society both outside and inside China. They are the province of the connoisseur and the art historian, peripheral rather than central to any attempt to understand the changes which it is generally accepted took place in Chinese society in the sixteenth and seventeenth centuries. Neither text, for example, finds a place in Wolfgang Franke's exhaustive work on the sources of Ming history,[1] even though he does give space to a number of works which cast light on the history of technology or of everyday life, both equally parts of Braudel's 'material life'. These include as a prime example Song Yingxing's *Tian gong kai wu, Heaven's Craft in the Creation of Things*, of 1637 which discusses, and illustrates by woodblock printing, many of the processes involved in the production of the material culture of Ming China; the ceramic industry, jade working, metallurgy and textiles are recorded, as well as the technology of wells, salt pans and mines.[2] Also listed by Franke is the *Nong zheng quan shu, Complete Book of the Regulation of Agriculture*, a manual of agricultural improvement compiled during the years 1625 to 1628 by Xu Guangqi (1562-1633; ECCP, 316-19), the most distinguished of the Christian converts made by the first, optimistic wave of Jesuit missionaries to the Chinese empire. This notable man's technological interests, as well as his engagement with the Christian missionaries, were shared by Wang Zheng (1571-1644; ECCP, 807-9), who attempted to improve the design of farm tools by his *Zhu qi tu shuo, Illustrated Explanations of the Various Implements*, of 1627 and to transmit to his contemporaries some of the mechanical devices of European culture in his *Yuan xi qi qi tu shuo*,

Illustrated Explanations of the Strange Implements of the Far West, of the same year. The respectful attention given to these works by Xu Guangqi and Wang Zheng in the present century is in strong contrast to the marginalization of the literature of luxury consumption.

Yet, while mindful of the many trenchant criticisms which cultural historians have directed over the years at the notion of a *Zeitgeist*, or indeed, any other underlying principle of cultural homogeneity, it can be argued that there *are* connections between this new-found interest in dams and looms and carts *as things* and the precision with which a writer like Wen Zhenheng treats beds and inkstones and hats. Song Yingxing, Xu Guangqi and Wang Zheng were members of the same elite status group as was Wen Zhenheng, with the same type of education and the same cultural resources at their disposal. Their work is in no sense the articulation of the views of a hitherto mute element of society; they were not engineers. All of them were operating in an intellectual climate in which one of the key issues raised to an overt status was that of the importance of concrete 'affairs' (*shi*) as opposed to abstract principles. Joanna F. Handlin has provided an important case study of how Lü Kun (1536–1618) used records, manuals and didactic literature of several kinds to forge a new style of Confucian moral leadership which was intended to be firmly anchored in the specific social conditions of the period.[3] The growth in the acceptability and use of objectified, fact-centred methods of cultivation among the elite can be seen as part of a larger picture which can encompass the technological treatise, the guidebook to interior decoration, the statistical compilation, the merchant route book, the householder's manual and the didactic work on norms of behaviour, under the very broad rubric of 'the commoditization of knowledge'. The clustering together of all these categories in time is very marked. The *Wanli kuai ji lu, Record of the Accounts of the Wanli Reign* of 1586 is, as far as we know, the first attempt to provide a concretely documented 'budget' of the empire's finances. The earliest extant route book was printed in 1570, and the first independent manual for merchants in 1626. The category of topographical and institutional gazetteers (i.e. guides to anything other than an administrative unit, like a temple, famous mountain or academy), which has been studied by Timothy Brook, flourished unprecedentedly after 1580.[4] Aggregating his figures on the production of these guides, which he sees as a product of the growth of gentry society and the involvement of the surplus degree holding elite in local institutions, we see that the years 1400 to 1579 produce 69 editions, while the half century from 1580 to 1639 saw as many as 152 editions. This is the same surge seen in almanacs, in reprints of antiquarian texts and in new works on taste, and it cannot be explained by anything internal to the publishing industry alone.

Texts like Wen's *Treatise*, whether described as guidebooks to elegant living, a literature of reassurance and the creation of social barriers or commodities which are themselves designed to open up a wider world of commodity enjoyment, have rarely been accorded anything other than a peripheral role in attempts to understand the society of Ming China. A part of this neglect must lie in the attitudes held by those most articulate members of the Chinese elite who survived the traumatic conquest of the empire by the Manchus, now better seen as a long and bloody process rather than the sudden and totally overwhelming *Blitzkrieg* of official Qing historiography. While some seem to have immersed themselves in a bittersweet nostalgia, writing loving recreations of the vanished world of upper-class prostitution in Nanjing, or like Zhang Dai writing examples of the *biji* form of literature which chronicle in detail the byways of elite life under the vanished Ming, others took a more rigorous, even puritanical, line.

The reasons for the dynasty's collapse were to be of obsessive interest to the alienated and disaffected intellectuals of the second half of the seventeenth century, excluded from political power but also to an extent culturally marginalized by the court's continuing suspicion of the lower Yangtze region as the heartland of tax evasion, Ming loyalism and general insubordination. Those who looked back into what were now known to be the closing decades of the Ming dynasty found much to reprehend in the actions of their peers and predecessors. Above all, there was the factional strife, which had prevented the whole-hearted implementation of any policy initiative, and the personalization of politics, which meant that any proposal was judged not on its own merits but in terms of the factional alignment of the official who brought it forward. There was also the sense that the late Ming, defined as the period from the accession of the Wanli emperor in 1573, was in some sense frivolous. This is seen most forcefully in the writings of Fang Yizhi (d. 1671?; ECCP, 232–3) and Gu Yanwu (1613–1682; ECCP, 421–6). Willard Peterson shows how in the early Qing the term 'man of culture' (*wen ren*) almost came to be used ironically, implying a class of self-absorbed, studiedly amateurish dilettanti who had, by putting theatricals or garden design on a par with government, brought about their own nemesis. Gu Yanwu might have been writing about Wen Zhenheng when he said in 1646:

> In the last twenty or thirty years, those in the local districts who were known as 'men of culture' (*wen ren*) without exception devoted

themselves to the attainment of empty reputation and unearned gain.[5]

It is their view of late Ming society, as a culturally exquisite bloom which was nevertheless in some sense rotten inside, which has prevailed. It was the view which became the state orthodoxy through the judgements made on Gao Lian, Zhang Yingwen and Wen Zhenheng by the editors of the catalogue of the imperial library in the mid-eighteenth century. Wen in particular is castigated for his attention to 'niceties and trivialities', the fripperies of late Ming social life among an elite now seen as essentially effete and unfit to govern. His work is worth preserving more for the noble nature of his lineage and for his own martyr's death (since by now the Manchu emperors lauded as paragons of loyalty those who had given their lives to oppose the conquest), rather than for its intrinsic value. This very effeteness and unfitness of the Ming elite, of which Wen Zhenheng was such an archetypal representative, in fact became an important plank of Qing state ideology; as in an extension of the venerable 'Mandate of Heaven' theory of state decline, it was argued that not just the Ming ruling house but the entire Han Chinese ruling class had lost the legitimate mandate through factionalism, internal dissension and an unseemly degree of attention to selfish aesthetic gratification at the expense of practical affairs.

This orthodox Qing view has continued to find echoes in the present century. The major catalogue of late Ming material from the Shanghai Museum produced by Chinese scholars in the United States is an attempt to rehabilitate the period by taking its aesthetic claims, even its aesthetic claims about 'minor' matters, seriously, but it seems to me that it does so only at the cost of entering into the world of late Ming aesthetics to a very great degree and, in fact, writing from within that tradition, accepting its basic premises as given.[6] It sees the aesthetic endeavours of the major figures around whom the discussion is structured as in some sense an escape from undesired social and political pressures, just as much of late Ming writing on aesthetics, especially painting, would claim that it was. And yet, challenged by Pierre Bourdieu's claim that 'art is one of the major sites of denial of the social', are we justified in viewing writing about these superfluous things as being merely a pleasant safety valve, as something taking place on the sidelines which has no claims on the attention of those historians who are after bigger game? I would argue we are not. Following the lead given by Appadurai, in his view that 'consumption is essentially social, relational and active, rather than private, atomic and passive', I would argue that the consumption patterns of the elite and their engagement with the luxury material culture of the day are not a byway of Ming history; they are one of the key areas of discourse which operated on its social fabric in a period of change.

At the very beginning of this century, Werner Sombart argued that in the case of early modern Europe, over a long time span from 1300 to 1800, the expansion of trade and manufacture was led by demand and, above all, not by demand for staples but by demand for luxury goods, the 'superfluous things' of early modern Europe so much desired by court and aristocratic societies, as well as by urban patrician elites.[7] More recently, Chandra Mukerji has given an even greater role to consumption by arguing that it was a distinctively materialist European culture, with patterns of desire attuned to the constant creation of new goods and products, which created the capitalist mode of production, rather than the other way round. She has written: 'The growth of materialism in early modern Europe is evidenced by Europeans' increasing preoccupation with objects . . .'[8] There is much for the student of China to ponder in Mukerji's work. I am clearly influenced by her idea that ideological attitudes to material culture can condition economic development, rather than (as orthodox Marxism would insist) the other way round. However, there is a danger in some of her views, which are in process of becoming an orthodox explanation for 'the Rise of the West', with 'modernity' and 'materialism' tending to appear as terms in a circular relationship of mutual explanation.[9]

It is piquant to recall that 'materialism' was a charge laid equally by the Jesuits in late Ming China at their host civilization (many of the upper classes being openly sceptical about the concept of the immortality of the soul) and by Chinese intellectuals at the Jesuits (who by their division of the universe into spirit and matter denied the all-pervasiveness of spiritual power, even in rocks and trees).[10] At a less philosophically exalted level, a close reading of the late Ming literature of material culture, such as has been attempted here, must cast doubt on the uniquely 'materialist' nature of civilization in the West. While Wen Zhenheng is specifying the materials, forms, decoration and precise dimensions of desirable goods, his European contemporaries (for example, his very close English contemporary Henry Peacham) seem by contrast obsessed with idealist generalizations and very unwilling to specify the actual types of luxury consumption around which they are constructing a discourse of gentility.

It was Quentin Bell who posited the existence of a system of fashion as a spin-off of class conflict, the necessary way in which elites could remain one step ahead of those seeking to replace them as brokers of cultural power.[11] Despite the fact that everything Bell has to say about China as a 'static' society without the concept of fashion is quite wrong and offered without any supporting evidence, it has become part of the general currency of consciousness about the distinctiveness of the West. Mukerji, for example, has again chosen to take this formulation as a uniquely European development and one, again, intimately connected with the rise of a distinctively 'materialist' society.[12] The evidence I have sought to present tends, in my view, to undermine the unique nature of early modern European consumption patterns, or even to show them as lagging behind equivalent developments in China. A number of other points of comparison have been raised above, which I would now wish to recapitulate. The creation of new types of luxury goods and their wide circulation, the idea of culture itself as a commodity, the degree of attention given to the specifics of luxury consumption over a broad range of writers, the decline of state sumptuary control, and the idea that there is positive benefit in such luxury consumption all point towards the conclusion that Europe may, judged solely on the basis of consumption, have been one of a number of complex pre-industrial societies, with the roots of its later distinctiveness having to be sought elsewhere. Peter Burke's comparison of the broad patterns of culture in the Netherlands and in Japan in the seventeenth century raises similarly intriguing possibilities.[13]

Perhaps one of the most striking recurrences of a broad cultural pattern in both Ming China and early modern Europe is what might be called 'the invention of taste'. For if the unequal distribution of cultural resources is necessary to the stratification of society, as Bourdieu has argued, and if those cultural resources are all full commodities, available to all who possess the relevant economic resources, what is to prevent the cultural and economic hierarchies collapsing into each other, till the rich *are* the cultured, and the cultured *are* the rich? Here, taste comes into play, as an essential legitimator of consumption and an ordering principle which prevents the otherwise inevitable-seeming triumph of market forces. In China, this happens contemporary with, or even prior to, its establishment in Europe. There can be little doubt that from the late seventeenth century in England the concept of taste was a crucial development in promoting an acceptance of the fact that a difference existed between mere possessors of luxury and connoisseurs, whose judgement was based on a set of morally grounded aesthetic principles. It was, then, not just possible, but absolutely necessary, for a gentleman also to be a connoisseur. As Richard Steele put it, 'The appellation of a gentleman is never to be affixed to a man's circumstances, but to his behaviour in them.'[14] It was arguments of this type which eventually took much of the heat out of the 'luxury debate' in England, but they were arguments which only really began to be put forward in the Augustan age, by writers like Jonathan Richardson (in his *Two Discourses* of 1719) and the Earl of Shaftesbury.[15] Yet, it seems coherent to argue that the same aim is at work in Wen Zhenheng's *Treatise on Superfluous Things*, written almost exactly a hundred years previous to this. Not only is he using the concept of 'elegance' and attaching more importance than hitherto to the manner of possessing (rather than the fact of possession) with regard to accepted categories of high-status goods, he is also bringing within him ambit types of luxury goods new to the sixteenth century, like Japanese lacquerware and the stoneware teapots of Yixing.

This and the other comparisons I have made are not offered in support of an argument that Ming China was 'just like' contemporary Europe. Nor are they intended to render China more 'familiar', more 'comprehensible'. China remains firmly fixed in the West as part of the Other, a place where things happen 'by contrast'. Thus, to draw attention, however arbitrarily, to patterns which appear to replicate in China and early modern Europe is here offered as part of a project to *de*familiarize notions of 'China' as the essential contrast to 'Europe'. It is certainly not meant to suggest a taking of sides in the now surely futile 'sprouts of capitalism' controversy by arguing that consumption patterns infallibly indicative of nascent capitalism were at work in the China of the period. In any case, a more sophisticated use of the heritage of Marx, as developed by Immanuel Wallerstein,[16] might be to suggest that, at a time when the hitherto separate worlds of Asia, the Americas and Europe were undergoing the first stages of integration into a world system, when decisions taken in Madrid might affect the price of rice in Fujian, when military actions fought on Taiwan might affect the Amsterdam bourse, major similarities can be observed in a crucial area of social activity at either end of Eurasia. Even if we are careful to avoid the imputation of a sort of vulgarly reductionist relationship between economics and culture, these similarities still do not have to be the result of mere coincidence. If we accept that overseas trade played a part in the creation of the buying power which engendered these patterns, then we are given a mechanism for grappling with, if not understanding, these similarities.

If we accept, too, the 'social, relational and active' nature of consumption, then we perhaps have a tentative way of grappling with the question of why, if sixteenth-century China exhibits so many consumption patterns paralleling those of Europe, eighteenth-century China yet 'feels' totally different from eighteenth-century Europe.

Firstly, the geographical restriction of those patterns of consumption discussed in this book to a small part of the empire, albeit the wealthiest and most populous part, was probably never overcome. It is no accident that the evidence of Ming writers quoted throughout this book is all drawn from the lower Yangtze region, for that is where it all comes from. Europe taken as a whole had at this time a number of competing cores and peripheries, while Ming China's most enduring miracle, its maintenance of a unified polity with a population of over 150 million, may have been its undoing in this aspect.

Secondly, the degree of dispersal of these consumption patterns down through society in China remained limited to what must have been only a small fraction of the population. Ming China's elite of consumers, even if in some ways their behaviour can be presented at least as, if not more, 'modern' than that of their Western contemporaries, were in no sense the midwives present at the birth of a consumer society. The vast majority of the population remained engulfed in the struggles of the subsistence economy. Future comparative work could with profit concentrate not just on the mechanisms of a 'consumer society', which can be demonstrated with equal facility for a number of points on the globe with very different subsequent histories, but on the extent to which these patterns had achieved a 'critical mass' which would ultimately transform the whole of society.

Thirdly, consumption as a motor of change, rather than a result of it, is particularly vulnerable to changes in cultural values, and even to direct political intervention, such as took place in China after 1644. Consumption went out of fashion; not that it ceased to exist, but it ceased to be a legitimate topic of concern for the elite, an object of discourse able to act as a site of power. Talking about things had become superfluous.

Appendix I

Editors of *Treatise on Superfluous Things*

1 Wang Liu (MRZJ, 50) came from a family with a long history of connections to the Wen clan. His father was Wang Zhideng (1535–1612; DMB, 1361–3), originally a talented young man from a humble background who enjoyed the patronage of Wen Zhenheng's grandfather and great-uncle and from them acquired the mantle of the poetic heir and guardian of the style of the great Wen Zhengming. Wang Zhideng himself lived to become extremely rich and famous and was one of the most sought-after writers of inscriptions and commemorative essays in the late Ming. The successful sale of his literary talents, which did not excluded the execution of a number of genteel calligraphic forgeries, from which one contemporary (Shen Defu, Vol. 3, 655) maintained that he obtained 'half his income', provided the wealth which enabled him to purchase in 1607 what was possibly the single most important work of calligraphic art in circulation at the time, the letter known as 'Clearing Weather after Sudden Snowfall' (*Kuai xue shi qing tie*), by Wang Xizhi (303–361), and to build a special pavilion to house this treasure in his Nanjing residence. The vendor was the son of its previous owner Feng Mengzhen, a frequenter of the West Lake mansion of Gao Lian in Hangzhou. Wang Zhideng was fifty years older than Wen Zhenheng, and the relations of patron and client which had once existed between the two families were now to an extent reversed in their case, with the older man taking the leading role. We know that he allowed the young Wen Zhenheng to examine his collection, and the memory of this was still fresh to Wen as he inscribed a colophon on 'Clearing Weather' when seeing it again in Nanjing in 1622 (*Shi qu bao ji*, 458–9). However, there were also familial ties over a number of generations. Wang Zhideng had at least two sons. The elder, Wang Zhengjun, was Wen Zhenheng's father-in-law. The second son, Wang Liu, was the commentator on Wen's text who we are concerned with here, while a sister of theirs was married to Wen's uncle, Wen Yuanshan. Wang Liu provided Wen Yuanshan's obituary. A son of Wang Liu, named Wang Qi, has the distinction of being the creator of the only work of art other than 'Clearing Weather after Sudden Snowfall' to bear the seals of Wen Zhenheng, his brother-in-law; Contag and Wang (1940). Wang Qi must have been older than Wen, as his earliest known work is dated 1600; Yu Jianhua (1981).

2 Pan Zhiheng (MRZJ, 775). Born in 1556 and dying in 1622, Pan was a scholar of a generation above Wen Zhenheng and was a personal friend of Wang Daokun, encountered already as the semi-professional author and provider of the obituary of Gao Lian's father. Pan's interest in popular material culture is confirmed by his authorship of at least two treatises on card games; Lo (1988).

3 Li Liufang (DMB, 838-9). Li, whose dates are 1575-1629, is best remembered as an artist, one of the 'Four Gentlemen of Jiading', and a member of the artistic tendency crystallized around the great artist, artistic theoretician and major politician Dong Qichang (1555-1636: ECCP, 787-9). In terms of the canons of Chinese painting as laid down in the late Ming and perpetuated into the Qing dynasty, he was thus part of a more advanced circle, the 'Jiading school', rather than the supposedly exhausted 'Wu' (i.e. Suzhou) school embodied by Wen himself; Li and Watt (1987). Li's participation in the project of the *Treatise* is thus important for establishing links between a quintessentially Suzhou figure like Wen Zhenheng and the group associated with the town of Jiading, near modern Shanghai.

4 Qian Xiyan. A figure about whom little as yet has been discovered, except in the negative sense that he was not a holder of the *jinshi* degree and has no surviving biography or tomb inscription. He was in Hangzhou in 1596, visited the Dongting Lake in 1599, published various works on drama in 1613, and was still alive in 1622; Zhang Huijian (1986), pp. 365, 375, 423, 461.

5 Shen Defu (DMB, 1190-1). Shen (1578-1642) was a wealthy member of an old-established family with a distinguished official history, who is best known as the author of one of the finest and most frequently quoted examples of Ming *biji* or 'note-form' literature, the *Random Gatherings of the Wanli Era* (*Wanli ye huo bian*) of 1606.

6 Shen Chunze (MRZJ, 172) is discussed above, p. 25.

7 Zhao Huanguang (MRZJ, 760). Zhao (1559–1625) was a native of Suzhou, noted for his practice of calligraphy in seal script and as a poet. His wife, also noted as a writer, was the daughter of Wen Zhengming's close friend Lu Shidao.

8 Wang Liu appears again, the only figure to be credited with the 'editing' of more than one chapter, which is perhaps symptomatic of the closeness of the ties between the two families.

9 Lou Jian (MRZJ, 611). As another member, together with Li Liufang, of the group known as 'Four Gentlemen of Jiading', the presence here of Lou Jian (1567–1631) strengthens the links between Suzhou and the nexus of interests centred on Dong Qichang.

10 Song Jizu (Yamane (1964), p. 515). There is very little known about Song, beyond his taking of the *jinshi* degree in 1553. He appears to have been a native of Changshu, near Suzhou, but the *Treatise* has him as from 'the capital'.

11 Zhou Yongnian (MRZJ, 315). A contemporary of Wen Zhenheng, Zhou (1582–1647) was like him a holder of the *zhusheng* degree.

12 Wen Zhenmeng (DMB 1467–71) was the author's elder brother and eventually a major political figure in his own right.

Appendix II

Selected prices for works of art and antique artefacts *c.* 1560–1620

Prices are arranged in ascending order in ounces of silver (*liang*). See pp. 125ff.

7/10–8/10 ounce: The price recorded by Zhan Jingfeng as standard for a modern fake painting attributed to Shen Zhou (1427–1509); Zhan Jingfeng, 2.70 [*juan* 2, p. 70].

4 ounces: 'Cloudy mountains' hanging scroll on paper by Mi Fu (1052–1107); Zhan Jingfeng, 1.57.

3–6 ounces: Set of the *Jiang tie* rubbings, Song-dynasty calligraphic specimens; Zhan Jingfeng, 1.57.

6 ounces: Wang Meng (1301–1385) 'Bamboo and rock' on paper; Zhan Jingfeng, 1.54.

6 ounces: Old copy of 'White eagle' by the Song aesthete – emperor Huizong (r. 1101–25); Zhan Jingfeng, 3.155.

7 ounces: Li Sixun (eighth century) small landscape. Recorded as a bargain price; Zhan Jingfeng, 2.104.

10 ounces: Horse in Tang style by Zhao Mengfu (1254–1322); Zhan Jingfeng, 2.94.

15 ounces: Recorded in a later colophon as being the price paid by Xiang Yuanbian for 'Land of the Immortals' by Chen Ruyan (*c.*1331 – before 1371), now in the Cleveland Museum of Art; Eight Dynasties (1980), p. 140.

16 ounces: Four calligraphic inscriptions by Zhao Mengfu; Zhan Jingfeng, 3.140.

20 ounces: Calligraphy by Zhang Xu (active *c.* 700–750); Zhan Jingfeng, 1.31.

20 ounces: Album of twenty Song-dynasty, landscape-album leaves, including the work of Ma Yuan, Xia Gui and Liu Songnian; Zhan Jingfeng, 1.27.

20 ounces +: Twenty ounces were turned down for an anonymous figure painting 'Ge Hong moves his dwelling', in the style of the Tang artists Wu Daozi or Zhang Sengyu; Zhan Jingfeng, 2.110.

20 ounces: 'Living in seclusion' by Ma Wan (active *c.* 1342–1366), purchased and remounted in 1577 by Xiang Yuanbian; Weng Tongwen (1979), p. 165.

20 ounces: Calligraphic tomb inscription by Zhao Mengfu; Weng Tongwen (1979), p. 165.

20 ounces: 'Living like an immortal' by Wang Meng; Wang Tongwen (1979), p. 167.

24 ounces: Albums of ten landscape leaves by Tang Yin (1470–1523); Weng Tongwen (1979), p. 163.

30 ounces: Anonymous 'Eighteen Scholars' scroll, of debatable age; Zhan Jingfeng, 1.27.

30 ounces: 'Dwelling in the mountains', handscroll by Qian Xuan (*c.*1275 – after 1301); Weng Tongwen (1979), p. 167.

40 ounces: Scroll with poems in the calligraphy of Zhao Mengfu and pictures by Shen Zhou, bought by Xiang Yuanbian in 1559; Wen Tongwen (1979), P. 167.

50 ounces: Landscape by Wang Meng; Zhan Jingfeng, 4.224.

50 ounces: 'Picking Oranges Letter', calligraphy by Wang Xianzhi; Zhan Jingfeng, 2.102.

50 ounces: Poems in the calligraphy of Yu Ji (1272–1348), bought in 1560 by Xiang Yuanbian; Weng Tongwen (1979), p. 170.

75 ounces: Text of the *Huangtingjing* in the calligraphy of Zhao Mengfu; Zhan Jingfeng, 1.62.

80 ounces: Painting By Huang Quan (903–968), 'Meetings and Partings'; Weng Tongwen (1979), p 170.

100 ounces: Poems in the handwriting of Mi Fu, bought by Xiang Yuanbian in 1563; Weng Tongwen (1979), p. 169.

100 ounces: Price almost paid by Gao Lian for a bronze *ding* tripod, until close examination showed it to be a fake; Gao Lian, p. 18b.

100 ounces: Unsigned scroll originally bought for 1 ounce but identified by Shen Defu as being by Li Sixun; Shen Defu, Vol. 3, p. 658.

100 ounces: Reputed price of two scrolls by Qiu Ying, commissioned by Zhou Fenglai; Laing (1979), p. 52.

150 ounces: Price paid by the Wanli emperor (r. 1573–1620) for an unusually large antique ceramic vase of Jun ware; Tan Qian, p. 339.

150 ounces: Anonymous painting 'The Red Cliff', attributed by Xiang Yuanbian to Zhu Rui; Weng Tongwen (1979), p. 167.

160 ounces: Small bronze *ding* tripod, attributed to the reign of King Wen of the Zhou dynasty; Zhan Jingfeng, 4.220.

180 ounces: Scroll containing four pieces of calligraphy, including a Wang Xizhi (303–361) tracing copy; Zhan Jingfeng, 3.88.

200 ounces: the price paid in the Zhengde reign (1506–21) for a ceramic incense burner of Ge ware, according to the *biji, Bi chuang suo yu*; Sayer (1951), p. 98.

200 ounces: 'Spring night in the Han palace' by Qiu Ying (*c.* 1494–*c.* 1552); Weng Tongwen (1979), P. 168.

200 ounces: Paid in 1564 for Wang Xizhi's 'Offering Oranges Letter', and the price inscribed on the work; Ledderose (1986).

300 ounces: The 'Offering Oranges Letter' sold for this price in 1617 by Xiang Yuanbian's descendants; Ledderose (1986). This is the only instance in the period when it is possible to see the movement in the price of a given object.

300 ounces: Album of sixty Song and Yuan dynasty album leaves, recorded as sold to Xiang Yuanbian; Zhan Jingfeng, 1.29.

300 ounces: Price of a jade cup, ostensibly from the Song dynasty imperial collections; Jiang Shaoshu, 1.6-7.

300 ounces: Price of the three decorated bronze vases from the tomb of Duke Jing of Qi; Zhang Dai, r. 84.

300 ounces: Paid for a modern fake set of the *Chunhuage tie* rubbing collection; Shen Defu, p. 656.

350 ounces: Particularly fine bronze *fu* vessel from the reign of King Wen; Zhan Jingfeng, 4.217.

350 ounces: Ceramic incense burner of Ding ware; Zhan Jingfeng, 4.217.

500 ounces: Offered by Xiang Yuanbian for a 'white Ding incense burner, a Ge ware vase and a Guan ware ewer for wine' belonging to the uncle of Zhang Dai; Zhang Dai, p. 80.

550 ounces: Paid in 1577 by Xiang Yuanbian for a version of the 'Orchid Pavilion Manuscript' in the calligraphy of the Tang writer Feng Chengsu; Weng Tongwen (1979), p.165.

800 ounces: Paid in 1572 by Xiang Yuanbian for a piece of calligraphy by Su Shi (1037-1101); Weng Tongwen (1979), p. 169.

800 ounces: Price of the *Jiang gan xue yi*, sold to a rich man of Huizhou following its attribution to Wang Wei (701-761) by Dong Qichang; Shen Defu, p. 658.

1,000 ounces: Paid in 1534 by the collector An Guo for the 'centre' copy of the rubbings of the archaic 'Stone Drums' inscriptions; DMB, p. 10.

1,000 ounces: Price, the value of an estate, of a set of four scrolls by Shen Zhou, paid by Wang Xiyuan to Wang Guxiang; Tang Zhixie, quoted in Yu Jianhua (1986), p. 1276.

1,000 ounces: 'Drunken Taoist' by Yan Liben, the copyist of which was paid 10 ounces; Shen Defu, p. 655.

1,000 ounces: Price of a Song-dynasty set of the rubbing collection *Chunhuage tie*, in the collection of Xiang Yuanbian; Shen Defu, p. 656.

1,000 ounces: The calligraphic 'Autobiography' of the monk Huaisu (737 – after 798) in drafting script; Zhan Jingfeng, 1.23.

1,000 ounces: Dong Qichang pawned 'Dwelling in the Fuchun Mountains' by Huang Gongwang (1269–1354) for this sum in or around 1630 (Plate 8); Riely (1975).

1,000 ounces: The price for which in around 1620 the grandson of Tang Houzheng sold the fake Ding incense burner by Zhou Danquan to an unnamed wealthy vulgarian; Jiang Shaoshu, 1.8.

2,000 ounces: Price paid by Xiang Yuanbian for the *Zhan jin tie* by Wang Xizhi. The work was sold again for this huge sum in 1619 by one of Xiang's sons; Weng Tongwen (1979), p. 163.

Notes

Chinese primary sources are referenced by the name of the author only or, in the case of anonymous works, by the name of the work. Full details of editions used will be found in the Bibliography of primary sources. Secondary literature in Chinese and other languages is referenced by author and date, or occasionally by an abbreviation in the case of frequently cited works. Full citations are in the Bibliography of secondary literature.

INTRODUCTION

1 Mukerji (1983), p. 15. The source of some of this lies in the ideas of Paul Ricoeur about 'meaningful action considered as a text', discussed by Henrietta Moore in Tilley (1990), pp. 97–9.
2 Goldthwaite (1987); Schama (1987).
3 St George (1988). While the American project appears concerned to define material culture studies as a discipline, Tilley (1990) p. vii sees a refusal of disciplinary allegiance as one of the 'series of refusals' which this 'developing field of enquiry' must inevitably embrace, along with the theory/practice and subject/object antitheses, and the reification of categories of analysis into separate spheres.
4 Appadurai (1986), p. 5.
5 Work which exists to a greater or lesser extent in response to the hypothesis of the 'birth of a consumer society' in early Georgian England, as contained in McKendrick et al. (1982).
6 Burke (1986).
7 Zhu Weizheng (1987). Spence (1990) also takes the years around 1600 as the starting point in his 'search for modern China'.
8 Liu Bohan and Wang Jieyun (1981) is a convenient collection of many of the key articles, dating back to the 1950s.

9 Four works in particular stand out. We now have a basic narrative of the political history of the dynasty in Mote and Twitchett (1988), to supplement the invaluable *Dictionary of Ming Biography*, already familiar to its users as DMB. We have a characteristically subtle and rich explanation of how the Ming state apparatus actually, as opposed to theoretically, functioned, in the form of Huang (1981). And we have a collective account of the cultural ideals of the elite by a distinguished group of contemporary Chinese scholars, in Li and Watt (1987).

CHAPTER 1   BOOKS ABOUT THINGS

1   van Gulik (1958), p. 51.
2   The origins of the *congshu* are discussed in Xie Guozhen (1981), p. 203.
3   Taam (1935), pp. 76–7.
4   ZGCSZL.
5   David (1971).
6   Ibid., p. 3.
7   Quoted in Appadurai (1986), p. 43.
8   David (1971), p. lvii.
9   Wang Daokun A, *juan* 47.
10 *Shi qu bao ji xu bian*, 6, p. 3167.
11 Feng Mengzhen, 48, p. 69b.
12 Fong (1977); Ledderose (1979a).
13 Edmond Yee, 'Kao Lien', in Nienhauser (1986), pp. 472–3.
14 Chen Meilin (1986), p. 84.
15 Tanaka (1985), p. 148.
16 Needham (1986), p. 361.
17 Wang Zhongmin (1983), p. 266.
18 Most of my citations come, in fact, from the 1928 edition of it contained in a specialist *congshu* of artistic texts, although I have also studied the two separate Ming editions of the *Eight Discourses* in the British Library and the Percival David Foundation.
19 Though not unique. It is used also by Gao's 'house guest', Tu Long.
20 Brook (1988a).
21 Wang Zhongmin (1983), p. 348.
22 Wylie (1922), pp. 144, 148, 150, 151, 154.
23 See the partial genealogy in Sirén (1958) vol. 4, p. 186. There is now a large literature on members of the Wen family as painters, though no one has yet encompassed their full social/cultural role.
24 Wakeman (1985), vol. 1, p. 133.
25 Liu Dunzhen (1979).
26 Hucker (1971) is a full translation and commentary on *The True Story of the Proclamation*, which is almost certainly by Wen Zhenheng,

and allots him the hero's role in the resistance to eunuch-led corruption.

27 The text is given in an appendix to the edition of Wen Zhenheng's *Treatise* specified in the Bibliography of primary sources.

28 *Zhong shu she ren*, rank 7b in the nine-rank structure; Hucker (1985) p. 193.

29 Wakeman (1985), p. 153.

30 *Ru ren*; Hucker (1985), p. 273.

31 A little information on him is preserved in a local gazetteer and in a late Ming/early Qing collection of painter's biographies, the *Ming hua lu*, *Register of the Painters of the Ming* of 1673; MRZJ, 172.

32 In Li and Watt (1987), p. 5.

33 Wen Zhenheng p. 153; Hucker (1985), p. 481.

34 Whitfield (1987), p. 19.

35 Wen Zhenheng, *Zhang wu zhi jiao zhu*, *'Treatise on Superfluous Things'*, *Edited and Annotated*, by the eminent botanist Chen Zhi (b. 1898). He is the collator and source of most of the biographical and bibliographical material used in this study, and it is this edition which is used throughout. Chen, a professor at the Nanjing Institute of Forestry, had principal research interests in the history of botany and in the garden in China, being responsible for a critical study of another key Ming text in this area, the *Yuan ye*, *The Craft of Gardens* of 1635, by Ji Cheng (fl. *c.* 1600–1640; DMB, 215–16: this text has been translated in full as Hardie (1988). A preface tells us that Chen's work on Wen Zhenheng was completed in 1965, but the bitter repression of scholarship which then ensued meant that, like so many other pieces of intellectual work, publication did not take place until 1984, after Chen Zhi's death. The political turmoil and the violence which shattered Wen Zhenheng's life have not, for Chinese scholars of the later twentieth century, simply been distant historical events of no contemporary resonance.

36 Mote and Chu (1989), pp. 189–92. This may well be the case with Chen Jiru's supposed editorship of an edition of Gao Lian's best-known play, *The Jade Hairpin*, as there is no independent confirmation of his connection with Gao at any stage.

37 DMB, p. 1326, entry on Tu Long by Chaoying Fang.

38 Weng Tongwen (1983).

39 *Si ku quan shu zong mu ti yao*, p. 2576.

40 Ibid., pp. 2576–7.

41 Ibid., p. 2714.

42 Ibid., p. 2577.

43 Beurdeley (1966), pp. 118–28 concerns Zhang Yingwen and his milieu.

44 The *Ping shi* is also translated into French and annotated in full in Vandermeersch (1964).

45 This, one of the largest of all Ming *congshu*, continued to appear on into the early Qing period, and has a particularly tangled publishing history; Chang Bide (1979).
46 Tadao (1970); Brook (1988b).
47 Wang Zhongmin (1983), p. 347.
48 Ruitenbeek (1989), p. 45.
49 Wu Jinming (1987).
50 Evans (1979), p. 389. This literature of domestic economy can be traced in Italy as far back as the mid-fifteenth century, with a text like Leon Battista Alberti's *La cura della famiglia*.
51 Y. W. Ma,'*pi-chi*', in Nienhauser (1986), pp. 650–2; Xie Guozhen (1981) gives more detail on the most important examples.
52 David Roy, '*Chin P'ing Mei*', in Nienhauser (1986), pp. 287–91. Early translations of this have either been severely abbreviated, or else depend on inferior Chinese recensions, and invariably preserve the erotic action at the expense of the density of texture which makes the novel an encyclopedia of Ming material culture and domestic life. André Lévy's masterly new French version redresses the imbalance with a full and fluent translation which omits none of the valuable detail; Lévy (1985). David Roy's own complete English version appeared too late to be used here.

CHAPTER 2   IDEAS ABOUT THINGS

1 Wen Zhenheng, p. 31.
2 Ibid., pp. 46–7.
3 Ibid., pp. 112–13.
4 Ibid., p. 123.
5 Ibid., p. 183.
6 Ibid., p. 225.
7 Ibid., p. 231.
8 Ibid., p. 247.
9 Ibid., p. 333.
10 Ibid., p. 345.
11 Ibid., p. 352.
12 Ibid., p. 369.
13 Ibid., p. 409.
14 More lengthy extracts drawn from Chapter 5, 'Calligraphy and painting' can be found in translation in van Gulik (1958). The material on furniture has been used extensively in Clunas 1988a), while further quotations from Chapter 7 'Vessels and utensils' can be found in Clunas (1984b) (dealing with attitudes to ivory as a material) and Li and Watt (1987), covering mostly ceramics. More extensive citation of this sort of Ming connoisseurship literature is available to those who do not read Chinese in a number of scattered sources; Waley (1925) translates Gao

Lian's section on ceramics from *Eight Discourses* (this material also occurs in a number of the other classic early Western works of scholarship on Chinese ceramics), while chunks of Tu Long (as we have seen, actually the work of Gao Lian, again) on goldfish and ceramics have been put into English by Moule (1950), and David (1937). There also exists an excellent and critically informed French translation of his contemporary Zhang Chou's treatise on flower arranging, the *Manual on Vases and Flowers*; Vandermeersch (1964).

15 Li and Watt (1987), p. 6.
16 *Zhi bu zu zhai congshu, Collectanea from the Studio of Knowing One's Inadequacies*, edited by Bao Tingbo (1728–1814; ECCP, pp. 612–13).
17 Shen Bang, e.g. pp. 154–62.
18 Bauer and Haupt (1976).
19 Baxandall (1985), p. 9.
20 An example of this in current practice is Clunas (1986b), where Wen's entry on 'Brush testers' from the 'Vessels and utensils' chapter is used to assign some degree of historic meaning to an object which had lain unidentified in a museum collection for over a hundred years.
21 Bonnaffée (1902) contains a complete French translation, and there are English extracts in Klein and Zerner (1966). Alsop (1982), pp. 419–25 calls the *Ricordi* 'a rare book by an obscure man', which seems to underrate both its fame in its own time and the degree of current awareness of it, especially among Renaissance art historians. I used the 1554 'Vinegia' edition, the earliest in the British Library.
22 Klein and Zerner (1966), pp. 23–5.
23 Guazzo (1586).
24 Peacham (1622).
25 Mote and Chu (1989), pp. 135–45; Fu Xihua (1980) is one of several recent compilations of illustrations to drama and other forms of *belles-lettres*.
26 Gu Yuanqing.
27 Forty (1986), p. 93.
28 Ibid., pp. 63–6.
29 Wen Zhenheng, pp. 241 (beds), 354 ('prettiness') and 25 (balustrading).
30 David (1971), p. 143.
31 Clunas (1988a), p. 94.
32 Weidner et al. (1988), cat. nos 14–16.
33 Ward (1977).
34 Clunas (1988b).
35 Brook (1981).
36 Wen Zhenheng, pp. 303 (brushes) and 307 (paper).
37 *Ju jia bi yong shi lei quan ji, juan* 5, p. 60b.

38 Schafer (1963) remains the classic account of this under the Tang dynasty (618–906).

39 Li Yangong and Hao Jie, p. 67. The 'sprinkled gold' describes the distinctively Japanese lacquering techniques of *nashiji* and *maki-e*.

40 Fairbank, Reischauer and Craig (1973), p. 178. The notion of an irrational 'hostility to alien things' remains an important element in orientalist discourse in general.

41 Wen Zhenheng, pp. 242–3.

42 Gao Lian, p. 231 (at the same place he relishes another 'exotic' import, Buddhist images from Tibet); Zhang Yingwen, p. 12a. Shen Defu, pp. 906–7 waxes enthusiastic about 'western ocean' agates, probably imported from the flourishing industry of South India.

43 Li Junjie (1987).

44 Whitfield (1975).

45 Zhou Gongjin (1986), p. 100 (Chinese text), p. 17 (English text).

46 Shen Defu, p. 663.

47 Wang Shizhen was widely recognized by contemporaries as the leading scholar of the day, but he is also identified by Shen Defu, p. 564, as the man whose example spread the mania for art collecting among the 'frivolous' of the Yangtze Valley region.

48 Wang Shizhen, quoted in Xie Guozhen (1980), vol. 1 pp. 289–90. This passage is also translated by James Watt in Li and Watt (1987), p. 9, where the reading 'Zhou Ye' is preferred. It is substantially the same as Shen Defu, p. 653.

49 Zhang Dai, pp. 11–12.

50 Ibid., p. 59.

51 Clunas (1987a); Gillman (1984).

52 Quoted in Clunas (1987b), p. 78.

53 Tsang and Moss (1984) translate the gazetteer entry; Li and Watt (1987), cat. no. 62 is the Hu Guangyu bronze.

54 Chen Shiqi (1955).

55 Shearman (1967), p. 44.

56 Burke (1986), p. 64, quoting H. Tietze, 'Master and Workshop in the Venetian Renaissance', *Parnassus*, 11 (1939), 34–5.

57 Sonenscher (1989); Clifford (1988). In recognition of this, and of the fact that it was likely to have been the case at a period much earlier than that for which any archival material survives, most scholars of British silver now tend to call what was once the 'maker's mark' by the more non-committal name of 'sponsor's mark', the mark of that concern which presented the piece to the Goldsmith's Company for ratification of its metallic content, rather than its aesthetic begetters.

58 Dillon (1976).

59 Jörg (1982); Clunas (1984b).

60 Zhang Dai, p. 80.

61 Clunas (1987a); Clunas (1988a), p. 71.

62　Translated in Kerr (1990), p. 24.
63　E.g. Bush and Shih (1985), pp. 75–8.
64　Stanley-Baker (1986), p. 58. I would, however, reject the notion at any point of a 'direct encounter between man and art', with which the Chinese social relationship can be juxtaposed.
65　Bush and Shih (1985), p. 99.
66　Shen Defu, vol. 3, p. 658.
67　Wen Zhenheng, p. 151.
68　Ibid., p. 138.
69　Ibid., p. 153.
70　Ho (1976); Cahill (1982), p. 87.
71　Barnhart (1983).
72　Wen Zhenheng, p. 142.
73　This has been translated in full in van Gulik (1958), pp. 4–6.
74　He Liangjun, p. 315.
75　Wen Zhenheng, p. 249.
76　Li and Watt (1987), p. 164. The privileging of 'ceramics' as a distinct category of artefact in this catalogue is a concession to modern curatorial and art-market practice in what is otherwise an attempt to deal seriously with the Ming hierarchy of objects.
77　Bourdieu (1984), p. 29.
78　Ibid., p. 479.
79　Wen Zhenheng, p. 10.

CHAPTER 3　WORDS ABOUT THINGS

1　van Gulik (1968).
2　Chaves (1983).
3　Bush and Murck (1983).
4　A stimulating exception is that of Cahill (1976), in which James Cahill teases out the implications of the word *fang*, 'imitation' as it bears upon the concept of originality in painting; also that of Li and Watt (1987), in which James Watt gives a broad survey of some key terms deployed across the whole range of concerns in late Ming aesthetics. There is also the example of Japan to show that this kind of historical lexicography can be approached with great success from inside a cognate culture, with some of the same problems of a seemingly unchanging set of graphic signifiers. Kuki Shuzo's pioneering study earlier this century on 'The Structure of *iki*', a word given dictionary equivalents such as 'stylish', 'chic' even 'sexy', cf. Kuki (1930), and the more recent work of Tanikawa Tetsuzo on the distinctive connoisseurly vocabulary of the tea ceremony, cf. Tanikawa (1980–1), have been major advances for which there is as yet no Chinese equivalent.
5　Baxandall (1985); Burke (1986).
6　Handlin (1983); the author points to the ambiguous nature of 'the

investigation of things', which also occupied a place in the most subjectivist schools of Ming philosophy.

7 For 'see all the things', see Feng Mengzhen, *juan* 59, p. 38b; for agates, see Shen Defu, p. 907.

8 Jiang Shaoshu, *juan* 1, p. 6; Zhang Dai, p. 84; He Liangjun, p. 315.

9 For 'academic painting', see Wen Zhenheng, p. 151; for archaizing jades, see Chen Jiru, p. 6b.

10 Wang Qi, p. 42.

11 Wen Zhenheng, p. 246.

12 Mather (1976), p. 22, with *pinyin* romanization.

13 Tian Yiheng, vol. 2, p. 810.

14 Wen Zhenheng, p. 247.

15 *Ju jia bi yong shi lei quan ji, juan* 5, pp. 74b and 85a.

16 Lynn (1983).

17 He Liangjun, p. 315.

18 Appadurai (1986), p. 38.

19 *Tian shui bing shan lu*, pp. 156a (zithers), 188b (paintings), 158a (inkstones), 170b (bronzes).

20 Gao Lian, p. 33a.

21 Shen Defu, vol. 3, p. 658 (paintings); Feng Mengzhen, p. 26 (books); Gao Lian, p. 14b (bronzes).

22 Yu (1983).

23 DeWoskin (1983), p. 202, where the term is also shown to mean 'uncomplicated', 'simple'.

24 Laing (1968).

25 Wang Daokun B, p. 7a.

26 Shen Defu, p. 653.

27 Wen Zhenheng, p. 10.

28 Zhang Dai, p. 79; Wen Zhenheng, p. 315.

29 Bush (1971), p. 175 translates it as 'beauty', in the context of a polemical quotation from Fan Yunlin (1558–1641; MRZJ, 361), a friend and partisan of Dong Qichang.

30 Chaves (1983), p. 347.

31 Wen Zhenheng, p. 262.

32 Tu Long, p. 1b; He Liangjun, p. 315.

33 Wen Zhenheng, pp. 269, 271, 276.

34 E.g. Shen Defu, pp. 653, 654.

35 Wen Zhenheng, pp. 272, 291, 307.

36 Sun Chengze, vol. 1, p. 56.

37 Jiang Shaoshu, *juan* 1, pp. 6 and 7; also used by Zhang Dai, p. 79, for two jades in the collection of the Zhu family (probably Zhu Jingxun).

38 David (1971), p. 133.

39 Jiang Shaoshu, *juan*, p. 6.

40 He Liangjun, p. 315; Wen Zhenheng, p. 310.

41 On Mi Fu, see Ledderose (1979a), pp. 59, 86 and 97; Barnhart (1983), p. 395, n. 67.

42   Ming examples of *jian shang* are Wen Zhenheng, p. 247; Gao Lian pp. 1b and 41a.
43   Zhang Chou, quoted in Yu Jianhua (1986), vol. 2, p. 1244.
44   Zhang Dai, p. 80; Wang Qi, p. 45.
45   Zhang Dai, p. 11.
46   *Ying lie zhuan*, 18 *hui*, p. 70.
47   Shen Defu, p. 653: Vandermeersch (1964), p. 120, translates *hao shi* as *passion*.
48   Zhang Dai, p. 43.
49   Shen Defu, p. 653, a passage which is heavily indebted to a much-repeated text of Wang Shizhen.
50   Jiang Shaoshu, *juan* 1, p. 8.
51   Long Qian'an (1985), pp. 646–7, quoting the texts *Du cheng ji sheng* of 1235 and *Meng liang lu* of 1274.
52   *Ci yuan* (1979), vol. 1, p. 459.
53   Zhan Jingfeng, *juan* 2, p. 95; Shen Defu, vol. 3 p. 655; Feng Mengzhen, *juan* 59, p. 38b.
54   Li and Watt (1987), pp. 4–5.
55   Chaves (1983), pp. 345–7 describes *qu* as 'the ineffable essence at the heart of things', and notes Yuan Hongdao's specific distaste for those who attempt to capture it through the collecting of antiques, a devotion to incense or the cult of tea in terms which suggest that Wen Zhenheng may have occupied just the kind of position to which he was most opposed.
56   Wen Zhenheng, pp. 251, 347 and 135.
57   Zhang Yingwen, p. 1b.
58   Li Huibing (1986).
59   Bush and Shih (1985), p. 23.
60   *Ju jia bi yong shi lei quan ji*, *juan* 5, p. 85b.
61   Lévy (1985), pp. 128, 271; p. 581 for the use of 'à la mode'.

CHAPTER 4   THINGS OF THE PAST

1   Murck (1976), p. xi.
2   Whitfield (1969); Clapp (1975).
3   Lowenthal (1985).
4   As Ibid., p. 78 points out.
5   Wen Zhenheng, pp. 294–5.
6   D'Elia (1942), vol. 1, p. 91.
7   On Vico see Andrew Burnett, 'Renaissance forgeries of ancient coins' in Jones (1990), pp. 136–7. Burnett also makes the point that 'authenticity' in relation to coins was a matter of everyday experience; J. Evelyn, *Numismata: A Discourse of Medals Antient and Modern . . .* (London, 1697), p. 209.
8   The following discussion of this early 'scholarly' phase of bronze study, centred on and supported by the imperial court, follows to

a large extent Rawson (forthcoming) and Kerr (1990). Full bibliographic details can be found in Poor (1965) and Balazs/Hervouet (1978).

9   Quoted in Kerr (1990), p. 16.
10 He Liangjun, p. 256.
11 Poor (1965).
12 Lawton (1988).
13 Bush and Shih (1985), p. 52.
14 See Rawson (1987) for a comprehensive and clear introduction.
15 Wen Zhenheng, pp. 316–17.
16 Rawson (forthcoming), quotes the relevant passage: 'The inscriber discourses about and extols the virtues and goodness of the ancestors, their merits and their zeal, their services and their toils, the congratulations and rewards given to them, their fame recognized by all under Heaven; and in the discussion of these things on spiritual vessels he makes himself famous.'
17 Wang Qi, p. 69.
18 Kerr (1990), pp. 50–5.
19 Wang Qi, p. 45; Zhang Dai, p. 79.
20 Rawson (forthcoming).
21 Zhang Dai, p. 84.
22 Vandermeersch (1964), p. 96.
23 Wen Zhenheng, p. 247.
24 Gao Lian, pp. 57a–59b.
25 The terminology is that of Binford (1962).
26 Shanghai (1972).
27 Jiangsu (1987).
28 Zhang Dai, p. 80.
29 Ye Zuofu (1989).
30 Treager (1982).
31 David (1971), pp. 139–43.
32 Wen Zhenheng, pp. 317–18.
33 Ibid., pp. 266, 310 and 361.
34 Tian Yiheng, vol. 3, p. 1273.
35 Muthesius (1988).
36 Shen Defu, p. 653.
37 Li and Watt (1987), pp. 15–16; both Chu-tsing Li and James Watt (p. 8) point to the essentially conventional, rather than personal or idiosyncratic, nature of this hierarchy.
38 Wang Qi, pp. 45–6, with altered punctuation in the list of names of *qin* zithers.
39 Zhang Yingwen, p. 12b.
40 Shen Defu, vol. 3, p. 654.
41 Ledderose (1979b).
42 Zhan Jingfeng, *juan* 1, p. 60.
43 He Liangjun, p. 255.
44 Zhang Dai, p. 80.

45 Chen Jiru, *juan* 4, p. 3a.
46 Tan Qian, p. 339; another such 'chance find' report is Chen Jiru, *juan* 3, pp. 3b–4a.
47 Craig Clunas, 'Faking in the East', in Jones (1990), pp. 99–101.
48 Alsop (1982), pp. 240–50.
49 Kerr (1990), p. 68.
50 Mote and Chu (1989), pp. 189–92.
51 van Wijk (1948); the leaf is translated into German in Klose (1983), and I am indebted to Renate Stephan of the Bayerische Staatsbibliothek for a copy of this article.
52 Li and Watt (1987), p. 31.
53 Wen Zhenheng, p. 148.
54 A good survey of the relevant sections of Gao Lian, Wen Zhenheng and other writers can be found in van Gulik (1958).
55 Stanley-Baker (1986); on the *Bao hui lu* see also Lovell (1973), p. 30.
56 Shen Defu, vol. 3, p. 655.
57 Weiss (1988), p. 190.
58 Zhan Jingfeng, *juan* 1, p. 40, states, 'The people of Suzhou often do this.' He is only one of many witnesses to the practice.
59 Jones (1990), cat. no. 109.
60 Zhan Jingfeng, *juan* 2, p. 70.
61 Yang Xin (1989).
62 *Ju jia bi yong shi lei quan ji*, *juan* 5, p. 75a.
63 Kerr (1990), p. 74.
64 Clunas (1987b).
65 Jiang Shaoshu, *juan* 1, p. 8.
66 Laing (1975), p. 228.

CHAPTER 5 THINGS IN MOTION

1 Appadurai (1986), p. 13.
2 Ibid., p. 14.
3 McDermott (1981).
4 Wakeman (1985), p. 871, n. 61; Levy (1966) is an annotated translation of *Diverse Records of Wooden Bridge*, by Yu Huai (1616–1696), one of the richest sources for the study of the sexual services industry in the late Ming.
5 Chin and Hsü (1981), p. 24.
6 Xu Zhengji (1988).
7 Celia Carrington Riely, 'Tung Ch'i-ch'ang (1555–1636) and the Interplay of Politics and Power', paper delivered at the conference, *The Scholarly Tradition in Chinese Art*, organized by the Friends of the Chinese University Art Gallery, Academy for Performing Arts, Hong Kong, 30 October – 1 November 1990. This paper remains unpublished.

8   Cahill (1978), pp. 216–17.
9   Li and Watt (1987), cat. no. 7.
10 Siggstedt (1982).
11 Laing (1979). There must either be a discrepancy in Zhou Fenglai's dates, or else the lady involved was the principal wife of his father and, hence, his honorary rather than biological mother.
12 Dubosc (1975).
13 McDermott (1985); the documentation discovered over the past few decades in the Huizhou region of Anhui province does hold out the promise of a much better understanding of the mechanisms of ownership, both of land and movable goods, through in particular the study of surviving wills.
14 Wen Zhenheng, p. 139.
15 Quoted in Yu Jianhua (1981), p. 1276.
16 Lovell (1973), pp. 18–20.
17 Weng Tongwen (1979).
18 Lovell (1976), pp. 68–9.
19 Ledderose (1986).
20 Quoted in Alsop (1982), p. 384. An even more striking reversal of our present hierarchies is the monetary equivalence in this inventory of a small Donatello with a featherbed and set of pillows.
21 Tinti, *La nobilta di Verona* (1592), quoted in Lowenthal (1985), p. 77, n. 18.
22 Wen Zhenheng, p. 141.
23 Yang (1952) and Peng Xinwei (1958) supply the broad framework.
24 Cribb (1977).
25 Atwell (1982).
26 Peng Xinwei (1958), pp. 677–98; a further series of price statistics for the Ming period is provided by Huang Wantang (1985), pp. 346–72.
27 Cartier (1981).
28 Wakeman (1985), vol. 1, pp. 6 and 35.
29 Huang (1981), p. 64.
30 The Ming bolt was standardized at 40 Ming *chi*, or feet, equivalent to 12.48 m.
31 *Tian shui bing shan lu*, pp. 249a–b (bolts) and 150a (garments).
32 Cai Guoliang (1984), pp. 247–60 in the chapter 'Ming urban economic life as reflected in *Jin ping mei*.
33 *Tian shui bing shan lu*, p. 155b, (furniture) and 259b (ceramics).
34 DMB, p. 828; James Watt, in Li and Watt (1987), p. 8, records that Li Rihua 'was friendly with the literatus potter Hao Shijiu', but this looks like a case of lustre by association.
35 Ye Mengzhu, p. 164.
36 Zhang Dai, p. 23.
37 Isobe Akira (1980). I am indebted to Professor T.J. Barrett for this reference.
38 Equivalent to 2–3 ounces per *mu*; Cai Guoliang (1984), p. 252.

39 Zhan Jingfeng, *juan* 2, p. 94.
40 Owyoung (1982).
41 Zhan Jingfeng, *juan* 2, p. 107 (uncle to nephew), and *juan* 2, p. 68 (two owners).
42 Shen Defu, vol. 3, p. 658.
43 Zhan Jingfeng, *juan* 3, p. 151 and *juan* 2, p. 74.
44 Ibid., *juan* 3, p. 119 and *juan* 3, p. 130.
45 Ibid., *juan* 4, p. 188 and *juan* 4, p. 205.
46 Ibid., *juan* 1, p. 31.
47 'Retold' in English in Mao (1975) and discussed in Hanan (1988), pp. 98–102.
48 Wakeman (1985), vol. 1, p. 149.
49 Zhan Jingfeng, *juan* 2, p. 104.
50 Feng's 'assignments' are translated by Wai-kam Ho in Li and Watt (1987), p. 28.
51 Zhan Jingfeng, *juan* 1, p. 53.
52 Laing (1975).
53 Li and Watt (1987), p. 30.
54 Zhang Dai, p. 94.
55 Ibid., p. 84.
56 Zhan Jingfeng, *juan* i, p. 22, *juan* 1, p. 31 and *juan* 2, p. 69.
57 Shen Defu, vol. 2, p. 613.
58 Liu Tong and Yu Yizheng, p. 161.
59 Sun Chengze, vol. 1 p. 56.
60 Jiang Shaoshu, *juan*, 1, p. 6.
61 Riely (1975); Fong (1977).
62 Riely (1975), p. 58.
63 Fong (1977), p. 13.
64 Ho (1976).

CHAPTER 6   ANXIETIES ABOUT THINGS

1 Watson (1964), p. 116.
2 Quoted in Yang Jinding (1987), p. 293.
3 Rawson (1987), *passim*.
4 Lu Yuanjun (1977), p. 713.
5 Brook (1981).
6 Zhang Han, pp. 76–80. All the following quotations are taken from the *Account of the Hundred Crafts*, Zhang Han, pp. 76–80.
7 Yang (1957).
8 McKendrick et al. (1982), p. 16.
9 Shen Defu, vol. 2, p. 484.
10 Appadurai (1986), p. 25.
11 *Da Ming hui dian*, vol. 2, *juan* 60–2.
12 *Ming shi*, vol. 6, p. 1672.
13 Legge (1885), p. 12.

14 Guazzo (1586), p. 94.
15 Burke (1982), p. 52, quoting R. Levi Pisetzky, *Storia del Costume in Italia*, III (Milan, 1966).
16 Elliott (1986), p. 11 shows Velazquez's 1623 portrait of Philip IV in this collar, the *golilla*.
17 Harte (1976).
18 Schama (1987), pp. 186–7.
19 Evans (1973), p. 131. I have not been able to pursue his Czech references.
20 *Da Ming hui dian*, vol. 2, *juan* 61, p. 37b.
21 There is an account of the analogous situation as prescribed in the regulations of the succeeding Qing dynasty in Cammann (1952) and a survey of the less tidy evidence for real practice in that same period, based on pictorial representation and surviving garments, in Wilson (1986).
22 Shen Defu, vol. 1, p. 20.
23 *Tian shui bing shan lu*, pp. 136a–154b.
24 Zhang Han, p. 140.
25 Tian Yiheng, vol. 2, pp. 604 (dwellings), 674 (singsong girls) and vol. 1, p. 74 ('Han-dynasty brocade').
26 Wakeman (1985), vol. 1, p. 95, n. 24.
27 Elliott (1986), pp. 90–1.
28 Tian Yiheng, vol. 1, pp. 158 and 162.
29 Mote (1977).
30 Beattie (1979), p. 44.
31 Wang Shixiang (1985), p. 15, the translation modified from that in the English edition of 1986.
32 Wang Daokun B, p. 7a.
33 *Ju jia bi yong shi lei quan ji, juan* 4, p. 3a.
34 Tian Yiheng, vol. 3, pp. 1107–36.
35 Ibid., vol. 1, p. 111.
36 He Liangjun, p. 315.
37 Huang (1981), p. 138.
38 Burke (1982).
39 Goldthwaite (1987), p. 166.
40 Cannadine (1982).
41 Tanaka (1985).
42 Zhang Dai, p. 75.
43 Wakeman (1985); Beattie (1979); Rawski (1985).
44 Quoted in Beattie (1979), p. 19.
45 e.g. Huang Wantang (1985), pp. 159–96, 'On the Question of Ming Aristocratic Estate Landholding'.
46 Boxer (1953), p. 107, chapter VIII of da Cruz's *Tractado* of 1556.
47 Wakeman (1985), p. 338.
48 Huang Renyu (1974).
49 Stone (1986), p. 131.

50 Wu Qizhen (active 1635–1677), translated in Chin and Hsü (1981), p. 22.
51 Shen Defu, vol. 3, p. 653.
52 Shen Defu, vol. 3, p. 664.
53 Wen Zhenheng, p. 11.

CONCLUSION

1 Franke (1968).
2 Sung (1966).
3 Handlin (1983).
4 Brook (1988b).
5 Peterson (1979), p. 155, quoted in Wakeman (1985), vol. 1, p. 644.
6 Li and Watt (1987).
7 Appadurai (1986), pp. 36–9 speaks highly of Sombart. There is, however, a disturbing undercurrent to the whole question of the 'origin of modernity' in his writing, in his acquiescence in the uses to which his identification of a 'modern', 'Jewish' commercial ethos were put by National Socialist polemic.
8 Mukerji (1983), p. 20.
9 e.g. Grant McCracken, *Culture and Consumption: New Approaches to the Symbolic Character of Consumer Goods and Activities* (Bloomington and Indianapolis, 1988), depends heavily on Mukerji and is quite at ease with the nature of 'materialism' as a purely Western concept.
10 Gernet (1985), pp. 203–4.
11 Bell (1947).
12 Mukerji (1983), pp. 170–9.
13 Burke (1986), pp. 242–3 quotes Marc Bloch's definition of two kinds of historical comparison, between things fundamentally alike and things fundamentally unalike. Italy/Netherlands is the former type; Italy/Japan is the latter. However, none of the terms of a comparison present themselves as natural objects, and we can legitimately wonder at what level of analogy similarities cease to matter. At the level of comparison with China, 'Europe' may be one, but take a closer look at 'Italy' and a new level of comparanda presents itself.
14 Quoted in Stone (1986), p. 19. For those writers like Guazzo and Peacham who were contemporaries of Wen Zhenheng, 'circumstances' were an indispensable component of 'gentility'.
15 Hoppit (1987). McKendrick et al. (1982), pp. 14–20.
16 Wallerstein (1974).

Bibliography of primary sources

Chen Hongmo (1474-1555), *Zhi shi yu wen*, preface dated 1521, Yuan Ming shiliao biji cong kan edn (Beijing, 1984)

Chen Jiru (1558-1639), *Ni gu lu*, completed before 1620, Meishu congshu 1 ji 10 ji (Shanghai, 1928)

Da Ming hui dian, preface dated 1587, Dongnan shubaoshe facsimile edn, 5 vols (Taibei, 1963)

Feng Mengzhen (1546-1605), *Kuai xue tang ji*, 1616 edn

Gao Lian, (fl. 1580-1600), *Yan xian qing shang jian*, compiled 1591, Meishu congshu 3 ji 10 ji (Shanghai, 1928)

Gu Yuanqing (1487-1565), *Shi you tu zan*, Shuo fu xu 1646 edn, diao 36

He Liangjun (1509-1562), *Si you zhai cong shuo*, preface dated 1569, Yuan Ming shiliao biji cong kan edn, second edn, (Beijing, 1983)

Jiang Shaoshu (fl. *c*.1640-1680), *Yun shi zhai bi tan*, Congshu jicheng chu bian edn, (Shanghai, 1935-7)

Ju jia bi yong shi lei quan ji, 10 juan, Jiajing period (1522-1566) edn, in the library of the Institute of Literature, CASS, Beijing (046 7337 (1-5))

Li Yangong and Hao Jie, *Riben kao*, Wanli period (1573-1620), Zhongwai jiaotong shiji cong kan (Beijing, 1983)

Liu Tong and Yu Yizheng, *Di jing jing wu lüe*, preface dated 1635, Beijing guji chubanshe edn, (Beijing, 1980)

Ming shi, completed 1739, Zhonghua shuju edn, 28 vols (Beijing, 1974)

Shen Bang (fl. 1567-1596), *Wan shu za ji*, compiled 1593, Beijing guji chubanshe edn, (Beijing, 1980)

Shen Defu (1578-1642), *Wanli ye huo bian*, preface dated 1606 with continuation of 1619, Yuan Ming shiliao biji cong kan edn, second edn 3 vols (Beijing, 1980)

Shi qu bao ji, completed 1745, Guoli Gugong Bowuyuan facsimile edn (Taibei, 1970)

Shi qu bao ji xu bian, completed 1793, Guoli Gugong Bowuyuan facsimile edn, (Taibei, 1970)

Si ku quan shu zong mu ti yao, abbreviated from the *Si ku quan shu zong mu* of 1782, Commercial Press punctuated edn, 4 vols (Shanghai, 1933)

Sun Chengze (1593–1675), *Tian fu guang ji*, preface dated 1671, Beijing guji chubanshe edn, 2 vols (Beijing, 1982)

Tan Qian (1591–1657), *Bei you lu*, completed 1656, Qingdai biji shiliao cong kan, second edn, (Beijing, 1980)

Tian Yiheng (1524–?1574), *Liuqing ri zha*, preface dated 1573, Gudi an zang Ming Qing zhanggu cong kan edn, 3 vols (Shanghai, 1985)

Tian shui bing shan lu, Zhou Shilin ed., *Zhi bu zu zhai congshu* edn, preface dated 1737

Tu Long (1542–1605), *Qi ju qi fu jian*, Meishu congshu 2 ji 9 ji (Shanghai, 1928)

Wang Daokun A (1525–1593), *Tai han fu mo*, preface dated 1591, Late Ming edn, Hangzhou University Library

Wang Daokun B, *Nian ping yu*, Shui bian lin xia congshu edn, Suzhou Municipal Library

Wang Qi (1433–1499), *Yu yuan za ji*, preface dated 1500, Yuan Ming shiliao biji cong kan edn, (Beijing, 1984)

Wen Zhenheng (1585–1645), *Zhang wu zhi jiao zhu*, compiled 1615–20, Jiangsu kexue jishu chubanshe edn, annotations by Chen Zhi, Yang Zhaobo ed. (Nanjing, 1984)

Ye Mengzhu (fl. mid-17th c.), *Yue shi bian*, completed *c*.1693, Shanghai guji chubanshe edn (Shanghai, 1981)

Ying lie zhuan, Baowentang shudian edn (Beijing, 1981)

Zhan Jingfeng (*juren* 1567), *Dongtu xuan lan bian*, preface dated 1591, Meishu congshu 5 ji 1 ji, Yiwen yinshuguan edn (Taibei, 1975)

Zhang Dai (1597–?1684), *Tao'an meng yi*, written before 1665, Xi hu shu she edn (Hangzhou, 1982)

Zhang Han (1511–1593), *Song chuang meng yu*, preface dated 1593, Yuan Ming shiliao biji cong kan edn (Beijing, 1985)

Zhang Yingwen (fl. 1530–1594), *Qing bi cang*, preface dated 1595, Meishu congshu 1 ji 8 ji (Shanghai, 1928)

Bibliography of secondary literature

Alsop (1982): Joseph Alsop, *The Rare Art Traditions: The History of Art Collecting and its Linked Phenomena* (New York, 1982)

Appadurai (1986): Arjun Appadurai, 'Introduction: Commodities and the Politics of Value', in Arjun Appadurai, ed., *The Social Life of Things: Commodities in Cultural Perspective* (Cambridge, 1986), pp. 3-63

Atwell (1982): William S. Atwell, 'International Bullion Flows and the Chinese Economy circa 1530-1650', *Past and Present*, 92 (1982), 68-90

Balazs/Hervouet (1978): *A Sung Bibliography (Bibliographie des Sung)*, initiated by Etienne Balazs, edited by Yves Hervouet (Hong Kong, 1978)

Barnhart (1983): Richard Barnhart, 'The "Wild and Heterodox School" of Ming Painting', in Susan Bush and Christian Murck, eds, *Theories of the Arts in China* (Princeton, 1983), pp. 365-96

Bauer and Haupt (1976): Rotrud Bauer and Herbert Haupt, 'Das Kunstkammerinventar Kaiser Rudolfs II, 1607-1611', *Jahrbuch der kunsthistorischen Sammlungen in Wien*, 72 (1976)

Baxandall (1985): Michael Baxandall, *Patterns of Intention: On the Historical Explanation of Pictures* (New Haven, 1985)

Beattie (1979): Hilary J. Beattie, *Land and Lineage in China: a Study of T'ung-ch'eng County, Anhwei, in the Ming and Ch'ing Dynasties* (Cambridge, 1979)

Bell (1947): Quentin Bell, *On Human Finery* (London, 1947)

Beurdeley (1966): Michel Beurdeley, *The Chinese Collector Through the Centuries: from the Han to the 20th Century* (Rutland, Vt., and Tokyo, 1966)

Binford (1962): Lewis Binford, 'Archaeology as Anthropology', *American Antiquity*, 28.2 (1962), 217-26

Bonnaffée (1902): Edmond Bonnaffée, *Etudes sur l'art et la curiosité* (Paris, 1902)

Bourdieu (1984): Pierre Bourdieu, *Distinction: A Social Critique of the Judgement of Taste*, trans. Richard Nice (London, 1984)

Boxer (1953): C.R. Boxer, ed., *South China in the Sixteenth Century*, The Hakluyt Society, Second Series, Vol. 106 (London, 1953)

Brook (1981): Timothy Brook, 'The Merchant Network in 16th Century China', *Journal of the Economic and Social History of the Orient*, 24 (1981), 165–214

Brook (1988a): Timothy Brook, 'Censorship in Eighteenth Century China: A View from the Book Trade', *Canadian Journal of History*, 23 (1988) 177–96

Brook (1988b): Timothy Brook, *Geographical Sources of Ming*–Qing History, Michigan Monographs in Chinese Studies 58 (Ann Arbor, 1988)

Burke (1982): Peter Burke, 'Conspicuous Consumption in Seventeenth-Century Italy', *Kwartalnik Historii Kultury Materialnej*, (1982), 43–56

Burke (1986): Peter Burke, *The Italian Renaissance, Culture and Society in Italy*, rev. edn (Cambridge, 1986)

Bush (1971): Susan Bush, *The Chinese Literati on Painting: Su Shih (1037–1101) to Tung Ch'i-ch'ang (1555–1636)*, Harvard–Yenching Institute Studies 27 (Cambridge, Mass., 1971)

Bush and Murck (1983): Susan Bush and Christian Murck, eds, *Theories of the Arts in China* (Princeton, 1983)

Bush and Shih (1985): Susan Bush and Hsio-yen Shih, *Early Chinese Texts on Painting* (Cambridge, Mass., and London, 1985)

Cahill (1976): James Cahill, 'Style as Idea in Ming-Ch'ing Painting', in M. Meisner and R. Murphy, eds, *The Mozartian Historian* (Berkeley, 1976), pp. 137–56

Cahill (1978): James Cahill, *Parting at the Shore: Chinese Painting of the Early and Middle Ming Dynasty, 1368–1560* (New York and Tokyo, 1978)

Cahill (1982): James Cahill, *The Distant Mountains: Chinese Painting of the Late Ming Dynasty, 1670–1644* (New York and Tokyo, 1982)

Cai Guoliang (1984): Cai Guoliang, *Jin ping mei kaozheng yu yanjiu* (Xi'an, 1984)

Cammann (1952): Schuyler Cammann, *China's Dragon Robes* (New York, 1952)

Cannadine (1982): David Cannadine, 'The Transformation of Civic Ritual in Modern Britain: The Colchester Oyster Feast', *Past and Present*, 94 (1982), 107–30

Cartier (1981): M. Cartier, 'Les importations des métaux monetaires en Chine: essai sur la conjoncture chinoise', *Annales*, 36.3 (1981), 454–66

Chang Bide (1979): Chang Bide, *Shuo fu kao* (Taibei, 1979)

Chaves (1983): Jonathan Chaves, 'The Panoply of Images: A Reconsideration of the Literary Theory of the Kung-an School', in Susan Bush and Christian Murck, eds, *Theories of the Arts in China* (Princeton, 1983), pp. 341–64

Chen Meilin (1986): Chen Meilin, 'Shi lun zaju "Nü zhen guan" he chuanqi "Yu zan ji"', *Wenxue yichan* (1986, no. 1), 79–87

Chen Shiqi (1955): Chen Shiqi, 'Mingdai gongjiang zhidu', *Lishi yanjiu* (1955, no. 6), 61–88

Chin and Hsü (1981): Sandi Chin and Cheng-chi (Ginger) Hsü, 'Anhui

Merchant Culture and Patronage' in James Cahill, ed., *Shadows of Mt Huang: Chinese Painting and Printing of the Anhui School* (Berkeley, 1981)

Ci yuan (1979): *Ci yuan*, rev. Shangwu yinshuguan edn, 4 vols (Beijing, 1979)

Clapp (1975): Anne de Coursey Clapp, *Wen Cheng-ming: The Ming Artist and Antiquity*, Artibus Asiae Supplementum 34 (Ascona, 1975)

Clifford (1988): Helen Clifford, *Parker and Wakelin: A Study of an 18th Century Goldsmithing Business with Particular Reference to the Garrard Ledgers, c.1760–1776*, unpublished Ph.D dissertation, Royal College of Art, London, 1988

Clunas (1984a): Craig Clunas, 'Ivory and the "Scholars' Taste"', in William Watson, ed., *Chinese Ivories from the Shang to the Qing* (London, 1984)

Clunas (1984b): Craig Clunas, *Chinese Export Watercolours*, Victoria and Albert Museum Far Eastern Series (London, 1984)

Clunas (1986): Craig Clunas, 'Object of the Month: Song Dynasty Jade Brush Washer', *Orientations*, 17.10 (1986), 32–4

Clunas (1987a): Craig Clunas, 'Some Literary Evidence for Gold and Silver Vessels in the Ming Period (1368–1644)', in Michael Vickers and Julian Raby, eds, *Pots and Pans: a Colloquium on Precious Metals and Ceramics*, Oxford Studies in Islamic Art 3 (Oxford, 1987), pp. 83–7

Clunas (1987b): Craig Clunas, 'Ming Jade Carvers and their Customers', *Transactions of the Oriental Ceramic Society*, 50 (1985–6), 69–85

Clunas (1988a): Craig Clunas, *Chinese Furniture*, Victoria and Albert Museum Far Eastern Series (London, 1988)

Clunas (1988b): Craig Clunas, 'Books and Things; Ming Literary Culture and Material Culture', in Frances Wood, ed., *Chinese Studies*, British Library Occasional Papers 10 (London, 1988), pp. 136–43

Contag and Wang (1940): Victoria Contag and Wang Chi-Ch'üan, *Maler- und Sammler-Stempel aus der Ming- und Ch'ing-zeit* (Shanghai, 1940)

Cribb (1977): J.E. Cribb, 'Some Hoards of Spanish Coins of the Seventeenth Century Found in Fukien Province, China', *Coin Hoards*, 3 (1977) 180–4

David (1937): Sir Percival David, 'A Commentary on Ju Ware', *Transactions of the Oriental Ceramic Society*, 14 (1936–7), 18–69

David (1971): Sir Percival David, *Chinese Connoisseurship: The Ko Ku Yao Lun* (London, 1971)

D'Elia (1942): Pasquale M. D'Elia, S.J. ed., *Fonti Ricciane . . .*, 3 vols (Rome, 1942)

DeWoskin (1983): Kenneth DeWoskin, 'Early Chinese Music and the Origins of Aesthetic Terminology', in Susan Bush and Christian Murck, eds, *Theories of the Arts in China* (Princeton, 1983), pp. 187–214

Dillon (1976): Michael Dillon, *A History of the Porcelain Industry in Jingdezhen* unpublished Ph.D. dissertation, University of Leeds, 1976

DMB: L. Carrington Goodrich and Chaoying Fang, eds, *Dictionary of Ming Biography*, 2 vols (New York and London, 1976)

Douglas and Isherwood (1979): Mary Douglas and Baron Isherwood, *The World of Goods: An Anthropologist's Perspective* (New York, 1979)

Dubosc (1975): Jean-Pierre Dubosc, 'A Letter and a Fan Painting by Ch'iu

Ying', *Archives of Asian Art*, 38 (1974–5), 108–12

ECCP: Arthur W. Hummel, ed., *Eminent Chinese of the Ch'ing Period* (New York, 1943)

Eight Dynasties (1980): *Eight Dynasties of Chinese Painting: The Collections of the Nelson Gallery – Atkins Museum, Kansas City, and the Cleveland Museum of Art*, ed. Sally W. Goodfellow, with essays by Wai-kam Ho, Sherman E. Lee, Laurence Sickman and Marc F. Wilson (Cleveland, 1980)

Elliott (1986): J.H. Elliott, *The Count – Duke of Olivares: The Statesman in an Age of Decline* (New Haven and London, 1986)

Evans (1973): R.J.W. Evans, *Rudolf II and his World: A Study in Intellectual History* (Oxford, 1973)

Evans (1979): R.J.W. Evans, *The Making of the Habsburg Monarchy 1550–1700* (Oxford, 1979)

Fairbank, Reischauer and Craig (1973); John K. Fairbank, Edwin O. Reischauer and Albert M. Craig, *East Asia: Tradition and Transformation* (Boston, 1973)

Fong (1977): Wen Fong, 'Rivers and Mountains after Snow (Chiang-shan hsüeh-chi), Attributed to Wang Wei (A.D. 699–759)', *Archives of Asian Art*, 30 (1976–7), 6–33

Forty (1986): Adrian Forty, *Objects of Desire: Design and Society 1750–1900* (London, 1986)

Franke (1968): Wolfgang Franke, *An Introduction to the Sources of Ming History* (Kuala Lumpur and Singapore, 1968)

Fu Xihua (1980): Fu Xihua, ed., *Zhongguo gudian wenxue banhua xuanji*, 2 vols (Shanghai, 1980)

Gernet (1985): Jacques Gernet, *China and the Christian Impact. A Conflict of Cultures* (Cambridge, 1985)

Gillman (1984): Derek Gillman, 'A Source of Rhinoceros Horn Cups in the Late Ming Dynasty', *Orientations*, 15.12 (1984), 10–17

Goldthwaite (1987): Richard Goldthwaite, 'The Empire of Things: Consumer Demand in Renaissance Italy', in F.W. Kent and Patricia Simons, with J.C. Eade, eds, *Patronage, Art and Society in Renaissance Italy* (Canberra and Oxford, 1987)

Guazzo (1586): *The Civil Conversation of Stefano Guazzo . . .* (London, 1586)

Hanan (1988): Patrick Hanan, *The Invention of Li Yu* (Cambridge, Mass., and London, 1988)

Handlin (1983): Joanna F. Handlin, *Action in Late Ming Thought: The Reorientation of Lü K'un and other Scholar-Officials*, (Berkeley, Los Angeles and London, 1983)

Hardie (1988): Ji Cheng, *The Craft of Gardens*, trans. Alison Hardie (New Haven, 1988)

Harte (1976): N.B. Harte, 'State Control of Dress and Social Change in Pre-industrial England', in D.C. Coleman and A.H. John, eds, *Trade, Government and Economy in Pre-industrial England* (London, 1976), pp. 132–65

Ho (1976): Wai-kam Ho, 'Tung Ch'i-ch'ang's New Orthodoxy and the

Southern School Theory', in Christian F. Murck, ed., *Artists and Traditions* (Princeton, 1976), pp. 113–30

Hoppit (1987): Julian Hoppit, 'The Luxury Debate in England, 1660–1760', paper delivered at the Workshop on Design, Commerce and the Luxury Trades in the Seventeenth and Eighteenth Centuries, Victoria and Albert Museum, 31.10.1987

Huang (1981): Ray Huang, *1587 A Year of no Significance: the Ming Dynasty in Decline* (New Haven and London, 1981)

Huang Renyu (1974): Huang Renyu, 'Cong "San Yan" kan wan Ming shangren', *Xianggang zhongwen daxue zhongguo wenhua yanjiusuo xuebao*, 7.1 (1974), 133–54

Huang Wantang (1985): Huang Wantang, *Ming shi guan jian* (Ji'nan, 1985)

Hucker (1971): Charles O. Hucker, 'Su-chou and the Agents of Wei Chung-hsien', in his *Two Studies in Ming History*, Michigan Papers in Chinese Studies 12 (Ann Arbor, 1971), pp. 41–83

Hucker (1985): Charles O. Hucker, *A Dictionary of Official Titles in Imperial China* (Stanford, 1985)

Isobe Akira (1980): Isobe Akira, 'Minmatsu ni okeru "Seiyūki" no shutaiteki juyōsō ni kansuru kenkyū', *Shukan toyogaku*, 40 (1980), 50–63

Jiangsu (1987): Jiangsu sheng Huai'an xian bowuguan, 'Huai'an xian Mingdai Wang Zhen fu fu hezang mu qingli jianbao', *Wenwu* (1987, no. 3), 1–15

Jones (1990): Mark Jones, ed., *Fake? The Art of Deception*, exh. cat., British Museum (London, 1990)

Jörg (1982): C.J.A. Jörg, *Porcelain and the Dutch China Trade* (The Hague, 1982)

Kerr (1990): Rose Kerr, *Later Chinese Bronzes*, Victoria and Albert Museum Far Eastern Series (London, 1990)

Klein and Zerner (1966): R. Klein and R. Zerner, *Italian Art 1500–1600: Sources and Documents*, Sources and documents in the history of art series (Englewood Cliffs, 1966)

Klose (1983): Wolfgang and Petra Klose, 'Nachricht über einen chinesischen Raubdruck des 16. Jahrhunderts', *Aus dem Antiquariat. Monatliche Beilage zum Borsenblatt für den Deutschen Buchhandel – Frankfurter Ausgabe* (29.4.1983), 131–2

Kopytoff (1986): Igor Kopytoff, 'The Cultural Biography of Things: Commoditization as Process', in Arjun Appadurai, ed., *The Social Life of Things* (Cambridge, 1986), pp. 64–91

Kuki (1930): Kuki Shūzō, 'The Structure of *iki*', an unpublished translation of *Iki no kōzō*, by John Clark, typescript deposited in the National Art Library, Victoria and Albert Museum. Translation copyright John Clark (1978)

Laing (1968): Ellen Johnston Laing, 'Real or Ideal: The Problem of the "Elegant Gathering in the Western Garden" in Chinese Historical and Art Historical Records', *Journal of the American Oriental Society*, 88 (1968), 419–33

Laing (1975): Ellen Johnston Laing, 'Chou Tan-ch'üan is Chou Shih-ch'en.

A Report on a Ming Dynasty Potter, Painter and Entrepreneur', *Oriental Art*, NS 21.3 (1975), 224–30

Laing (1979): Ellen Johnston Laing, 'Ch'iu Ying's Three Patrons', *Ming Studies*, 8 (Spring 1979) 49–56

Lawton (1988): Thomas Lawton, 'An Imperial Legacy Revisited: Bronze Vessels from the Qing Palace Collection', *Asian Art*, 1 (1987-8), 51–79

Ledderose (1979a): Lothar Ledderose, *Mi Fu and the Classical Tradition of Chinese Calligraphy* (Princeton, 1979)

Ledderose (1979b): Lothar Ledderose, 'Some Observations on the Imperial Art Collection in China', *Transactions of the Oriental Ceramic Society*, 43 (1978-9), 33–46

Ledderose (1986): Lothar Ledderose, 'Chinese Calligraphy: Its Aesthetic Dimension and Social Function', *Orientations*, 17.10 (October 1986), 35–50

Legge (1885): James Legge, *The Sacred Books of China. The Texts of Confucianism Parts III and IV*, Sacred Books of the East, 27 and 28 (Oxford, 1885)

Levy (1966): Howard S. Levy, *A Feast of Mist and Flowers: The Gay Quarters of Nanking at the End of the Ming* (Yokohama, 1966)

Lévy (1985): *Fleur en fiole d'or (Jin ping mei cihua)*, trans. André Lévy, 2 vols (Paris, 1985)

Li and Watt (1987): Chu-tsing Li and James C. Y. Watt, eds, *The Chinese Scholar's Studio: Artistic Life in the Late Ming Period*, (New York, 1987)

Li Huibing (1986): Li Huibing, '"Cha jing" yu Tangdai ciqi', *Gugong bowuyuan yuankan* (1986, no. 3), 55–8

Li Junjie (1987): Li Junjie, 'Zhe shan ji qi shanmian yishu', *Shanghai bowuyuan jikan*, 4 (1987), 101–10

Liu Bohan and Wang Jieyun (1981): Liu Bohan and Wang Jieyun, eds, *Ming Qing zibenzhuyi mengya wenti yanjiu lunwen ji* (Shanghai, 1981)

Liu Dunzhen (1979): Liu Dunzhen, *Suzhou gudian yuanlin* (Nanjing, 1979)

Lo (1988): Andrew Lo, 'Dice, Dominoes and Card Games in Chinese Literature; A Preliminary Survey', in Frances Wood, ed., *Chinese Studies*, British Library Occasional Papers 10 (London, 1988), pp. 127–35

Long Qian'an (1985): Long Qian'an, *Song Yuan yuyan cidian* (Shanghai, 1985)

Lovell (1973): Hin-cheung Lovell, *An Annotated Bibliography of Chinese Painting Catalogues and Related Texts*, Michigan Papers in Chinese Studies 16 (Ann Arbor, 1973)

Lovell (1976): Hin-cheung Lovell, 'Yen-sou's "Plum Blossoms": Speculations on Style, Date and Artist's Identity', *Archives of Asian Art*, 29 (1975-6), 59–79

Lowenthal (1985): David Lowenthal, *The Past is a Foreign Country* (Cambridge, 1985)

Lu Yuanjun (1977): Lu Yuanjun, *Shuo yuan jin zhu jin yi* (Taibei, 1977)

Lynn (1983): Richard John Lynn, 'Alternate Routes to Self-Realization in Ming Theories of Poetry', in Susan Bush and Christian Murck, eds, *Theories of the Arts in China* (Princeton, 1983), pp. 317–40

Mao (1975): *Twelve Towers: Short Stories by Li Yü*, retold by Nathan Mao (Hong Kong, 1975)

Mather (1976): Richard B. Mather, *Shih-shuo hsin-yu: A New Account of Tales of the World* (Minneapolis, 1976)

McDermott (1981): Joseph P. McDermott, 'Bondservants in the T'ai-hu Basin During the Late Ming: A Case of Mistaken Identities', *Journal of Asian Studies*, 90 (1981), 675–701

McDermott (1985): Joseph P. McDermott, 'The Huichou Sources: A Key to the Social and Economic History of Late Imperial China', *Asian Cultural Studies*, International Christian University Publication III-A, 15 (1985), 49–66

McKendrick et al. (1982): Neil McKendrick, John Brewer and J.H. Plumb, *The Birth of a Consumer Society. The Commercialization of Eighteenth-century England* (London, 1982)

Momigliano (1950): Arnaldo Momigliano, 'Ancient History and the Antiquarian', *Journal of the Courtauld and Warburg Institutes*, 13 (1950), 285–315

Moss (1983): Paul Moss, *Documentary Chinese Works of Art in Scholar's Taste* (London, 1983)

Mote (1977): Frederick W. Mote, 'Yüan and Ming', in K.C. Chang, ed., *Food in Chinese Culture* (New Haven and London, 1977), pp. 195–257

Mote and Twitchett (1988): Frederick W. Mote and Dennis Twitchett, eds, *The Cambridge History of China*, Volume 7: *The Ming Dynasty, 1368–1644,* Part I (Cambridge, 1988)

Mote and Chu (1989): Frederick W. Mote and Hung-lam Chu, *Calligraphy and the East Asian Book* (Boston and Shaftesbury, 1989)

Moule (1950): A.C. Moule, 'A Version of the Book of Vermilion Fish', *T'oung Pao*, 39 (1950), 1–82

MRZJ: *Ming ren zhuan ji ziliao suoyin*, compiled by Taiwan zhongyang tushuguan, reprinted Zhonghua shuju edn (Beijing, 1987)

Mukerji (1983): Chandra Mukerji, *From Graven Images: Patterns of Modern Materialism* (New York, 1983)

Murck (1976): Christian F. Murck, 'Introduction', in Christian F. Murck, ed., *Artists and Traditions; Uses of the Past in Chinese Culture* (Princeton, 1976), pp. xi–xxi

Muthesius (1988): Stefan Muthesius, 'Why Do We Buy Old Furniture? Aspects of the Antique in Britain 1870–1910', *Art History*, 11 (1988), 231–54

Needham (1956): Joseph Needham, with the research assistance of Wang Ling, *Science and Civilisation in China,* Volume 2: *History of Scientific Thought* (Cambridge, 1956)

Needham (1986): Joseph Needham, with the collaboration of Lu Gwei-djen, *Science and Civilisation in China,* Volume 6: *Biology and Biological Technology,* Part I: *Botany* (Cambridge, 1986)

Nienhauser (1986): William R. Nienhauser, Jr, ed., *The Indiana Companion to Traditional Chinese Literature* (Bloomington, 1986)

Owyoung (1982): Stephen D. Owyoung, 'The Huang Lin Collection',

Archives of Asian Art, 35 (1982), 55-70

Peacham (1622): Henry Peacham, *The Compleat Gentleman* . . . (London, 1622)

Peng Xinwei (1958): Peng Xinwei, *Zhongguo huobi shi* (Shanghai, 1958)

Peterson (1979): Willard Peterson, *Bitter Gourd: Fang I-chih and the Impetus for Intellectual Change* (New Haven and London, 1979)

Poor (1965): 'Notes on the Sung Dynasty Archaeological Catalogues' *Archives of the Chinese Art Society of America*, 19 (1965), 33-43

Rawski (1985): Evelyn S. Rawski, 'Economic and Social Foundations of Late Imperial Culture', in David Johnson, Andrew J. Nathan and Evelyn S. Rawski, eds, *Popular Culture in Late Imperial China* (Berkeley, Los Angeles and London, 1985), pp. 3-33

Rawson (1987): Jessica Rawson, *Chinese Bronzes: Art and Ritual* (London, 1987)

Rawson (forthcoming): Jessica Rawson, 'Artifact Lineages in Chinese History', in W.D. Kingery and S. Lubar, eds, *Learning from Things: Working Papers on Material Culture* (forthcoming)

Riely (1975): Celia Carrington Riely, 'Tung Ch'i-ch'ang's Ownership of Huang Kung-wang's "Dwelling in the Fuchun Mountains"', *Archives of Asian Art*, 28 (1974-5), 57-68

Ruitenbeek (1989): K. Ruitenbeek, *The Lu Ban Jing; A Fifteenth-Century Chinese Carpenter's Manual*, unpublished Ph.D. dissertation, University of Leiden, 1989

St George (1988): Robert Blair St George, ed., *Material Life in America 1600-1860* (Boston, 1988)

Sayer (1951):, Geoffrey R. Sayer, *Ching-tê-chên T'ao Lu, or the Potteries of China* (London, 1951)

Schafer (1963): Edward H. Schafer, *The Golden Peaches of Samarkand: A Study of T'ang Exotics* (Berkeley and Los Angeles, 1963)

Schama (1987): Simon Schama, *The Embarrassment of Riches: An Interpretation of Dutch Culture in the Golden Age* (London, 1987)

Shanghai (1972): Shanghai shi wenwu guanli daoguzu, 'Shanghai faxian yipi Ming Chenghua nianjian keyin de changben, chuanqi', *Wenwu* (1972, no. 11), 67

Shearman (1967): John Shearman, *Mannerism* (London, 1967)

Siggstedt (1982): Mette Siggstedt, 'The Life and Paintings of a Ming Professional Artist', *Bulletin of the Museum of Far Eastern Antiquities, Stockholm*, 54 (1982), 1-240

Sirén (1958): Osvald Sirén, *Chinese Painting: Leading Masters and Principles*, 7 vols (London, 1958)

Sonenscher (1989): Michael Sonenscher, *Work and Wages: Natural Law, Politics and the Eighteenth-century French Trades* (Cambridge, 1989)

Spence (1990): Jonathan D. Spence, *The Search for Modern China* (London, 1990)

Stanley-Baker (1986): Joan Stanley-Baker, 'Forgeries in Chinese Painting', *Oriental Art*, NS 32 (1986), 54-66

Stone (1986): Lawrence Stone and Jeanne C. Fawtier Stone, *An Open Elite?*

England 1540-1880, abridged edn (Oxford, 1986)

Su Huaping (1977): Su Huaping, 'Wuxian Dongtingshan Ming mu chutu de Wen Zhengming shuhua', *Wenwu* (1977, no. 3, 65-8

Sung (1966): Sung Ying-hsing, *T'ien-Kung K'ai-Wu: Chinese Technology in the Seventeenth Century*, trans. E-tu Zen Sun and Shiou-Chuan Sun (University Park and London, 1966)

Taam (1935): Cheuk-woon Taam, *The Development of Chinese Libraries Under the Ch'ing Dynasty, 1644-1911* (Shanghai, 1935)

Tadao (1970): Sakai Tadao, 'Confucianism and Popular Educational Works', in Wm. Theodore de Bary, ed., *Self and Society in Ming Thought*, Columbia University Studies in Oriental Culture 4 (New York and London, 1970), pp. 331-66

Tanaka (1985): Tanaka Issei, 'The Social and Historical Context of Ming – Ch'ing Local Drama', in David Johnson, Andrew J. Nathan and Evelyn S. Rawski, eds, *Popular Culture in Late Imperial China* (Berkeley, Los Angeles and London, 1985), pp. 143-60

Tanikawa (1980-1): Tanikawa Tetsuzo, 'The Aesthetics of Chanoyu: Parts 1-4', *Chanoyu Quarterly*, 23-7 (1980-1) [a translation and adaptation of the same author's *Cha no bigaku* (Tokyo, 1977)]

Tilley (1990): Christopher Tilley, ed., *Reading Material Culture: Structuralism, Hermeneutics and Post-Structuralism* (Oxford, 1990)

Treager (1982): Mary Treager, *Song Ceramics* (London, 1982)

Tsang and Moss (1984): Gerard Tsang and Hugh Moss, 'Chinese Metalwork of the Hu Wenming Group', *International Asian Antiques Fair* (Hong Kong, 1984), pp. 33-68

Vandermeersch (1964): L. Vandermeersch, 'L'arrangement de fleurs en Chine', *Arts asiatiques*, 11 (1964), 79-140

van Gulik (1958): R.H. van Gulik, *Chinese Pictorial Art as Viewed by the Connoisseur*, Serie Orientale Roma 19 (Rome, 1958)

van Gulik (1968): R.H. van Gulik, *The Lore of the Chinese Lute* (Tokyo, 1968)

van Wijk (1948)): Louise E. van Wijk, 'Het Album Amicorum van Bernardus Paludanus', *Het Boek*, 29 (1948), 265-86

Wakeman (1985): Frederic Wakeman, Jr, *The Great Enterprise: The Manchu Reconstruction of Order in Seventeenth-century China*, 2 vols (Berkeley, Los Angeles and London, 1985)

Waley (1925): 'The Tsun Sheng Pa Chien, A.D. 1591, by Kao Lien, translated by Arthur Waley, with Introduction and Notes by R.L. Hobson', *Yearbook of Oriental Art and Culture* 1 (1924-5), 80-7

Wallerstein (1974): Immanuel Wallerstein, *The Modern World System*, 2 vols (New York, 1974)

Wang Shixiang (1985): Wang Shixiang, *Ming shi jiaju zhenshang* (Hong Kong, 1985)

Wang Zhongmin (1983): Wang Zhongmin, *Zhongguo shanbenshu tiyao* (Shanghai, 1983)

Ward (1977): Barbara E. Ward, 'Readers and Audiences: An Exploration of the Spread of Traditional Chinese Culture', in R.K. Jain, ed., *Text and*

Context (Philadelphia, 1977), pp. 181–203

Watson (1964): *Han Fei Tzu: Basic Writings*, trans. Burton Watson (New York, 1964)

Weidner et al. (1988): Marsha Weidner, Ellen Johnston Laing, Irving Yucheng Lo, Christina Chu and James Robinson, *Views from Jade Terrace: Chinese Women Artists 1300–1912* (Indianapolis and New York, 1988)

Weiss (1988): Roberto Weiss, *The Renaissance Discovery of Classical Antiquity*, 2nd edn (Oxford, 1988)

Weng Tongwen (1979): Weng Tongwen, 'Xiang Yuanbian Qian Wen bianhao shuhua mu kao', *Soochow Journal of Chinese Art History*, 9 (1979), 157–80

Weng Tongwen (1983): Weng Tongwen, 'Xiang Yuanbian ming xia "Jiao chuang jiu lu" bian wei tanyuan', *Gu gong jikan*, 17.4 (1983), 11–26

Whitfield (1969): Roderick Whitfield, *In Pursuit of Antiquity: Chinese Paintings of the Ming and Ch'ing Dynasties from the Collection of Mr and Mrs Earl Morse* (Rutland, Vt., and Tokyo, 1969)

Whitfield (1975): Roderick Whitfield, 'Tz'u-chou Pillows with Painted Decoration', in Margaret Medley, ed., *Chinese Painting and the Decorative Style*, Percival David Foundation of Chinese Art Colloquies on Art & Archaeology in Asia 5 (London, 1975), pp. 74–94

Whitfield (1987): Roderick Whitfield, *Chinese Rare Books in the P.D.F.* (London, 1986)

Wilson (1986): Verity Wilson, *Chinese Dress*, Victoria and Albert Museum Far Eastern Series (London, 1986)

Wu Jinming (1987): Wu Jinming, 'Taicang Nanzhuancun Ming mu ji chutu guji', *Wenwu* (1987, no. 3), 19–22

Wylie (1922): Alexancder Wylie, *Notes on Chinese Literature* (1867; Shanghai, 1922)

Xie Guozhen (1980): Xie Guozhen, ed., *Mingdai shehui jingji shiliao xuanbian*, 3 vols (Fuzhou, 1980)

Xie Guozhen (1981): Xie Guozhen, *Ming Qing biji tancong* (Shanghai, 1981)

Xu Zhengji (1988): Xu Zhengji, 'Zheng Banqiao de run ge', *Meishuxue*, 2 (1988), 157–70

Yamane (1964): Yamane Yukio, *Nihon genson Mindai chihō-shi denki sakuin-kō* (Tokyo, 1964)

Yang (1952): Lien-sheng Yang, *Money and Credit in China* (Cambridge, Mass., 1952)

Yang (1957): Lien-sheng Yang, 'Economic Justification for Spending – An Uncommon Idea in Traditional China', *Harvard Journal of Asiatic Studies*, 20 (1957), 36–52

Yang Jinding (1987): Yang Jinding, ed., *Zhongguo wenhuashi cidian* (Hangzhou, 1987)

Yang Xin (1989): Yang Xin, 'Shangpin jingji, shifeng yu shuhua zuowei', *Wenwu* (1989, no. 10), 87–94

Ye Zuofu (1989): Ye Zuofu, 'Sichuan Tongliang Ming Zhang Shupei fu fu mu', *Wenwu* (1989, no. 7), 43–7

Yu (1983): Pauline Yu, 'Formal Distinctions in Chinese Literary Theory', in Susan Bush and Christian Murck, eds, *Theories of the Arts in China* (Princeton, 1983), pp. 27-56

Yu Jianhua (1981): Yu Jianhua, ed., *Zhongguo meishujia renming cidian* (Shanghai, 1981)

Yu Jianhua (1986): Yu Jianhua, ed., *Zhongguo hualun leibian*, 2 vols, 2nd edn (Beijing, 1986)

ZGCSZL: *Zhongguo congshu zonglu*, 3 vols (Shanghai, 1982)

Zhang Huijian (1986): Zhang Huijian, *Ming Qing Jiangsu wenren nianbiao* (Shanghai, 1986)

Zhou Gongjin (1986): Zhou Gongjin (Julie Chou-Ling), 'You jin sanshi nian lai chutu Songdai qiqi tan Songdai qi gongyi', *Gu Gong jikan*, 4 (1986), 93-104 (with English translation, pp. 1-22)

Zhu Weizheng (1987): Zhu Weizheng, *Zouchu zhong shiji*, Sixiangzhe wencong (Shanghai, 1987)

Index

agates, 33, 43, 61–2, 78, 187 n. 42
agriculture, 77, 140–2, 146, 155, 160, 166–7
almanacs, 37, 46, 118, 167
amber, 33, 47
An Guo, Ming collector, 180
Anhui province, 38, 57, 61, 66, 100, 108, 109, 162–3; Changzhou, 58; Huizhou, 62, 66, 162–3, 193 n. 13; Shexian, 61, 163; Tongcheng, 155; Xin'an, 139, 163; Xiuning, 163; Xuanzhou, 58
Appadurai, Arjun, 2, 81, 116–17, 128, 147, 169
aristocracy, 137, 141, 143, 148–9, 159, 161
art market, and forgery, 113–14; in Ming dynasty, 87–8, 100, 107, 113, 116–40 *passim*, 150, 162
art market, modern, 3, 8–9, 11, 45, 50, 64, 75, 133
artisans, 46, 60–7, 76; attitudes to, 141–7; workshop practices, 65–7
'Asiatic Society', 91

bamboo, 62, 63, 150
Bao hui lu, Records of Precious Painting, by Zhang Taijie, 112, 134
Bao Tiancheng, Ming rhinoceros horn carver, 61
Bao yan tang bi ji, 29, 35

biji, 'note-form' literature, 38, 61, 93, 96, 97, 98, 121, 154, 157, 168, 175, 179
Biondo, Flavio, 92, 96
birds, 26; parrots, 41–2, 54; turkeys, 42, 58
boats, 44
Bohemia, 151
books, 29, 48, 82, 101, 106, 118, 136; illustrated, 51–2, 135, 148, 156, 166; prices of, 132; shops, 135; of the Song period, 33, 105; storage of, 55; *see also* publishing
Bourdieu, Pierre, 2, 73, 90, 120, 169, 171
bronze coinage, 48, 128, 130, 139
bronze vessels, antique, 9, 11, 15, 18, 33, 35, 48, 81, 82, 88, 91–114 *passim*, 137; antiquarian study of, 95–100, Plate 3; as flower vases, 100, 109; forgery of, 110–11, 114, 179; as incense burners, 43, 100, 156; inlaid, 98–9; inscriptions on, 98–9, 110; from Japan, 58–9; prices of, 126, 179–81; in tombs, 101
bronze utensils, Ming dynasty, 42, 43, 44, 48, 60, 61, 62, 63, 64, 67, 72, 80, 104, 137; Song dynasty, 101; Tang dynasty, 101
brushes, 29, 38, 57–8; from Korea, 58

buildings, 41, 48, 54, 130, 132, 148-9, 150, 154, 156, 158-9; in Europe, 159
burials, 37, 56, 93, 100-1, 108-9, 120, 131, 148; grave-robbing, 93, 109; *see also* excavation, archaeological

Cai Xiang, calligrapher, 104
Cao Zhao *see Ge gu yao lun*
calligraphy, 9, 11, 14, 16, 23, 26, 29, 33, 48, 70, 82, 88, 93, 94, 104-5, 106, 107, 131, 136, 137, 176; prices of, 125-7, 177-81
Castiglione, Sabba di, 50-1, 186 n. 21
ceramics, 11, 18, 33, 38, 43, 45, 48, 49, 52, 57, 61, 66, 72-3, 80, 94, 117, 132, 143, 158, 166, 188 n. 76, 193 n. 34; Chai ware, 102, 104, 111; Chenghua ware, 61, 102, 103, 104, 137; Cizhou ware, 102; Dehua, 72; *Ding* ware, 43, 101, 102, 104, 105, 111, 115, 180, 181; Dong ware, 102; faking of, 87, 103, 110-11, 115, 181, Plate 6; *Ge* ware, 43, 61, 101, 102, 103, 105, 111, 179, 180; *Guan* ware 43, 101, 102, 103, 105, 106, 111, 180; Jian ware, 43; Jun ware, 102, 179; Korean, 102; Longquan ware, 43, 102; pillows, 60, 93; prices of, 131-2, 179-81; Ru ware, 61, 105, 111; Song dynasty, 93, 101; *shufu* ware, 102; Tang dynasty, 93; tiles, 90, 110; Xiang ware, 102; Xuande ware, 43, 61, 102, 103, 137; Yixing stoneware, 132, 136, 172; Yongle ware, 61, 102
Cha jing, Tea Classic, by Lu Yu, 89-90
Changshu, 25, 35, 176
Chen Jiru, Ming writer, 29, 31, 35, 110, 184 n. 36
Chen Ruyan, Yuan painter, 177-8
Chen Youliang, Yuan warlord, 98-9, 145
Cheng shi cong ke, Master Cheng's Collected Prints, 35
Chong ding xin shang pian, Recompiled Texts on Connoisseurship, 36

collecting, 32, 33, 35, 36, 190 n. 55; size of collections, 105-6
collectors, 21, 34, 35, 86, 95, 106-8, 124, 163
colophons, 15, 16, 85, 112, 113, 139, 174
commodity economy, 4-5, 12-13, 116-17
Confucius, 79; Confucian classics, 19, 149-50; *see also Li ji; Shu jing; Zhou li*
congshu, 10, 11, 20, 26, 29, 30, 34-6, 37, 46, 52
conspicuous consumption, 51, 156-9; in Europe, 159
'consumer society, birth of', 3, 173, 182 n. 5
Cruz, Gaspar da, 161
crystal, 33, 43

Da Ming hui dian, Collected Statutes of the Great Ming, 148, 151
Dai Song, Tang painter, 69, 111
dealers, in antiques, 88, 108, 109, 112, 133-8, 163
decoration, 43, 44, 54, 59, 71-2, 142-51; prohibitions on, 149, 152-3
Ding lu, Record of Tripods, by Yu Li, 35
Dong Qichang, Ming painter, 26-7, 70, 108, 111, 119, 125, 127, 175, 176; ownership of 'Dwelling in the Fuchun Mountains, 138-9, 181, Plate 8; of 'Rivers and Mountains after Snow', 139, 180
Dong Yuan, Five Dynasties painter, 111
Dong tian qing lu ji, Record of the Pure Registers of the Cavern Heaven, by Zhao Xigu, 9, 32, 35, 59
Dongtu xuan lan bian, Compiled Hermetic Connoisseurship of Dongtu, by Zhan Jingfeng, 123-4, 125-7, 133-5, 177-81
drama, 17, 52, 57, 76, 112, 159, 175, Plate 7

dress, 26, 29, 45, 47, 48, 55, 63, 82, 101, 105, 130-1, 145, 163, 195 n. 21; European, 51, 54, 150-1; hats, 47, 96, 151; and sumptuary laws, 148, 150, 152-5

economy, Ming, 128-30, 161-2, 167, 172-3; *see also* 'sprouts of capitalism'
enamels, cloisonné, 55, 137
eunuchs, 21, 22, 132, 133, 135, 157
Europe, early modern, 170-3
Evelyn, John, 94
examination system, 5, 15, 16, 21, 49, 118, 160, 167
excavation, archaeological, 37, 56, 59, 93, 101, 109, 120, 128; *see also* burials

factionalism, in court politics, 21-2, 23, 25, 168-9
Fan Chao, Ming writer, 155-6
Fang Yizhi, Qing writer, 168
fans, 60, 61, 65; imported from Japan, 59, 85, 137; by Wen Zheng-ming, 101
fashion, 61, 90, 163-5, 170-1
Feng Chengsu, Tang calligrapher, 180
Feng Fang, Ming writer, 110
Feng Mengzhen, Ming writer, 16-17, 136, 139, 174
festivals, 17, 85, 146, 159-60
fiction, 38, 52, 76, 118; *Shui hu zhuan*, 88; *Ying lie zhuan*, 86; *see also Jin ping mei*
fish, 26, 29, 30, 156
flower arranging, 35, 36, 44, 100
flower shops, 135
flowers, 26, 29, 105, 156; camellias, 41; Epidendrum, 20; orchids, 35
food and drink, 18, 20, 26, 33, 34, 35, 36, 45, 101, 105, 156; feasts, 49, 72, 81, 158; restaurants, 131, 155; sumptuary laws on, 151
forgery, 12, 32, 87, 109-15, 135; of bronzes, 110, 114; of calligraphy, 109, 174; of ceramics, 87, 105, 115; in Europe, 94; of Lake Tai rocks,

41; of literary texts, 29, 110; of painting, 109-14 *passim*, 177; Mat-teo Ricci on, 94
furniture, 18, 26, 35, 42-3, 44, 48, 50, 52, 63, 67, 71, 90, 145, 149, 155-6, 163, Plate 2; as dowry, 54-5; from Japan, 59; prices of, 131

games and gambling, 35, 155, 175
Gao Jigong, Ming merchant, 14
Gao Lian, Ming writer, 13-20, 28, 36, 67, 70, 81, 175, 179; as dra-matist, 17, 184 n. 36; name of studio, 83; *see also Zun sheng ba jian*
gardens, 22, 24, 26, 82, 107, 159, 184 n. 35
Ge gu yao lun, Essential Criteria of Antiquities, by Cao Zhao, 11-13, 33; on ceramics, 102; on forgery, 110
Ge zhi cong shu, Investigation of the World, 34
gender distinctions, 54-6, 154-5; *see also* women
gentry society, 160-1, 167
gold, as currency, 133; ingots, 47; jewellery, 154; vessels, 47, 61, 72, 80, 81, 149, 158
Gu Ling, Qing writer, 23, 24
Gu qi qi lu, Record of Curious Ancient Vessels, by Lu Sheng, 13, 146
Gu Yanwu, Qing writer, 168-9
Gu Yuanqing, Ming writer, 34, 36
guanxi, 'connections', 21, 119, 139, 153
Guazzo, Stefano, 51, 150
Guo Zhongshu, Five Dynasties painter, 16

Hai Rui, Ming official, 158
Han dynasty, 78, 80, 81, 82, 93, 94-5, 96, 97, 100, 110
Han Fei, Warring States philo-sopher, 141-2

Han Gan, Tang painter, 69, 111
Han Shineng, Ming collector, 107, 124
Hangzhou, 14, 16, 28, 135, 136, 139, 146, 155, 174, 175; antique market in, 136; brush-making centre, 57; as Southern Song capital, 57, 60, 87, 102
He Liangjun, Ming writer, 97, 108, 158
Hegel, Friedrich, 91
householder's manuals, 46, 155, 167; *see also Ju jia bi yong shi lei quan ji*
Hu Guangyu, Ming bronze-worker, 64
Hu Wenming, Ming bronze-worker, 62, 64, 65, 67, 147
Hu Yinglin, Ming writer, 30
Huaisu, Tang calligrapher, 181
Huang Daozhou, Ming official, 23, 24
Huang Gongwang, Yuan painter, 'Dwelling in the Fuchun Mountains', 127, 138-9, 181, Plate 8
Huang Quan, Five Dynasties painter, 179
Huang Tingjian, Song calligrapher, 104, 111
Huizong, Song emperor, 177

imperial collections, Ming dynasty, 137; Qing dynasty, 97, Plate 8; Song dynasty, 95, 111, 180, Plate 5
imperial court, 20, 21, 47, 107, 144, 152-3; politics at, 21
imperial library *see Si ku quan shu*
imports, to Ming China, 58-60, 105; from Americas, 58; from Europe, 59-60, 137; from Islamic world, 55, 110; from Japan, 42, 44, 58-9, 85, 137; from Korea, 58-9, 85; from Malacca, 58; from Tibet, 59, 137, 187 n. 42
incense, 20, 24, 25, 29, 35, 36, 44, 47, 59, 89, 190 n. 55; shops for, 135; storage of, 72
incense burners, 43, 55, 71, 72, 89

ink, 29, 33, 49, 80
inkstones, 9, 11, 20, 29, 33, 35, 36, 48, 52, 81, 105; forgery of, 110; sources of, 57
inventories, in Europe, 49; *see also Tian shui bing shan lu*
Italy, 2, 4, 50-1, 54, 78, 86, 92, 96, 126-7, 185 n. 50, 196 n. 13; architecture in, 158-9; painting in, 64, 68, 121, 122; sumptuary laws, 150
ivory, 47, 137, 149

jades, 11, 33, 43, 52, 63, 67, 78, 88, 137, 143, 149, 189 n. 37; antique, 81, 89, 93-114 *passim*; belts, 47; forgery of, 111, 114-15; by Lu Zigang, 61, 64; prices of, 126, 180; vessels, 47; storage of, 59; water-pots, 84
Japan, 4, 67, 171, 188, 196 n. 13; fans from, 85; lacquer from, 58-9; tables from, 42, 44
Jesuits, in China, 59, 93, 166, 170
Ji gu lu, Records on Collecting Antiques, by Ouyang Xiu, 95
Jiading, 175, 176; Jiading school of painters, 70, 175
Jiang Baoyun, Ming bronze-worker, 61-2
Jiang Shan, Ming officer, 158
Jianyang, 18
Jiao chuang jiu lu, Nine Records from a Banana-shaded Window, falsely attributed to Xiang Yuanbian, 29, 110
Jiaoshan, 136
Jiaxing, 62, 136
Jin ping mei, The Golden Lotus, 38-9, 72, 76, 90, 135, 156, 185 n. 52; price data in, 131, 132
Jin shi lu, 'Collection of Texts on Metal and Stone', by Zhao Mingcheng and Li Qingzhao, 95-6, 114
Jing Hao, Five Dynasties painter, 123
Jingdezhen, 38, 57, 66, 131-2
Ju jia bi bei, Necessities for the Householder, 36-7

Ju jia bi yong shi lei quan ji, Complete and Categorized Essentials for the Householder, 37–8, 58, 80, 114, 157
Juran, Five Dynasties painter, 111

Kao gu tu, Researches on Archaeology Illustrated, 95, 97, Plate 3
Kao pan yu shi, Desultory Remarks on Furnishing the Abode of the Retired Scholar, by Tu Long, 28–31, 32, 34–5, 110; sources of, 29–30
Kopytoff, Igor, 138
Korea, 58–9, 85

lacquerware, 11, 18, 48, 56, 62, 72, 136, 143; carved, 104, 106, 136, 137, 149, 155; Japanese, 58–9, 172, 187 n. 39; Song dynasty, 60, 104
landholding, 5, 20, 22, 36, 48–9, 117, 121, 142, 147, 159, 161–2, 193 n. 13
language, 49, 75–90, 158, 188 n. 4; spoken, 45, 87, 90
lanterns, 85, 146, 160; from Korea, 59; *see also* festivals
Li ji, Record of Rites, 98, 149–50, 191 n. 16; *see also* ritual, handbooks of
Li Liufang, Ming painter, 26, 63, 70, 175, 176
Li Rihua, Ming writer, 104–5, 120, 131–2
Li Shiying, Ming Taoist priest, 14, 19
Li Sixun, Tang painter, 111, 135, 177, 179
Li Xianggong, Ming collector, 123
Li Yu, Qing writer, 31, 135, Plate 7
Li Zhaodao, Tang painter, 111, Plate 5
lineage organizations, 159–60
Liu Jin, Ming eunuch, 157
Liu Songnian, Song painter, 178
Liuqing ri zha, Daily Jottings of Liuqing, by Tian Yiheng, 96, 154, 155, 157–8
Lou Jian, Ming painter, 70, 176

Lowenthal, David, 91–2
Lu Aishan, Ming goldsmith, 61
Lu Ji, Ming writer, 146
Lü Kun, Ming writer, 167
Lu Zigang, Ming jade-worker, 61, 64, 65, 67, 84, 147
Luoyang, 161
luxury debate, in Augustan England, 171–2

Ma Hezhi, Song painter, 16
Ma Wan, Yuan painter, 178
Ma Xun, Ming fan-maker, 61
Ma Yuan, Song painter, 105, 178
Mandeville, Bernard, 147
Mao Jin, Qing publisher, 35
Marx, Karl, 116; Marxist scholarship, 4, 57, 160, 170, 172
material culture studies, 2, 182 n. 3
materialism, 170–1
Medici, Lorenzo de', 113, 126–7; inventory of possessions, 193 n. 20
medicine, 18, 32, 52, 84; storage of, 59
merchants, 5, 14, 15, 57, 66, 105, 108, 111, 118, 119, 136, 149, 159, 162–3, 167; attitudes to, 141–7; European, 128, 162
Mi Fu, Song painter and calligrapher, 35, 86, 88, 105, 177, 179
military officials, 24, 130, 149, 158, 161
Ming shi, Ming History, 148–9
Minor Writings on Elegant Leisure, Xian qing xiao pin, 35
Mo Shilong, Ming artist, 155, 163
Mu Zong, Ming official, 133
Mukerji, Chandra, 2, 170–1
music and musicians, 23, 48, 61, 107, 146, 154; *see also* drama; *qin* zithers
museums, 1–3, 8–9, 11, 50, 59, 75, 133, 186 n. 20; British Museum, 99; Cleveland Museum of Art, 178; Freer Gallery, 124; Percival David Foundation of Chinese Art, 27; Shanghai Museum, 120, 169

Nanjing, 11, 23, 28, 87, 90, 107, 138-9, 168, 175; site of Southern Ming court, 24

Netherlands, 2, 110, 151-2, 171, 172, 196 n. 13; sumptuary laws in, 151

Ni Zan, Yuan painter, 61

officials, 5, 17, 21, 24, 46, 81, 119, 135, 146, 147, 149, 151, 155, 156, 160-1; as collectors, 107-8; salaries of, 130; and sumptuary laws, 152-4; wives of, 154

orientalism, 91, 187 n. 40

Ouyang Xiu, Song writer, 59, 95

paintings, 9, 11, 15, 16, 18, 22, 29, 33, 35, 36, 48, 75, 78, 81, 82, 84, 85, 89, 90, 93, 97, 104-5, 106, 107, 109, 136, 138-40, 156; export, 66; forgery of, 109-14 *passim*, 119, Plate 5; market for, 119-27; mounting of, 32; prices of, 121-7, 138, 177-81; signatures on, 67-71; Song dynasty, 61, 105, 122, 127; storage of, 42, 59; in tombs, 101; Yuan dynasty, 127

Paludanus, Bernardus, 110

Pan Zhiheng, Ming writer, 26, 36, 175

paper, 29, 33, 49, 57, 80, 112, 137, 158; for bed-curtains, 43; from Korea, 58

Paris, luxury trades in, 65

pawnshops, 15, 135, 162

Peacham, Henry, 51, 96, 170

pearls, 33, 47, 137, 154

peasants, 46, 51, 76, 109, 130, 141, 142, 145, 146, 161; in rebellion, 23, 160-1; *see also* landholding

Peking, 23, 26, 130, 134, 135, 139, 144, 159; markets in 136-8

pewter vessels, 48, 49, 61-2, 149

Ping hua pu, Manual on Vases and Flowers, by Zhang Chou, 35

Ping shi, History of Vases, by Yuan Hongdao, 35, 86, 89

poetry, 14, 22, 52, 76, 80, 105, 157, 176; Gong'an school, 28, 77, 84, 88-9

population, of Ming China, 4-5, 162

Portugal, 158, 161

prices, of books, 132; of ceramics, 131-2; of fans, 60; of furniture, 131; of land, 132; of mansions, 130, 132, 161; of paintings, 108, 111, 118, 121-7, 177-81; of rice, 129, 172; of textiles, 130-1

prostitution, 36, 87, 117, 146, 154, 155, 156, 168

publishing, 10, 14, 18, 25, 26, 31, 34, 51-2, 97, 110, 167; pirated editions, 20, 29, Plate 4; size of editions, 19-20; *see also* books

Qian Ning, Ming general, 158

Qian Qianyi, Qing politician, 139

Qian Xiyan, Ming writer, 175

Qian Xuan, Yuan painter, 178

Qian Zeng, Qing bibliophile, 27

qin zithers, 9, 11, 23, 29, 33, 47, 61, 77, 81, 105, 106, 108, 156; forgery of, 110

Qing bi cang, Pure and Arcane Collecting, catalogued in *Si ku*, 32, 169; by Zhang Yingwen, 31, 32, 33-4, 59, 106

Qing dynasty, 28, 29, 31-2, 97, 108, 110, 114, 118, 168-9, 195 n. 21; imperial library, *see Si ku quan shu*

Qing zhai wei zhi, Placing and Arrangement of the Pure Studio, by Wen Zhenheng, 27, 35

Qinghe shu hua biao, Qinghe's Listing of Calligraphy and Painting, by Zhang Chou, 32

Qiu Ying, Ming painter, 111, 121, 127, 179

Qun fang qing wan, Pure Enjoyment of a Myriad of Fragrances, 35

rhinoceros horn, 47, 61

ri yong lei shu, 'encyclopedias for daily use', 37, 38, 118

Riben kao, Study of Japan, by Li Yangong and Hao Jie, 58
Ricci, Matteo, 59, 93–4
Richardson, Jonathan, 172
Ricoeur, Paul, 182 n. 1
ritual, 142–3; handbooks of, 96, 98, 100
rocks, 9, 11, 26, 33, 105; Lake Tai, 41; *lingbi*, 41; *ying*, 41
route books, 37, 118, 167
rubbings, 9, 11, 29, 33, 48, 177, 180, 181; of bronze inscriptions, 95–6; forgery of, 180

seals, 15, 33, 63, 68, 94, 113, 139, 148, 175; ceramic, 103
servants, 41, 44, 55, 117–18, 154
Shaftesbury, Earl of, 172
Shan zhai zhi, Record of my Mountain Studio, by Gao Lian, 36
Shang dynasty, 78, 81, 94, 98, 99, 108
shang gu, 'High Antiquity', 92, 94–5, 97
Shang zheng, Regulations of the Goblet, by Yuan Hongdao, 36
Shao Changheng, Qing writer, 110
Shaoxing, 160
Shen Chunze, Ming writer, 25, 74, 83, 164, 184 n. 31
Shen Defu, Ming writer, 26, 175; *see also Wanli ye huo bian*
Shen Gua, Song writer, 68
Shen Wansan, Yuan plutocrat, 157
Shen Zhou, Ming painter, 61, 105, 119, 123, 177, 178, 181
Shi shuo xin yu, New Account of Tales of the World, 78–9
Shi you tu zan, Illustrated Praises of my Ten Friends, by Gu Yuanqing, 52, 106
shops, 117; antique, 78, 111, 134–6; *see also* pawnshops
Shu jing, Classic of Documents, 56
Shui bian lin xia, By the Waters, Beneath the Trees, 36
Shuo fu, Tales Within a City Wall, 10, 27, 35, 52

Shuo yuan, Garden of Tales, by Liu Xiang, 143
Si ku quan shu, 27, 28, 29, 31–2, 169
silver, as currency, 5, 47, 125, 128–9; in Britain, 65, 187 n. 57; imported from Japan and Americas, 128–9; jewellery, 67, 154; vases, 44; vessels, 47, 61–3, 73, 78, 80, 149
Sombart, Werner, 170, 196 n. 7
Song dynasty, 11, 43, 57, 60, 67, 69, 104–5, 109–10, 114, 142; antiquarian studies in, 52, 95–7; Hangzhou as capital of, 57, 60, 87; imperial collection, 95, 111, 180, Plate 5; imperial painting academy, 69, 123
Song Jizu, Ming official, 27, 176
Song Yingxing, Ming writer, 166–7
Songjiang, 11, 43, 60, 64, 139, 155–6
Spain, 154–5, 158, 172; sumptuary laws in, 150–1
'sprouts of capitalism', 4, 57, 116, 148, 162, 172
Steele, Richard, 171–2
studio, scholar's, 9, 20, 29, 37–8, 41, 44, 59, 79, 89, 156
Su Shi, Song calligrapher, 104, 111, 180
sumptuary laws, 147–55, 171; in Europe, 150–1
Suzhou, 21, 22, 24, 33, 35, 44, 57, 61, 62, 70, 78, 92, 106, 111, 112, 120, 134, 155–6, 158, 163, 164, 175; fall to Manchus, 23; shops in, 136
swords, 79; connoisseurship of, 9, 33, 105; from Islamic world, 110; from Japan, 58–9

Taicang, 37, 64
Tang dynasty, 59, 70, 80, 86, 89, 93, 104
Tang Houzheng, Ming official, 115, 181
Tang Yin, Ming painter, 111, 178
Tang Zhixie, Ming writer, 122–3
Tao Zongyi, Yuan writer, 63
taxation, 5, 64, 129–30, 142, 162

tea, 26, 29, 33, 34, 35, 36, 41, 45, 57, 105, 190 n. 55; ceremony, 188 n. 4; pots for, 132

technology, Ming writing on, 166-7

textiles, 11, 33, 43-4, 47, 48, 54, 57, 71, 99, 117, 137, 143, 150, 152-5, 166, 193 n. 30; banana cloth, 44; cotton, 43, 47, 105; *gaiji*, 47, 130, 152; gold-patterned, 47; gauze, 44, 47, 130; *kudzu* cloth, 47; pongee, 43; prices of, 130-1; shops, 135; silk tapestry (*kesi*), 75, 106; velvet, 47; *see also* dress

textual studies, 31, 110, 153

Tian gong kai wu, Heaven's Craft in the Creation of Things, by Song Yingxing, 166-7

Tian shui bing shan lu, A Record of the Waters of Heaven Melting the Iceberg, 46-9, 67, 80, 98, 105, 130-1, 133, 151-3

Tian Yiheng *see Liuqing ri zha*

tools, 46, 79, 141, 166-7

Tu Long, Ming writer, 16, 19, 28, 70

Vico, Enea, 94

Wan shu za ji, Miscellaneous Records of the Administration of Wanping County, 49

Wang Anshi, Song politician, 134

Wang Boluan, Song painter, 123

Wang Daokun, Ming writer, 14, 157, 163, 175

Wang Fu, Han writer, 142

Wang Fuyuan, Ming dealer, 136

Wang Guxiang, Ming collector, 123, 181

Wang Liu, Ming writer, 174-5, 176

Wang Meng, Yuan painter, 177, 178

Wang Qi, Ming painter, 175

Wang Qi, Ming writer, 98-9, 102, 106, 108

Wang Shimou, Ming official, 124

Wang Shizhen, Ming official, 30, 61-2, 64, 104, 107, 124, 163, 187 n. 47

Wang Wei, Tang painter, 134; 'Rivers and Mountains after Snow', 16, 138, 139-40

Wang Wenlu, Ming writer, 110

Wang Xianchen, Ming official, 123

Wang Xianzhi, Jin calligrapher, 179

Wang Xiaoxi, Ming agate-worker, 61-2

Wang Xizhi, Jin calligrapher, 111, 122, 179, 180; 'Clearing Weather after Sudden Snowfall Letter', 16-17, 112, 174; 'Gazing Nearby Letter', 125-6, 181

Wang Yuanqi, Ming writer, 129

Wang Zheng, Ming writer, 166-7

Wang Zhideng, Ming writer, 24, 26, 28, 33, 35, 36, 112, 174

Wanli kuai ji lu, Record of the Accounts of the Wanli Reign, 167

Wanli ye huo bian, Random Gatherings of the Wanli Era, 38, 60, 68, 86-7, 104, 107, 112, 134, 147, 152-3, 175, 179

Wei Zhongxian, Ming eunuch, 21

Wen Boren, Ming painter, 69

Wen Dong, son of Wen Zhenheng, 24

Wen Guo, son of Wen Zhenheng, 24

Wen Jia, Ming painter, 69, 119, 120

Wen Peng, Ming painter, 119, 138

Wen Shu, Ming painter, 56

Wen Yuanshan, uncle of Wen Zhenheng, 175

Wen Zhengming, Ming painter, 21, 69, 91, 101, 105, 119, 120, 136, 164, 175, 176, Plate 5

Wen Zhenheng, Ming writer, 17, 20-5, 33, 56, 64, 106, 112, 174-6; as property owner, 24; *see also Zhang wu zhi*

Wen Zhenmeng, Ming official, 21-2, 27, 176

Wenzhou, 60

woman, as commodities, 118; domestic work of, 85; language of, 76; literacy of, 56; quarters and dwellings, 42, 55

wood, 11, 155-6; *huali*, 42, 43, 156, Plate 2; *tieli*, 42; *xiangnan*, 42; *zitan*, 43
writing accessories, 9, 29, 48, 79, 84, 101; ceramic, 103; *see also* brushes; ink; inkstones; paper
Wu Daozi, Tang painter, 111, 178
Wu Mingguan, Ming potter, 62, 66
Wuxi, 136

Xia dynasty, 81, 94, 98, 99
Xia Gui, Song painter, 105, 178
Xiang Yuanbian, Ming collector, 15, 29, 101, 107, 124-5, 127, 133, 177-81
Xianyu Shu, Yuan calligrapher, 104
Xie Shichen, Ming painter, 123
Xu Chengrui, Ming writer, 25
Xu Guangqi, Ming writer, 166-7
Xuan he bo gu tu lu, Drawings and Lists of all the Antiquities Stored in the Xuan he Palace, 95, 97
Xunzi, Warring States philosopher, 154

Yan Liben, Tang painter, 181
Yan Shifan, Ming official, 135
Yan Song, Ming official, 46, 107, 120-1, 135, 158; inventory of possessions *see Tian shui bing shan lu*
Yangzhou, 118, 134
Yansou, Yuan painter, 124
Yixing, 138-9
Yu gong, Tribute of Yu, 56
Yu Ji, Yuan calligrapher, 104, 179
Yu zan ji, The Jade Hairpin, by Gao Lian, 17, 184 n. 36
Yuan dynasty, 37, 85, 99, 145; painting in, 69-70, 101, 105
Yuan Hongdao, Ming writer, 36, 86, 89, 190 n. 55
Yuan xi qi qi tu shuo, Illustrated Explanation of the Strange Implements of the Far West, by Wang Zheng, 79, 166-7

Zhan Jingfeng, Ming writer, 123-4; *see also Dongtu xuan lan bian*

Zhang Chou, Ming writer, 30, 32, 33, 35, 36, 86
Zhang Dai, Ming writer, 61, 66, 67, 86, 99, 100, 101, 108-9, 132, 136, 160, 168
Zhang Fengyi, Ming writer, 112
Zhang Han, Ming writer, 143-6, 153-4
Zhang Juzheng, Ming official, 107, 130
Zhang Sengyu, Tang painter, 134, 178
zhang wu, 'superfluous things', explanation of term, 78-9
Zhang wu zhi, Treatise on Superfluous Things, by Wen Zhenheng, 1, 9, 20, 24, 25-8, 34, 40-6, 49, 52-74, 81, 103, 118, 148, 150, 154, 158, 166, 167, 170, 172; on bronzes, 98, 100; on ceramics, 100, 102; catalogued in *Si ku*, 32, 169; date of, 25-7, 35; editions of, 27-8, 184 n. 35; editors of, 25-7, 174-6; language in, 78-90; on painting and calligraphy, 69-70, 127, 156; preface to, 74, 164; on prices for painting and calligraphy, 122; sources, 28, 30
Zhang Xu, Tang calligrapher, 178
Zhang Yanyuan, Tang writer, 97
Zhang Yingwen, Ming writer, 30, 32, 33
Zhao Huanguang, Ming poet, 176
Zhao Liangbi, Ming craftsman, 61-2
Zhao Mengfu, Yuan calligrapher, painter, 104, 177, 178, 179
Zheng Xie, Qing painter, 118-19
Zhou Chen, Ming painter, 120-1
Zhou Danquan, Ming Taoist priest, 115, 136, 181
Zhou dynasty, 78, 81, 94, 96, 98
Zhou Fenglai, Ming patron, 121, 179, 193 n. 11
Zhou li, Rites of Zhou, 149
Zhou Shunchang, Ming official, 22, 24
Zhou Yongnian, Ming writer, 176
Zhou Zhu, Ming inlay-worker, 61

Zhu Bishan, Yuan silversmith, 61–3
Zhu Chenggong, Ming collector, 107
Zhu Jingxun, Ming collector, 108
Zhu qi tu shuo, Illustrated Explanation of the Various Implements, by Wang Zheng, 166
Zhu Rui, Song painter, 179
Zhu Xi, Song writer, 106
Zhu You, calligrapher, 111

Zhu Yunming, Ming calligrapher, 105
Zun sheng ba jian, Eight Discourses on the Art of Living, by Gao Lian, 1, 9, 13, 17–21, 28, 29, 30, 31, 34, 59, 81, 100, 148, 166, Plate 1; catalogued in *Si ku*, 31–2, 169; editions of, 20, 183 n. 18; on fake bronzes, 114; illustrations to, 52